Secondhand Scotch

How One Family Survived In Spite Of Themselves

A Memoir

by

Cathy Curran

Author's Note

"Secondhand Scotch" found its way onto paper through my memory. I've done my best to recreate events and conversations so that they depict the original sentiment of each situation. The family history contained in this book was passed on to me through word-of-mouth, mainly by my parents and grandparents. To maintain the integrity of my family history, whenever possible, I referred to records and documents to verify the accuracy of verbal assertions and to reconfirm my own recollection of some of the occurrences herein.

For the sake of brevity, some events contained in this book are consolidated and may be presented in different time frames, give or take a couple of years of the actual occurrences.

Please note that some names and foreign words are spelled phonetically in English. For example, I changed the spelling of Yia Yia, the Greek word for grandma, to Yaya.

The numerous aspects of human characteristics touched upon in "Secondhand Scotch" may be of interest and great value to the unknown score of others who've experienced similar circumstances. All things considered, this was the main factor in the decision to publish.

I have changed names and omitted current identifying characteristics of a handful of people in my memoir, and as well, withheld many of the negative occurrences I have experienced in an effort to focus on family dynamics and human characteristics, and to maintain balance and lightheartedness as much as possible.

As I convey within the pages of this book, my siblings and I were regarded on various class levels to the extreme, therefore, our beliefs and perspectives differ greatly, as do our experiences and remembrances.

Those who disagree with my perspective or recollections are free to write a memoir of their own.

As a final note, please keep in mind that the individual stories within my memoir are not meant to stand alone. "Secondhand Scotch" is the sum of all its parts.

The author's parents, Joseph Low and Armenouhe (Lillian) Kartalian, married on January 29, 1949.

Additional photos along with a glossary and a family tree, can be found on the author's website: secondhandscotch.com.

Dedication

This book is dedicated to the memory of my mother, who brought sanity to our crazy world, who gave her all, who loved, laughed and deserved so much more. It is also dedicated to the memory of my father, who shared the unembroidered story of his life with me, and in doing so, redeemed himself. And to all future generations of Joseph and Lillian Low, here, and yet to come.

Table of Contents

PART FOUR: ANOTHER FRESH START

PART FIVE: SIDES TAKEN

PART ONE: SOMEDAY NEVER CAME

The Noblest Deed of All

I was born wanting to live, but I lived wanting to die, and now that most of my life is gone, I want to live again.

I'm the second of nine children, a baby boomer—old enough to remember adjusting the wire hanger on my father's television while doubling as his human remote control. By age nine I could chew gum, change diapers, and sing "Hello, Dolly" all at once. I was quickly pegged as the family caregiver, and there was no escaping my duties. After all, my father was the family czar who thought nothing of curing me with a good dose of medicine, whether I needed it or not. So by the time I was little more than ten, my spirit was chiseled down to its bones, and I wished that I had never been born.

I appeared to be an average, lower class, all-American kid, but I was stuck in a Russian time warp without a Cossack's hat to keep my head warm. In school, when the air raid bell sounded, all of the children scrambled beneath their desks; and while they were hiding from the Russians, I was hiding from myself.

As an adult, I was expected to maintain my role as family caregiver, even as I created and cared for my own family. I stayed the course with uncommon devotion until I was forty-six years old—that's when my father disowned me for a disagreement I had with my older sister. It wasn't just the dispute that got me canned; it was because I finally stood up for myself in a way that was long overdue, and by doing so, I had stepped out of the role my father had assigned me.

It never mattered to Dad whether or not my sister was right. She was one of Dad's favored children, and that was the deciding factor in every squabble we had throughout our lives.

My family was everything to me. Being rejected devastated me to the core, but in order to be accepted, I'd have to jump back into the box where I would always be a loser at the game my father and sister played. If I wasn't willing to do that, I could just sit at the curb and wait to be scooped up by the shit-wagon.

I crawled into a dark corner, fetal, the way I did as a child, so no one would see my sadness. For the longest time I was numb and hollow until a few simple words, evolved from a poem by Henry David Thoreau, swooped into my void and echoed: "Most men lead lives of quiet desperation and go to the grave with the song still in them."

The words funneled through a familiar voice, one that I'd heard only in my head, one that never shouted or cursed like my father. But this time it bellowed, making me feel as though I'd been rapped on the side of my head by Dad's huge hand. I was stunned into thinking: *If I don't stand up for myself, I might as well die.*

Throughout my childhood my older sister audibly wished that I'd drop dead, and the words would shoot off her tongue with passion and contempt. I adored her as much as I loved my father, and somewhere along the way I embraced their sentiments of me. I believed that I just wasn't good enough for this world. Since I never had the courage to do myself in, I languished in my subservient role for almost half a century before finally realizing that my flexibility would never satisfy my sister, nor would it ever save me from my father's injustice.

From as far back as my memory stretches, my life was steeped in turmoil. What else could I expect? A high-strung man who thrived on controversy raised me. Joe Low was no graceful butterfly; he came flapping at me like a three-hundred-pound barfly leaving behind a path of destruction.

Dad's rules changed more often than the stock market, but I didn't know about the new ones until I broke them. And they were different for each of us Low kids. If I didn't like the way he did things, "too damn bad." It was his job to teach me that "life ain't fair and it ain't no goddamned picnic."

If his rough demeanor was contagious, it also came in handy. Some of my siblings weren't afraid of anyone but Dad—not monsters or ghosts, not even the neighborhood bullies. One day, when she was only ten, my sister, Joanne, was on the front lawn having a fistfight with two boys. Dad decided to "end this goddamned bullshit right now." He opened the window, stuck out his head and roared.

"Heeeeeey! One at a time, goddamn it!"

So the boys took turns and Joanne beat the hell out of both of them—one at a time.

Good thing, because if she had run back into the house crying, Dad might have whipped off his leather belt and really given her something to cry about. He could unbuckle that thing and draw it from his loops in one slick motion. No matter how many times he used it to straighten me out, he couldn't seem to mold me to his liking, but he kept trying, which is probably why I gravitated toward Mom.

She was more like a carousel—calm and predictable, and as honest as the freckle on the tip of my nose. Between Dad and us kids, we had a way of making her go round in circles, but her coping mechanism was humor. When Dad came home from work and found toys on the floor, he demanded to know what the hell Mommy did all day.

"I've been to London to visit the queen," she insisted, "in my fur coat, with the man next door." Then she'd wipe the baby puke off her shoulder and slide a plate of stuffed cabbages in front of him.

And when he pounded the kitchen table with his fist proclaiming to "rule the roost," Mom would salute him with a "cock-a-doodley-doodley-doots." Then she'd laugh, and her eyes would sparkle in a way that made you think she was breathing in sunshine instead of air.

It was fashionable to have lots of kids in the 1950s, so Mom kept popping them out until she could brag that she had her own baseball team. The years went by and up we grew, in a three-ring-circus—we Low kids. And that's a miracle, for in spite of my father's injustice and the sibling rivalry he nurtured, we made it into adulthood together. All but one of us got married and had kids of our own. The unmarried one would eventually have a mental collapse.

By the late 1980s our family had mushroomed to thirty-six members, spouses and children included, so our weekend get-togethers were like a field day at the nut house. (My unmarried brother had a ball.) Mom and Dad would sit and watch their grandchildren at play, admiring the outcome of their lifelong struggles. Friends who joined us envied our camaraderie. Perhaps they wouldn't have had they known that our hardscrabble lives created our uncommon bond. We seemed to be the lucky few to have come to such a place: a place of knowing that the contract of life includes adversity. But that was long before I truly understood the verbiage in Dad's ever-changing amendments.

When I first opened my neonate eyes and saw Joe Low gazing down at me with a Kool cigarette dangling from his lips, smelling like smoked-scotch, breathing like a pissed-off bear, I must've sensed I was looking into the eyes of adversity. It was impossible to turn away because my contract with my father was written and signed in family blood.

Dad was toughened up on New York City streets during the Great Depression, hard-bitten by the hand of his father's raw, untamed emotions. Free-flowing bathtub gin triggered his mother's intermittent absence, leaving him with a cavity that filled itself with heartache and uncertainty. Dad's childhood was miserable and throughout most of his adult life he'd point his finger back at his father and Russia and its czars and plenty of other people who had nothing to do with his screwed-up childhood. When Dad spoke of the misery of his yesteryears, he appeared to be reliving them as they were happening, as if he was little Joey, four years old, being beaten by his father for grabbing a morsel of food from the table. It didn't matter that his mother had forgotten to feed him. It didn't count that she was in a drunken stupor, or that his father had turned their apartment into a speakeasy. It didn't matter that it was just too noisy for a scared and hungry four-year-old to sleep. Joey knew he'd get a lickin' if he was caught snatching a hunk of *kielbasa*. Hunger trumps fear, but it doesn't diminish it.

For the rest of his life, starvation and fear would lie just beneath Joey's quilt of anger.

More than anything else, Dad was sick and tired of being poor, of scratching any and everything out of nothing. He loathed poverty and craved prestige. His ambition was to make a million dollars. He equated that number with happiness and did a lot of shady things in his pursuit of it. I watched him all my life as he struggled to give his family all the things he didn't have as a kid. He figured his restlessness would end when he made it big, and by the time I was grown, he did. He made more than the extra million he'd hoped for, which bought a lot of stuff in the mid-70s, but it didn't equal happiness.

When the golden door opened, it revealed to Dad the same discontent that caused him to hunt down a million dollars in the first place. In his pursuit he had forgotten why he was on the chase—that his family was more important to him than anything. Well, he didn't totally forget. If you asked him what's the most important thing in a person's life, he'd say family, then he'd tell you to hold up three fingers.

"At the end of your life, if you have three people who are willing to give up their right arms or jump into a fire for you, consider yourself the luckiest person alive," he'd proclaim.

Lucky for Dad, he didn't have enough fingers to hold up, but his misguided notion of success blinded his heart-sight. His discontent festered and plagued those most likely to jump into the fire for him— his family. It affected all of us, and some adopted his discontent, while others tiptoed around it. But eventually all volcanoes erupt, and this one blew at the worst possible time—during the last year of my mother's life.

Mommy tried to remain neutral, but she got caught in the crossfire and died on the battlefield—a fate she least deserved.

My family was split in half like the North and South, engaged in our own civil war. Our weapons were words, born of emotion and nurtured with rage. They were venomous darts that tore us to shreds.

Dad blamed me for splitting up the family, for ruining the empire he created. He stormed through the final stretch of his life blinded by rage, treating me like an enemy, yet I shouldn't have been surprised. His volatile emotions overshadowed reason and truth, and his legacy of anger was so powerful, it thrived upon his passing. Which is why I was shocked when my brother, Joseph, came to me with questions about our father. But even in the midst of Joseph's anger, he realized the sixteen years I had on him were loaded with historical information. He needed some facts because there would be only one eulogy—and he was going to deliver it. If all of us Low kids offered individual eulogies, observers might have thought nine fathers died, not one.

Truthfully, nine fathers did die—in the final beat of one man's heart.

Joseph confessed that he didn't know much about Dad's life, but he wanted me to assess what he had come up with thus far. His ideas sounded more like a fairytale. He had created a tenth father, one more like Santa Claus, and I wondered if he had had a mental lapse.

"People will know you're lying," I said.

"What do you mean by that?" he asked.

I knew I was risking an argument. After all, he was on the South, I was on the North, and when surrounded by the southern regime, Joseph's cruelty toward me was incomprehensible. But there were no other siblings present, so he was kind. I could see love in him and I had hope that he'd permanently set aside his anger. Whether or not he ever would, at that moment he did, so I felt I could be honest.

"There'll be plenty of people in the pews who've gone out drinking with Dad, many who've seen him shit-faced, and maybe a few who got punched in the face by him, or were in on one of his shady schemes," I said.

He looked at me for a long moment. *He'd rather tell the fairytale.* Beneath the layers of fantasy and anger, he knew I wasn't making this up. Although Joseph was also a favorite of Dad's, he'd been on the shit-end of his stick—the end I was most familiar with. Those of us Low kids on the shit-end grew up with a different perspective than the favored ones. Since Joseph had a sneak preview of our perception, it was all a matter of his willingness to remember.

We sat quietly, face to face, staring into each other's souls. I waited to see if I had pissed him off or jarred his memory.

"I don't want to disrespect our father," he shrieked.

"You don't have to paint a portrait of every detail," I said, "just a rough sketch, but of Dad's life, not Walt Disney's."

Surprisingly, Joseph took my advice and turned Dad's blunders into a humorous and heartfelt eulogy. Although we were still at odds, I was proud of him, and he knew it. What he didn't know is that the guidance I had given him about how to tell the story was something our father taught me. Joseph also didn't know about the secret Dad and I shared—the one that developed because of my refusal to embrace Dad's anger.

While my siblings on the southern side were obsessed with the family war, Dad grew weary of it, and just before autumn turned into what would be a very short winter for Dad, he began sneaking across the border. He didn't want the South to know he was socializing with the North. All he wanted was a peaceful visit, someone to talk to, and someone to listen to what he had to say. So he zigzagged over to my house, parked his car two feet from the curb, and limped toward my porch with regret and sorrow dripping from his face. I was almost fifty, yet I turned into a ten-year-old pile of mush as he wept with remorse and embraced me with a very belated hug.

My physically strong father had become feeble. With the little time we had left, he began to rehash the stories of his tumultuous childhood, and of his parents' chaotic lives, filling in the blanks while adding new and candid tales of his own mischievous and unscrupulous behavior. He did all the talking, and I, the listening—that's the way it was with him and me. I always knew his favorite color was blue, like his mother's eyes, but he would never know that mine is green, like the shade of grass just before sunset.

"Tell me more about your father," I'd say.

"You think you had it bad?" he'd growl. "Your life was a piece of cake compared to mine. My father was a mean son-of-a-bitch. Pop was a bastard! I could've written a book about Pop's life, and mine. I regret not writing it," he lamented. "Maybe someday I will."

Someday never came. In the midst of our family war Dad died without having written a single chapter, but my heart recorded his emotional narrative, and ironically, the man who so emphatically silenced my voice as a child, made amends by passing his story on to me.

The drama of his life cracked open his harsh cloak, revealing a man whose intentions were nobler than many of his deeds. And some of those things that seemed unfair, like our one-way conversations, may have been among his noblest deeds of all.

Dad's recollections, sprinkled with bits of European and American history, took me on an unexpected journey, one that gifted the pair of us with an understanding that led to acceptance of the past rather than denial.

Denial, it seems, nurtures that which could only be laid to rest through recognition.

Realizing that we are all simply a collection of experiences and memories, some made by our own hands, and some by the power of those who came before us, Dad acknowledged what was; and his simple act of recognition laid the foundation of a new course with a clear view.

Dad's fresh path was a short one, but long enough to understand that memories, even bad ones, are good. Without a memory, we wouldn't know each other, we wouldn't even know ourselves; nor would we have hindsight, the component that allows us to extract wisdom from our experiences. As broken as I was, it became clear to me that Dad's heart was broken long before I came into the world, as was his father's heart; and that alone begs forgiveness.

Thus, in appreciation of what was, I concede that the story of my life began long before I existed, in the 1800s, across the sea, under a czar—where the DNA that saturates my flesh and blood was alive and well and yearning to escape a life of misery.

PART TWO: CONNECTING THE DOTS OF MY LEGACY

From Russia to America

Russia is a mean-spirited land, swarming with peasants who know all too well that hope grows like wheat, yet spoils and rots just the same. Merciless living conditions are typical, but not for the nobles. Lucky for Sarah Chinska, she is born into nobility, and sheltered from the misery of life as a peasant. When she falls in love with Anthony Lukashchuk, a poor grain farmer with nothing to offer but a life of hardship, she marries him anyway and her parents disown her because the upper crust will not mingle with the crumbs.

Sarah and Anthony bring twelve sons and a daughter into the world. Their seventh son, Onouphry, is born under the reign of Alexander III during the 1891 Russian Famine. He will someday be my father's father.

Soon after Onouphry learns to walk, he works. Alongside his family he toils in the field with chapped hands till the disappearing sun suggests he get some rest. He's a rebel at heart, like his mother, like my father will be, as I will be. Our family will say it's in our blood. Onouphry hates the monotony of farming, but in order to produce enough grain for the Lukashchuks to barely survive, his share of the labor is needed.

To keep his sons in line, Anthony whacks them with a leather belt. He wastes no time explaining to the children why they must work like slaves, why they must keep their mouths shut. So they work, year in, year out, but unrelenting years of arduous labor does not lift the family from poverty—it fuels anger and diminishes hope.

The weather controls the crops and the nobles control the peasants. With each harvest the nobles dispatch their middleman to the village on a horse-drawn wagon. From time to time the farmers bicker with him, hoping for a better deal, yet nothing changes. As they become more complacent, Onouphry impulsively hatches a bold plan that will alter his destiny.

To get to the village, the middleman's horse-drawn wagon must be driven slowly over an old bridge a mile or so away. Onouphry takes careful note of the middleman's schedule, and when the time is right, he journeys to the bridge and waits beneath it. Just as the entire wagon is trapped on the wooden slats of the rickety overpass, Onouphry climbs up, jumps the middleman from behind, and pounds him into mincemeat. Then he leaves him draped on the bridge like an old rag doll.

Unfortunately, Onouphry does not think ahead. The trodden man cannot buy any yield of crops, and when he heals, he makes purchases from every farmer in the village, save the Lukashchuks. He'll never buy anything from them as long as Onouphry is around. Anthony and Sarah can barely care for their large brood of children as it is. Since the middleman keeps his word, the Lukashchuks fear that the nobles will force them off the land, leaving them homeless and starving. For the good of the family Anthony and Sarah have to get rid of Onouphry. They'd like to send him to America but they don't have the fare, so the other farmers pitch in what little they have, and collectively, their generosity makes it possible for the young Russian rebel to set sail across the Atlantic.

He arrives in Boston Harbor around 1907, exits the ship as Onouphry Lukashchuk, but enters America as Frank Low. He wanders the streets of Boston amid countless other immigrants who share his passion to succeed. His broken English and tattered clothing do not diminish his handsome features, yet his looks do nothing to land him a suitable job. Boston does not fulfill his needs, but there's talk on the street of a job opportunity with good wages at a factory way up north at the Canadian border. Frank heads north. He arrives at the work camp and is given a room in the company dormitory, and credit for merchandise in the company store. All goes well until he receives his statement of wages. Along with his earnings is a list of expenses for store purchases, room and board. The expenses exceed his wages, putting him in debt to the company. He can't leave the work camp unless his debt is paid, but the longer he works, the more he owes. He could try to escape, but brawny guards who tower over him are posted around the camp.

There are no laws protecting laborers like Frank in the early 1900s. It will not be until 1935 when labor-friendly President Franklin D. Roosevelt signs the Wagner Act giving a voice to American workers that things will change for the better. So Frank is a casualty of his place in time. He once despised injustice, but his experiences have taught him something new: To be honest is to be a victim of greed and corruption.

His thirst for freedom drives him to devise a plan of escape. He'll need money for food and travel so he steals gold jewelry from the company store, wraps the gold pieces in rags, ties them up, and hides them in the outhouse, which he calls the shitter. He watches the night guards on patrol, noting the times of their positions. When he's sure he has enough goods to hock, he makes his way to the shitter in the dark of morning. By candlelight, he sticks his bare hands into the fetid pool of excrement and fishes around for his gold. He unwraps it to find it discolored, blackened and mottled with rust. It's gold-plated metal—worthless junk, another symbol of how the company cheats its laborers.

Frank wants to get back at the company—ten times—but all he can do is try to escape. He scrubs his hands with dirt then rubs them clean in the dew on the grass. He creeps past the dormitories and factory, managing to dodge the guards, and is almost free when he's grabbed from behind by "a big son-of-a-bitch" who begins to pound him. But size has nothing on fury. The revelation of how badly he was cheated out of his hard-earned pay fuels a rage that pours into Frank's fists—the same ones that fished around in the shitter ten minutes earlier.

A right hook splits open the guard's lips and loosens his teeth. A left one cracks his nose, another jab gets him square in the gut and when he keels over, Frank snaps him in the jaw. He pummels the guard's face into cherry pie, knocking out his entire set of teeth.

When men assemble at a dormitory window to view the spectacle, Frank yells up to them.

"I beat da livingk shit out of da son-of-a-bitch. I didn't know I wuz so strrrongk. I knocked out da bastarrrd's teeth all at once, in one piss!"

But time enlightens him. In years to come, when he recounts these events, he will add, "I tingk maybe I'm strrrongker den I know, but den I find out dey wuz false teeth. I didn't know derrre wuz such a tingk. Could yuns imagine dey could invent such a tingk?"

With the guard lying helpless on the ground, Frank takes off, leaving behind the company that shamelessly exploited him and so many others. He works his way south, settling for short periods in various communities where he is able to find employment, steering clear of companies that resemble work camps. To him, they are nothing more than "prrrisons."

If he has to fight, cheat, and steal to get by, that's what he does.

He believes the only thing wrong with cheating and stealing is getting caught. He's certain big business is the bigger thief. It's a lesson he'll never forget and he'll be sure to pass his wisdom on to my father.

After many nomadic years Frank settles in Pennsylvania where he works as a coal miner. He's five-foot-six, strong and trim. He has brown hair and dark, steely eyes overflowing with dominance. The command in his gaze will only attract the most care-free, easy-going spirit as a mate. Rose Niovich, young and innocent, fits that profile.

The Words Not Spoken

The traditional Polish wedding of Catherine Kobylaz and Martin Niovich in the 1800s involves drinking wine and eating salted rye bread. The salt will remind them to endure when life becomes difficult, and the bread and wine symbolize hope that they never go hungry or thirsty.

Fertility gods smile on them, but the hope of their bread and wine shatters. By the latter part of 1899, with seven children to care for, desperation causes Martin and Catherine to join the four million Polish citizens migrating to America.

They perch in Tyler, Pennsylvania, where Martin works as a coal miner and Catherine as a maid. Their existence is sparse but they manage, even when Catherine finds herself pregnant with her eighth child. When the infant comes forth on a cold November morning in 1901, they name her Rose—and my grandmother's life will surely blossom among the thorns.

Catherine goes right back to work because she's got a secret plan. In preparation, she saves bits of her measly salary, and near the end of 1902 her resolve pays off. She packs a bag for her and Rose, then sails across the Atlantic, leaving Martin to care for their other children.

She arrives in Poland to reunite with her mother, but after a fleeting visit, Catherine takes Rose and makes her way to the train station for the first leg of her journey home. She hops on board, but she does not take her baby. She brazenly makes her way back to Martin and her other children, leaving Rose alone at the mercy of an unknown fate.

Coincidentally, a neighbor of Catherine's mother rambles through the train station. He hears a crying child and recognizes the blue-eyed, redheaded baby as the granddaughter of Mrs. Kobylaz. He scoops her up and delivers Rose to her grandmother, who takes her in without question. Now, Mrs. Kobylaz sends countless letters to Catherine letting her know that Rose is safe, that she should come and get her. Catherine never responds.

Rose lives in Poland for more than eleven years until her grandmother dies. Now alone with no family to care for her, she is saved when the poor villagers join forces and arrange to send her back to her mother. Those who have a little money throw it in a pile, and those who don't, sell treasured possessions to raise the fare needed for Rose's passage to America. They make contact with her family, notifying them of her arrival date, then off they send her.

With a ticket in hand, Rose boards a ship destined for New York in 1914, shortly before World War I, before Poland is invaded by Austria-Hungary. By that time Rose will be safe in America but struggling with a different kind of war—poverty.

Although Rose was born in America, she has no documentation to prove it, and without her records, she will need a sponsor. She arrives on Ellis Island hoping to see her mother. After three days of waiting, as she is about to be shipped back to Poland, her older sister, Agnes, arrives to find Rose dirty, disheveled and infested with lice. She undresses Rose, throws her into New York Harbor to bathe, washes out her clothing, combs out her matted hair, then pins a note on her saying, "Rose Niovich, Destination: Tyler, Pennsylvania." Agnes puts Rose on a train and sends her on her way.

Rose speaks only Polish, making communication difficult, but luckily, strangers, some probably just as destitute as she is, help the twelve-year-old to maneuver her way with train connections. When Rose arrives in Tyler with her meager belongings stuffed under her arm, she exits the train and glances around searching for anyone who might be looking for her. No one is. Forlorn, she enters a small general store near the station and approaches a man at the counter who, fortunately, knows her family. He sends word to them and soon her father arrives at the store. When Martin calls out her name, Rose presumes that the stranger is her father. She's elated to see him and believes she's finally going home. Instead, Martin leads her into a boarding house, where he arranges for her to work as a cook and maid in exchange for room and board. He's just following Catherine's instructions—she still wants nothing to do with Rose.

In short order, Catherine gives birth to her ninth child. The baby is healthy, but Catherine becomes gravely ill. Rose goes to see her, to tell her, "I love you Mama."

But her mother turns away.

Not long after that, Catherine dies. She passes on without giving her abandoned daughter an ounce of recognition, robbing her of a priceless treasure that even the poorest among us can afford to give —words. Catherine takes them to her grave: words that answer questions, that can soothe a weary heart. Words that only Catherine could have shared, and that Rose Niovich had every right to hear. Now Rose will live the rest of her life with unanswered questions—and they will haunt her—but she will find many ways to forget.

With Catherine gone, Martin finds it difficult to care for his infant so he quickly remarries. He and his new wife, Ena, send for Rose—and for the first time in her young life Rose feels wanted and embraced, particularly when her father rushes her off to a doctor after she's hit in the eye with a rock. Unfortunately, it's too late. Rose loses the vision in her left eye, yet the grateful gleam in her right one abundantly makes up for the other—especially when Ena turns into her very own fairy godmother.

Rose longs to attend an upcoming dance but she has nothing to wear. Ena, sensing her stepdaughter's sorrow, invites Rose to sit beside her. She grabs a book and turns a few pages until she comes to a dollar bill, then continues turning pages until she pulls out five bills and offers them to Rose. Many years from now when Rose is old and I am just a kid, she will tell me, "Dat's da firrrst time I had money to buy sometingk nice."

Five dollars is more than enough for a decent dress in 1917. She buys herself a pretty one, slips it on, spruces up her red locks and rushes off to the dance feeling like "Cinderrrella." She's fifteen, shy and waiting to be noticed. Frank Low, more than ten years her senior, saunters across the wooden floor to grab a dance with her as if he's entitled to it. An upbeat polka steals them away, and by the end of the evening Frank and Rose blend like scotch and water.

They flee Pennsylvania, set up house on Eliot Street in Boston, Massachusetts, and before long Rose looks as though she swallowed a watermelon. So off they go to City Hall to apply for a marriage license. Sixteen-year-old Rose tells the clerk she's eighteen. Frank drops the letter "r" from crook and lists his occupation as a cook. It's July 5, 1918. They tie the knot with shreds of emotional baggage that will never be unpacked. Instead it is just passed on to my father, and to me. That's how life is, and there's no looking back, no crying.

Two months later Rose gives birth to their first child, Anna.

Between 1920 and 1926 five more children are added to the Low clan. By this time Frank and twenty-five-year-old Rose, along with their six children, settle in an old farmhouse in Woodbridge, New Jersey.

Lucky Seven

My redheaded, blue-eyed father comes into the world on January 23, 1928. He's the seventh child of a seventh son and is later told that this is lucky. But Joey isn't blessed with a silver spoon. When Rose introduces him to food, she chews it until it's mush then transfers it directly from her mouth to his.

While she's in the kitchen, Frank's out back making gin—a lucrative enterprise during Prohibition. He also gambles on cockfights, and together he and Rose grow vegetables and raise chickens. They enlist the help of Anna, their firstborn, who assumes the role of maid and nanny. Good thing, because Rose finds herself pregnant for the eighth time. She gives birth to Andrei with the help of a midwife in 1929, and now that the Lows have eight children to feed, the stock market tanks and the American economy ends up in the toilet.

The Depression grips everyone, but the poorest of the poor end up on the streets along with their worn-out furniture. Some may remain honest—but *not* the Lows. Life handed them a hardball and they play the game accordingly. And as if life isn't fast and hard enough, by 1931 it pitches them another curve.

To celebrate Anna's thirteenth birthday, Frank and Rose take her shopping for shoes, leaving eleven-year-old Frances to mind the younger children. Joey scampers in the yard with Andrei, Helen and Edna, but the frolicking children aren't mindful of the deep hole that serves as a well. Andrei, age two, falls into it. He drowns. His life begins and ends before Rose finds the time to register his birth, so it just doesn't fit to report his death to the Woodbridge registrar.

The little brother Joey played with everyday vanishes like an amputated arm, leaving him with a cavity that his mother attempts to fill by ignoring his misconduct and protecting him from his father's wrath.

By the year's end Frank packs up his family and heads to New York City. He wants a fresh start and he gets it at 50 Clinton Street on the Lower East Side of Manhattan. And while the Depression takes center stage in America, bootlegging steals the show in the Low house. Although Joey's mother adores him, come the weekend, *every* weekend, she gets good and drunk—and Joey, not yet old enough for school, finds himself temporarily motherless.

Frank requires all the children to pitch in with the making of bathtub gin. He sends them out to buy heavy sacks of sugar that can only be lugged home like a dead mutt. While mixing, storing and delivering the gin the children get saturated with its odor and reek of alcohol, but the cops turn their heads and graciously accept Frank's hush money. Every Friday night Frank transforms his apartment into a speakeasy. He charges a cover fee, Rose sets out a plate of *kielbasa,* and the party begins. Guests come and go. Some stay, nap, and then awaken to catch their second wind. Thick swirls of cigarette smoke mingle with the stench of alcohol, slurred chatter, off-key Russian-Polish sing-a-longs and intermittent arguments. The cycle never ends and Joey is forbidden to come to the table during these parties. But he gets hungry, and when Rose is shit-faced she forgets to feed him. So he sneaks up to the table for a morsel of whatever he can find. When Frank catches him, he gives Joey some good medicine: a lickin' he'll never forget. Only this time the usual five-minute lickin' is too much trouble for Frank, so Joey is sentenced to kneeling on raw rice for hours until the kernels dig into his knees and torture him.

During the parties Frank curbs his drinking. After all, he's on the job. But Rose never quits until she's so intoxicated that she's hardly aware of the male guests with roving hands who get fresh with her, hoping for more than just a feel. Joey witnesses this while his father sits in the corner sleeping. Frank, however, sleeps with one eye open. He sees everything, but he's patient. On Sunday night when the makeshift speakeasy shuts down, like clockwork, Frank beats the hell out of Rose for getting sloppy drunk and letting other drunks take advantage of her. When he's done sweeping the floor with Rose, giving her a full dose of medicine, he gives the children theirs. Without fail, every Sunday ends the same.

When the Lows are forced out of their Clinton Street apartment, they move to Second Street, then Third, Orchard, Fourth, Fifth and Sixth streets, back to Orchard, out to Staten Island a couple of times, to the Bronx, Brooklyn, and back to Manhattan. Frank doesn't pay the rent. Well, he pays up front to get into an apartment, but that's it. When landlords come knocking at the door looking to get paid, it's Rose who contends with them. And she soon learns that her new landlord is not very patient. Antonio is tired of asking for the rent.

"When I comma back I wanna my money," he roars with his finger pointed at her face like a loaded gun. "If you no gotta money, you gonna be sorry!"

The next time Antonio comes looking for his rent, he arms himself with a kitchen knife just in case Rose comes up empty again. Sure enough she does, so he stabs her in the arm with a blade that his wife uses to shave *parmigiano*.

Before dawn Frank wakes up the family.

"We'rrre movingk! Get up and get yuns tingks."

He says it just once and everyone is up and packed.

He's too cheap to rent a horse and buggy so the children carry all the family possessions on their backs. They walk many city blocks, stopping intermittently as Frank tries to cut a deal with a new landlord. By sundown their arduous journey ends. Someone takes pity on the couple with seven children, and the Lows have a new address yet again.

When Joey is five, Frank determines it's time for him to contribute to the family. He takes him to a five-and-dime store and gives his son a nickel to purchase five tote bags, then shows him how to get to avenues where the rich shop. It doesn't take Joey long to maneuver his way around. He becomes a champ at selling penny tote bags for two cents to rich ladies who take pity on him. He brings Frank the profit but furtively builds his own stash. Instead of rushing home, he buys additional penny bags, sells them, takes his own cut and carefully hides it in his socks because he's sick of choking on Frank's medicine. When Joey needs relief from the guilt and from his enormous responsibility he hops a bus to Coney Island, rides every ride, eats enough hot dogs and *knishes* to hibernate all winter, then he washes it all down with celery soda.

Prohibition ends when Franklin D. Roosevelt moves into the White House in 1933. Now Frank's gin isn't bringing in the cash it used to. He has so many mouths to feed he can't just wait around for the New Deal to kick in. Since jobs are scarce, he invents new business schemes for his children. To show them the ropes, Frank puts them on the subway, lines them up in the seats and watches them like a hawk as they head downtown. They're not allowed to make a peep. If they do, he'll hand their heads to them when he gets them home. He's like an elephant. He never forgets. When he tells Joey he's getting a lickin', Joey knows it's coming, even if it's a whole day later. To remain quiet and still, Joey pretends he's the Lincoln Monument until the train reaches its destination, relieving him of his agonizing stillness. He and his siblings rise and exit the train, quietly and dutifully following Frank up the stairs. As they spill out of the subway and onto the city sidewalk, a band of Gypsies are making their way through the streets. Frank pays no mind to their colorful presence and loud music. His sights are set on putting his kids to work, so he isn't aware of the Gypsy woman snatching up his youngest daughter and loading her onto a wagon like a bag of groceries. But the Low kids notice.

"The Gypsies took Helen!" they scream.

Frank runs after the Gypsy caravan. "Yuns got-dem sons-a-bitches. Yuns pisses-a-shit!   Give herrr back, yuns scrrrewy bastarrrds!" he howls as he dashes through the street.

The traffic and changing lights slow their getaway, making it possible for Frank to catch up with them on foot. He scrambles onto one of the wagons, still swearing, and when the Gypsies realize the madman isn't backing down, they let Helen go.

If this is life's way of forcing Frank to stop and think, it doesn't work. He only sees what's in the spotlight—anything outside of the light doesn't count. It's business as usual. He sends his girls out to buy candy and resell it in the subway—without a permit. When the cops approach their traveling candy store, the girls scatter in a fright. The cops nab Anna, and a photographer snaps her picture and slaps it on the front page of the newspaper. Anna symbolizes the millions of needy cases across America, and because of the article, local charities take pity on the Lows. Clothes and food arrive at their doorstep, and the Low kids get to enjoy a couple of weeks at summer camp sponsored by the Fresh Air Fund.

****

Frank is Joey's primary physician and dentist. When Joey has a rotten tooth, Frank ties a string from his tooth to a doorknob, then slams the door. When the tooth is a molar, Frank grabs his pliers and yanks it out mercilessly, leaving Joey seeing stars for hours.

When Joey's infested with lice, Frank puts on the barber's hat and shaves "everrry got-dem hairrr off his head."

And when Joey's appetite becomes insatiable, Frank figures out that "he's eating forrr two—himself and da got-dem tapeworrrm."

Once again, he puts on his doctor's hat. While Joey lies on the floor folded in half like a lawn chair, the tapeworm rears its greedy head. Frank grabs it with the same pliers he uses for yanking molars. Very slowly, Frank pulls out the slimy creature.

Many years from now, when Joey is an old man, I will ask him, "How long was the tapeworm, Dad?"

He'll wince, then spread his arms the way he did when he bragged about the biggest bluefish he ever caught.

Joey turns eight in 1936, which means it's time for him to shine some shoes. His older brothers, Johnny and Frankie, are already out on the streets shining shoes and bringing Frank the profits. Frankie takes Joey out to the streets to teach him about territory. It has a language of its own—your fist is your deed. With the Depression at its height, there are no vacant territories. Too many kids are on the streets trying to make a buck for their families, but that doesn't hinder a Low kid. Frankie sets up Joey in someone else's spot. The rightful owner comes by and lunges at Joey, who fights back with a vengeance. The kid is twice his size but Joey only needs a little help. Frankie, three years his senior, jumps in, and together they sweep the streets with the kid. He never comes back.

****

The days of making bathtub gin are long gone, but Frank and Rose still tip the bottle, and they continue moving around as if life is a game of musical chairs. Frank rents a rotted out house on Staten Island. No one else will rent it because it's haunted. But Frank isn't afraid of ghosts. It's more likely that he'll "scarrre da livingk shit outta dem." So the Lows move in and sure enough, footsteps creak across the wood floor and clatter echoes from the attic.

But Frank insists, "Derrr's no such tingk as ghosts, got-dem it!"

To prove it, he crawls under the house and finds a huge snake's nest. They're hitting their heads on the floorboards, hence the footsteps. The overhead sounds are squirrels in the attic. It's infested, but the cost of renting was a bargain until Frank is forced to endure the constant shrieking of his frightened daughters. When he hires them out as maids to rich families, they're glad to go—until they learn that their employers are sending their paychecks directly to Frank.

The money the kids are bringing in isn't enough, so he finds a way to stretch the cash. For pennies on the dollar, Frank acquires some counterfeit money, and with a week's worth of his daughters' salaries, he buys "an old piss-a-shit" as a get-away car.

"If it rrruns," he declares, "who gives a got-dem what da hell it looks like?"

Since Rose is pregnant with her ninth child, Frank's got a perfect front. He makes his outings in the old jalopy a family affair. He's the getaway driver, Rose sits up front with the cash, and Joey and Helen sit in the back. If the cops stop Frank, they won't suspect a thing.

Frank pulls up to a store, Rose runs in, buys a cheap item, pays with a counterfeit ten, grabs the change, runs back to the car, and Frank speeds off. They get away with their antics for a while, but soon word gets out that the Feds are looking for a pregnant lady shopping with funny money. Frank pays no mind. He continues his daily jaunts. But

32

during one trip Frank sees flashing lights in his rearview mirror. He races up and down the streets trying to lose his pursuers.

"Go fasterrr Frrrank!" Rose yells, "Step on da gas!"

She leans into the back seat and stuffs the counterfeit money under Joey's shirt.

"Keep goingk Frrrank!"

The cops don't let up. And when Frank realizes there's no escaping, he pulls over, rolls down his window and innocently asks, "How can I help yuns, officerrr?"

Officer Jones demands to see Frank's license and orders everyone out of the car. Rose and Frank are frisked, the "piss-a-shit" is searched, and the police find nothing—until Jones notices the odd shape of Joey's belly. He orders Joey to lift his shirt, the counterfeit money is exposed, and that's the end of Frank's new profession. Frank and Rose are arrested for possession and distribution of counterfeit bills in Port Richmond, Staten Island, on July 2, 1938. The police confiscate six phony tens and two fives. They're taken to FBI headquarters, and while they're being booked, another agent is feeding Joey and Helen peanut butter and jelly sandwiches because the kids are famished. Frank and Rose go off to jail and the kids are sent to stay with their nineteen-year-old sister, Anna.

With Frank still behind bars, Rose gets an early release to deliver her ninth child. Several days later, Frank and Rose, along with their infant daughter, Dolores, appear in a Brooklyn court and plead guilty to the charges. Rose is sentenced to two years' probation and Frank is sent to Lewisburg Federal Penitentiary in Pennsylvania for a year.

The Depression is almost over, and F.D.R's New Deal kicks in, but there's no relief for the Lows. With Frank in jail, Rose moves her family in the middle of the night to avoid paying rent and to escape the city's social workers, who constantly implore her to give up her children.

Joey goes back to shining shoes for a buck while dabbling in grown-up activities. He tried his first cigarette at age nine and now he's a full-fledged smoker. The extra money from shining shoes is a pittance, so he joins a gang. Their main goal is to make quick cash.

They steal cards, dice and anything else illegal gambling halls will buy in a dash. He has no guilt. The men who buy his merchandise know damned well they're stolen goods, and if they didn't buy his take, he'd have "no goddamned reason to steal it in the first place."

Joey spends his cash on booze, cigarettes, back-alley dice, and dating. He's much too young for these activities, but there's no turning back now. He takes his little girlfriends to the movies, where they raffle off toys like BB guns to reckless wise guys like Joey. Now he breaks windows, dents cars, and when folks come looking for restitution, Rose covers for him.

"My Joey doesn't own a BB gun! Some otherrr kid must've done da damage," she swears.

Joey's IQ is remarkably high and he's a speed-reader. While everyone else is stuck doing homework, he's out carousing or pursuing his little girlfriends. He falls head over heels for Harriet Lipschitz and follows her around like a stalker, even when her mother's at her side. But Mrs. Lipschitz doesn't *futz* around. One crack on Joey's head with her handbag instantly cures her problem. Joey gives up on Harriet, but he will *never* forget his first love.

His disappointment over losing Harriet is eclipsed by the news of his father's homecoming. As gruff as Frank is, Joey misses him. With only a year of probation, Frank is released from jail on August 10, 1939. By this time, Rose has moved her family to Washington Avenue in the Bronx. Frank arrives home, and when Joey's recklessness with the BB gun leaks out, Frank smashes it "into a million goddamned pieces."

No one knows what happened in jail, but Frank is suddenly terrified of the law. He tries to get legitimate work, but his resume now includes a year in Lewisburg Federal Penitentiary. Rose works at home making artificial flowers. Since her wages aren't enough to make ends meet, Frank resumes his role as family foreman.

Joey continues running with his gang, stealing and turning over merchandise. Soon, greed prompts him to hunt for bigger game—a Western Union bike. He has no luck selling it, so he brings it home. When Frank sees the bike, he panics. Stealing from Western Union is a Federal offense and Frank already had his share of medicine from the

Feds. To keep the Feds off his back, Frank devises a plan to return the bike. He has Joey follow him through the dark city streets, and when they near the precinct Frank instructs his son to put the bike on the top step, but not until Frank gives him the signal.

He crosses the street to a phone booth and shouts to his son.

"Joey! Drrrop da bike on da stoop!"

With the bike in place, Frank dials the precinct and a dispatcher answers the call.

"I'm rrreturrrningk da stolen Westerrrn Union bike," Frank tells him. "It's on yuns frrront steps."

He hangs up, pops his head out of the booth, and yells, "Rrrun Joey, rrrun!"

Joey flies home like a buzzard chasing a shit-wagon, and many years later when he's an old man, he'll tell me for the thousandth time, "Times were tough back then. I just did whatever the hell I had to do in order to survive."

As for Rose, forever the abandoned child, survival is more than food and shelter. It's keeping your family together, no matter what. But social workers show up on her doorstep yet again. As always, she shoos them away like stray cats. But this time she's so incensed, the unwanted child inside of her awakens as a mad hyena.

With her youngest children all cleaned up and in tow, she marches into New York City Mayor Fiorello LaGuardia's office as if she owns the joint.

"Dey want my kids becuz I'm poorrr? I'm neverrr givingk dem my kids! Stop sendingk dose peoples! If yuns werrre smarrrt, yuns would give derrre fatherrrs worrrk, den yuns wouldn't have to carrre forrr half da kids in da city!"

Mayor LaGuardia nods his head in agreement.

Rose drops to her knees, folds her hands as if in prayer, and pleads, "Nobody will give Frrrank worrrk. Pleees find him a job, Mayorrr. I beg yuns!"

Still staring into Rose's good blue eye, Mayor LaGuardia says, "I will. I promise."

And that's just what the mayor does. He sends Frank to a chemical company where he's hired to do menial tasks. The pay isn't great, but Frank finally has a real job and that keeps social workers off their backs for a while.

The Charmer

The Depression ends. World War II begins. The Japanese drop bombs on Pearl Harbor and Joey drops the "y" in his name. Johnny, Joe's oldest brother, enlists in the service and sends his paychecks home to Frank for the good of the family. As the war rages on, Frankie enlists in the service and *his* wages are sent home.

Joe's older sisters run off to get married—shotgun style. The rhythm method is the only legal form of birth control, but it doesn't work so it doesn't count. Young girls are doomed to marry the fathers of their unborn babies and they're expected to live happily ever after whether they like it or not. In many cases, it doesn't matter if the father of the baby is a drunk, a bum, or both. You sleep in the bed you make "until death do you part."

Joe cuts school so often, he finally quits in the tenth grade. But soon Frank has enough of his goofing off. He marches Joe down to the chemical company to complete a job application and aptitude test. Joe's results profoundly impress company executives, who immediately put him to work in the chemical lab. And when Rose remarks about her flowers not holding their shape because of the chintzy materials her company provides, Joe dips them into an array of wet compounds that he's experimenting with. He achieves success when one of his potions dries clear and remains pliable. It's the perfect solution for Rose's problem. But when her employer refuses to buy the idea, Joe puts his brainchild on the back burners. Soon afterward, he quits the job.

Joe *loves* New York City. To him it's the whole world compressed into one small package, bursting at its own seams with vibrancy and opportunity, and he's enjoying all of it. He's smart enough to go to college, to expand his God-given talents, but he never looks ahead. He wants to make fast money, the more the better—and he needs more than the average kid because he's still required to give Frank a large cut of everything he earns or finagles.

As WWII rages on, Joe, barely seventeen, resents being too young to enlist in the Army. Until he's old enough, he works hard and plays hard, he gambles, drinks, goes through novels like water on a hot summer day, and he swings to the beat of big bands. Often, his nights out end with a bang. When mixed with booze, his behavior can only be tamed with a billy club—but the cops have a bad aim. They crack Joe on the nose and break it.

"It serrrves yuns got-dem rrright," Frank spews. "Yuns arrre nothingk but a got-dem rrrebel. Next time I hope dey crrrack some sense in yuns brrrains, got-dem-it!"

No matter what Frank says or does, he can't tame his son. Unlike Frankie and Johnny, Joe feels entitled to do as he pleases. He's living it up, and he'll scratch his itch to fight the Nazis and Japs with booze and whatever the hell else he wants until he finally turns eighteen.

American bombs are devastating Japan's industries, but Japan shows no signs of surrendering. July 16, 1945 the United States' top-secret Manhattan Project successfully tests the first nuclear bomb, prompting President Harry Truman's threat to use "the most terrible bomb in the history of the world." America and its allies, Britain and China, insist that Japan "surrender or face prompt and utter destruction." Japan refuses, and Truman gives the order that will forever change the world. Albert Einstein's mathematical theory is brought to life on August 6, 1945 and instantly flattens Hiroshima. Japan still doesn't bow. Three days later Truman's second order obliterates Nagasaki. Five days after that Japan surrenders and cheats Joe out of the good fight he'd been anticipating.

Joe finally turns eighteen in January 1946. The war is over but the United States still occupies Japan. Joe decides to enlist anyway. His eyesight is poor so he studies the eye chart, passes the exam, and is inducted into the Army. They send him off to Fort Dix, New Jersey, for

G.I. clothing and shots, then down to Polk, Louisiana, for basic training. Joe's Army buddies call him "Red." Red is a member of the 1st Platoon, Company A, 32nd Training Battalion. The 1st Platoon is the least compliant. They have the dirtiest rifles and are the last to fall in and the first to fall out. The sergeant dubs the brawling, heavy-drinking members of the 1st Platoon "Individuals." To teach them a thing or two, he has them do double time to the barracks, take off their shirts, return, fall into formation, fall out, do double time back to the barracks, put on their shirts, return, and fall in again—thirteen times! They learn squat. Now they're ordered to march through the grimy swamp with heavy packs weighing them down, but that's chocolate cake for guys who've hauled sacks of gin-making sugar, who've knelt on rice for hours, who've played Johnny-on-the-pony and ended up beneath a pile of twenty roughnecks. So the 1st Platoon sloppily tramps through the mucky mosquito-alligator-snake-infested swamp, while their thunderous voices burst with joy in song— "and those caissons go rolling along."

From Louisiana, Private Joseph Low is shipped off to Gifu, Japan, where he distributes Army supplies to the rank and file. Like his brothers before him, his pay is sent home to Frank, but Joe quickly learns that it's just as easy to drum up extra cash in Japan as it is on the streets of New York. He ends up with more cash than he can spend, but he tries. He drinks *sake* and a shit-load of scotch, he smokes opium, and he wines and dines Japanese beauties as if he's a millionaire.

After a thirteen-month stint in the Army, Joe receives an honorable discharge. He still has a load of yen, so he decides to purchase a rare black pearl. Before departing Japan, he puts the pearl in a special box and buries it under a wooden structure on base because he has every intention of returning to Gifu to reclaim his buried treasure.

He travels home to Staten Island to reunite with his family only to learn that Frank spent all of his Army pay on chickens and pigs. Unfortunately, the pigs became diseased and all that's left are the chickens. Joe is bitter, but he puts away his resentments in an effort to move forward. He makes repairs around Frank's shithouse, he feeds chickens, and schemes up ways to earn some extra pocket change.

To supplement his side schemes, Joe takes work as a New York City cabbie, but in no time he moves from job to job until he realizes that his niche is in chemicals. When he's not working, he transforms himself into Red the Charmer and heads into Manhattan where all the action is. Besides drinking and raising hell, dancing is among his favorite activities, and he tries to fit that in every weekend.

Come Friday night Joe is at the ballroom. He looks across the dance floor and sees a trim, beautiful woman with long, dark curly hair. She's dressed exceptionally well. She can dance, too. But the dance ends before he gets the chance to skate her across the floor.

Although he tries, Joe can't get that woman off his mind. His heart does the "Beer Barrel Polka" every time he thinks of her— constantly. He hopes to run into her the following week when the ballroom hosts their special Veterans dance because he's lovesick, and he's scaring the shit out of the chickens as he dances among them dispersing their grain.

To prepare for the upcoming dance, he buys a new suit and spit-shines his shoes. When Friday rolls around he bathes in the silver bucket, adorns himself with a few dabs of aftershave, shimmies into his suit, and he's out the door, off to Manhattan.

He slips in line in front of a woman—the one who stole his heart. She doesn't know she's a love-thief. She begins to laugh, then taps him on the shoulder.

Joe turns around, and Lil looks up to see a handsome redhead. His blue-gray eyes appear larger behind his dark, thick-rimmed glasses. He's five-foot-ten, a solid mass of a hundred and seventy pounds, strong and steady, but too weak to prevent his heart from doing the polka.

By the time the line moves into the ballroom, Joe Low and Lillian Kartalian know each other's names. Joe charms Lil into dancing every dance, and thus begins a new-fangled chapter in his life —brimming with Armenians, *pilaf* and *shish kabob*.

Walking on the Floor of Hell

It isn't easy for Armenians to live peacefully under the reign of the Ottoman Empire, yet Charles Kartalian and Mary Janazian give happiness a shot. They marry and have two sons. John, their first, appears in 1887. He will someday be my mother's father.

Armenians are forced to pay unjust taxes, but when they press for political reform between 1894 and 1896, Sultan Abdul Hamid II responds by slaughtering thousands of them. In 1913 a group of men hailed as the Young Turks oust the sultan, overthrow the government, then go on to reveal their pompous plan to expand the borders of the Ottoman Empire eastward to Central Asia, and to unite their people with one language and one religion: Turkish-Muslim.

When all eyes become focused on World War I, the Ottomans seize the diversion as an opportunity to implement their deportation order. Their interpretation of the order results in the torture and death of Armenian professionals from Constantinople (present-day Istanbul) on April 24, 1915. Before long, Armenians from rural villages are forced to relocate. They form caravans and proceed toward the desert, only to be attacked by Kurdish bandits and hardened criminals known as the Turks' Special Organization. They've been ordered to do as they please with the infidels. They command some to march nude in the hot sun, many are beaten and tortured, and babies are cut from their mothers' wombs, beheaded and flung onto rocks. Women are raped, forced into harems, and tattooed. Eyewitnesses report "the Euphrates River is red with Armenian blood." By 1918 up to 1.5 million Armenians perish. The few survivors are grief-stricken and haunted, yet sturdy, and defiantly, they will recover and multiply.

When John Kartalian's village is raided, the men are separated from women and children before being ordered to march toward the desert. Without food, water or shelter from the sun, John's wife and children, along with his brother's family, succumb to the torture and die. Among the dead is a little girl, John's daughter, Armenouhe. Many years from now John will name another daughter after her—my mother.

The countryside is littered with corpses and body parts: legs, heads, arms, all decomposing in the hot sun. The chance to flee arises, but in order to escape the same fate, John, his brother Harry, and their cousin Peter, must walk among the wickedness on the floor of hell. Dehydrated, emaciated, and laden with grief, they head for the home of a Turkish friend without knowing what to expect. They could be turned away, or turned in. Yet without question, the Turkish-Muslim woman takes them in, feeds them, and hatches a clandestine plan for their escape, even though she risks being hanged and burned for doing so.

She learns of a ship in port in need of bakers and sends the trio down there under cover of darkness. The Kartalians are hired. They board immediately, leaving behind the ashes of their stolen wives and children, and the chance to bid farewell to their valiant savior.

The Kartalians go to work baking, and with practice, they become skilled at their new profession.

They end up in Detroit, Michigan, where John opens a bakery. He does well, but loneliness prompts him to advertise for a wife within the Armenian-American community. He receives an encouraging response, wires the stranger her fare, and awaits the arrival of his new bride-to-be.

In the Eye of the Storm

The German Consulate in Constantinople put George Hanlian in charge of the German Kawassen Turkischen Military Police. Concurrently, the German Embassy engages him as their interpreter for his fluency in Armenian, Greek, French, German, Turkish and English. George also owns a candy store because he loves chocolate.

Despite the hostility against Armenians and Greeks in Constantinople, George and his fiancée, Christina Christoulidi, marry and bring two daughters into the world. Vartonoush, their second, born in 1899, will someday be my grandma, Yaya.

The Hanlian girls bud amid their ominous setting, yet prior to full bloom, George sends Vartonoush to a French School and Convent where she studies to be a seamstress. Her sister Alice is sent to the Academy of Paris in France to become a corsetiere, and when the 1915 deportation order is given, both girls are safe "in the eye of the storm."

They return home in 1917 to join their mother on a long-awaited trip to the countryside for a visit with extended family. As an aristocrat, Vartonoush is accustomed to using linens, china, and silverware. She detests the sight of her relatives, crowding around a community pot while eating with dirt-stained hands.

Because of his obligations at the embassy, George couldn't make the family trip—a disappointing circumstance, but a fate that will save the Hanlian bloodline. At the embassy a German friend tells George that the Turks are about to cut off and raid the area his family is visiting. George can't leave his post so he sends a confidant, who retrieves them just in time. Once again, Vartonoush is spared from having to witness anything worse than her relatives' eating rituals.

WWI finally ends in 1918, and simultaneously, the bankrupt Ottoman Empire crumbles like a stale cookie. But hostility toward Armenians prevails. George and Christina make the difficult decision to send their daughters off to Piraeus, Greece, to board the Patris, a ship bound for America.

The girls purchase second-class fares, but end up below deck, like canned sardines, encased in a stench of vomit and feces. This won't do for the Hanlian sisters. They return to the captain to request an upgrade. Noting the girls' poise and grace, the captain obliges, and up they go, to first class, where clean air and blue skies are dripping with music and where people are dancing their way to America.

As the voyage nears its end, the music is replaced with hallowed silence when the sight of a green-tarnished lady rises from between the sea and the sky. Triumphantly holding up her torch, she lights their way to the golden door. The long, still moment is broken with joyful sobbing as some fall to their knees, clenching their fists, exclaiming, "I'm alive! I made it!"

No one denounces God for the unspeakable atrocities they endured. They thank Him aloud, and in a multitude of foreign accents "America, America" resounds in waves, infusing the air with gratefulness—the kind that can only be articulated by the most wretched refuse. They fix their eyes on the statue, for if they look away, they might awaken from their dream.

The Patris arrives at Ellis Island on November 2, 1920 during a brave new era—the Roaring Twenties, a time of social and political upheaval.

Women's fashions depict the changing times. Hemlines rise to just below the knee and dresses, looser fitting than an earlier era, have fewer seams, but detailing on the garments is intricate, boasting jewels, beads and appliqué.

This fashion is no problem for Vartonoush. She's instantly employed by one of New York's top fashion designers who serve only the rich. She's paid a minimum of five dollars for each one-of-a-kind, hand-sewn dress she completes. This generous salary affords her more independence than most women have. She buys herself fine hats, shoes and handbags to match her handmade wardrobe.

She's a sharp dresser, and someday, when she's in her nineties, she'll straighten up her back, causing her colossal boobs to rise like dough from around her waist, and she'll brag.

"When I was young, I was big sport. Now I'm old—I look just like monkey!"

She may be as wrinkled as a raisin, but she is beautiful to me, and when I tell her that, she'll say, "You need glasses, my dear *kgaulaw?*"

Yaya's question will throw me into fits of laughter, because her pronunciation of girl in English means that she just called me an ass *(kolo)* in Greek. When my fit ends, I'll ask Yaya where she met her first husband, and she'll explain how she came across an ad: "Baker seeks Armenian wife."

Without delay she writes a letter of acceptance to John Kartalian telling him all about her big sporty self. To prove it, she encloses her photograph—a bust shot—and mails it to her future husband.

Depression and Abandonment

Vartonoush arrives in Detroit and is greeted by John and his brother, Harry. She's drawn to the tall, dark handsome one, but she gets John. He's short, with average looks that only fill the cup half way—but the cup is far too small for his wit and humor. After appraising John's qualities, she keeps her promise and marries him in the spring of 1921.

By 1927, with two children in tow, John moves his bakery to Niagara Falls, New York, where Vartonoush gives birth to a girl who reminds John of his stolen daughter—and without a second thought, my mother is named after her dead half-sister, Armenouhe.

It isn't long before the Kartalians move back to Detroit, where two more children are born in the wake of the Great Depression. With banks failing and businesses closing, fifteen million Americans find themselves unemployed. John's customers can no longer pay him, so he gives them bread in exchange for written promises of future payment. Never turning anyone away, he forwards the kindness of his Turkish friend who fed him at the risk of losing her life. He survived the odds, was given a second chance, a new family, a new career, and a stash of cash to fall back on. But his resilience in hard times makes him a perfect target in Detroit.

One morning, two gentlemen saunter into John's bakery just as his first batch of bread is being pulled from the oven. As they lean in to speak to John, the odor of garlic overpowers the sweet aroma of his *kata.*

"For a small weekly fee, we'll make sure no harm comes to you," the big one whispers.

A familiar feeling sickens John—Armenian Christians were forced to pay unjust taxes to the Ottomans, and in turn, were permitted to conduct their business.

"Protection from what?" John shouts. "From nothing! Get the hell out of my store and don't come back!"

They leave peacefully, just as you'd expect from a couple of gentlemen. But that night a bomb explodes in the Kartalian bakery. Before dawn, when John arrives at the bakery ready for work, he finds the storefront window shattered, and as he rummages through charred remains, the gentlemen return.

"We can get you help cleaning up this mess," the big one mutters with a smile that reveals a missing tooth. "For your own good, you should take the offer."

"Keep your offer! You're animals!" John spits. "Now get the hell out!"

John isn't going to sit around to see what happens next. To protect his family from the clutches of greed and insanity, he packs them up and moves to New York City.

There he opens another bakery, but soon, more and more folks are signing for their bread. Eventually, all the fresh bread goes to the needy and only the stale bread is brought home to his growing family. Cash flow comes to a halt soon after Vartonoush gives birth to her sixth child. In short order the Kartalians are evicted from their apartment. All of their belongings are thrown onto 29th Street, leaving eight people homeless.

By the time John procures a new apartment on 28th Street, Armenouhe is five. She speaks Armenian and Greek, intermingling the languages, along with some Turkish words, just as her mother does. Prior to attending New York City's public schools, she's sent to Armenian school to learn to read and write Armenian—but she'd rather be playing ball. She's so athletic she can outrun everyone in her age group, and someday, she will outrun the wind.

Finding extra money for material is difficult in the 1930s, so Vartonoush takes flour sacks from the bakery, bleaches them and turns them into respectable blouses and shirts. She's so meticulous when it comes to the appearance of her children and the cleanliness of her home, cockroaches think twice before they enter.

John works long grueling hours at the bakery, and when Armenouhe comes home from school, he's often asleep because he awakens early every day to begin baking bread. On Saturdays, to squeeze in some family time, Vartonoush takes her children to the bakery to visit John. From there, he joins them for lunch in the park. Armenouhe, or Arms, as her family calls her, loves her father's optimism. Together she and her father brag of how rich they are because of all the dough John makes—and their laughing eyes offer no signs of Depression.

John's heart is bigger than any pile of troubles life has in store for him. When George Ehmalian, a survivor of the Armenian Genocide, approaches him looking for work, John gives him a job. George is tall, strong and fit. He has a good work ethic, but he's an embittered man who incessantly curses the Turks. John tries to reason with George about his negativity, but it's futile. Except for one brother, George lost his entire family in the genocide so he's not about to relinquish his right to be angry. George's constant piercing convictions prompt others to dub him "the Baron." Now, when the Baron goes overboard, no one argues. Their silence, misconstrued as agreement, muffles him sooner than admonishment.

Summer arrives and the Church of the Incarnation in Manhattan sends Arms and her siblings to Incarnation Camp in Ivoryton, Connecticut, where they get to swim in a lake instead of the street in a puddle from a gushing fire hydrant. Arms loves every minute of it, but like the other children, she's homesick. Father Farringer, the Episcopal priest who oversees camp, knows all the children by name, but there are so many, it's impossible to comfort them individually. To overcome this obstacle, every night as the children hop into bed, he pours his wise old soul into the ivory keyboard, and out it floats, on a loving lilt, comforting dozens of young souls all at once. Like his other recitals, he always ends with his favorite song, "Danny Boy." And the children sleep.

Weather-wise, the next morning is a perfect 1935 summer day. Arms plays on the swings, pumping her legs to and fro, holding her face up to the warm sun, in a backdrop of irises and a chorus of birds —until her serenity is interrupted by a faint sound, growing louder.

"Your father's deh-ed!" a boy gleefully sings over and again.

"He is not dead!" she shouts back.

"He is too-ooo, he is too-ooo," the boy sings merrily.

She refuses to believe him. Nobody called for her. No one sent word to her. *He can't be dead.* It's too much to ponder. So she fills her head with "Danny Boy."

When summer ends, she travels home, steps off the train, looks up and sees her mother draped in black, standing next to the Baron, her father's employee—the grouchy one who hates Turks. He's holding her three-year-old sister, Louise! This sight burns into her core. She runs to Vartonoush anticipating an explanation—but her mother says nothing. She isn't told that high blood pressure stole her father's last breath at the age of forty-eight, or that it happened on a city sidewalk on his way home from the bakery. She isn't told of his perseverance, of his faith and courage. But no one has to tell her of his kindness, of his grateful attitude, his cheerful nature. His absence is agonizing, yet she refuses to become cynical like the Baron. Instead, she buries her pain —the same way a treasure is buried—out of sight, but never really out of mind.

Arms returns to school to begin third grade. She doesn't take kindly to teachers because in addition to mangling her name, they repeatedly whacked her hands for being a southpaw. She's finally ambidextrous, but she still has the same name. As her teacher reads names from a list, getting alphabetically closer to hers, Armenouhe Kartalian squirms. When her new teacher reaches the Ks, she pauses, then motions Arms to step up to her desk. Expecting the worst, Arms approaches her teacher who leans in and whispers, "What's your name, honey?"

Arms doesn't tell her the translation because people will call her *I-am-Armenian* or *To-be-Armenian.* That would be worse than butchering Armenouhe. She likes the name Lillian. She first learned of it when she saw it on her birth certificate—that was the registrar's name.

"Lillian," she says proudly.

Without question, her teacher crosses out Armenouhe and writes in Lillian. Now she can go out into the world with a normal name. Only her sisters will call her Arms—a perfect nickname for a girl who can throw a ball farther and faster than any boy.

School is better this year, but at home life is different. The Baron is *always* there. To avoid him, Lillian drops off her books after school, then she zooms out the door to play. One day, a friend of her father's from the bakery introduces her to a new game—flipping nickels for keeps. He gives Lillian her first nickel and teaches her to flip it by making a fist with her thumb facing up, and laying the nickel flat on her thumbnail. She takes the nickel home and practices until her muscle-memory takes over. Now she calls a flip so often, her father's friend loses at his own game.

Many years from now, when she tells me about her grown-up friend, I will say, "You must've won a lot of money, Mommy."

She'll say, "No."

"Why not?"

"Because," she'll tell me, "he lost his head."

"Did he go crazy?"

"No," she'll laugh, "he was on a train. He opened a window, stuck out his head to see the view, hit it on a post, and severed it."

To mask her woe she'll jokingly add, "I guess he wasn't the *head* of his class."

That's how she deals with pain. It's what you do when your flipping partner disappears, when your dad dies, when food is scarce, when the Baron comes to breakfast too often, insisting that you should hate the Turks—and you think the devil himself meandered in from Hell's Kitchen just to taunt you. You laugh. You don't hate Turks at all. The only thing you really hate is *hate*. And you're so tired of *hate* that you wish the Turks had finished off the Baron, too.

Shortly, the Baron becomes a fixture in the Kartalian household. He's like a big piece of furniture in a tiny room. So when the Baron storms out the door amid an argument with Vartonoush, Lillian and her sister, Louise, lock the door and wedge a chair under the doorknob.

"If he comes back, he won't be able to get in and that oughta fix him good," Lillian says as she and Louise split in a fit of giggles.

When Vartonoush hears him pounding on the door in the middle of the night, to the children's dismay, she lets him in.

Vartonoush can barely support her family, and the Baron offers little financial help, so she applies for public assistance. When given her options, she chooses to send her children to a social service agency in Yonkers, New York. Buck and Mary are too old so they get to stay home. But Lillian, her sisters Chris and Louise, and her brother, George, are sent off to Leake and Watts. The name sounds nice, but to Lillian, it's an orphanage. She bunks with numerous other children, some parentless, some from single-parent homes, and most, dirt-poor like she is. Her siblings bunk in different quarters, but during the day, she makes herself available to fend off hardhearted kids who quickly learn that messing with Lillian's younger sisters might buy them a left hook.

At the end of the school year Lillian reunites with all of her siblings at camp, where they remain all summer. Come September, Lillian, Chris, Louise and George head back to Leake and Watts. They forget what home is.

When Vartonoush marries the Baron, they set up house on 333 Third Avenue at 25th Street. Lillian, now sixteen, is sent home to live with them. She's so thin she can run through raindrops without getting wet, save her feet, because her shoes are Swiss cheese. Cardboard doesn't prevent water, sand or stones from creeping in, so she swallows her pride and asks the Baron for five dollars for a pair of leather shoes.

"No," he spits.

She glances toward her mother who shrugs her shoulders.

"What can I do?" she says. "He's the boss."

Lillian scoots out the door teary-eyed, yet determined. She takes a job in a bobby pin factory, slipping pins onto cardboard holders. She's so quick, she earns more money than most of the other factory workers, as they are all paid by the piece. With that, she buys her own shoes and material, makes her own dresses and coats, and she never asks her mother or the Baron for anything again.

Without notice, Louise is prematurely sent home from Leake and Watts; and shortly afterwards, Vartonoush announces she's going to California with the Baron for a couple of weeks—but weeks turn into years. While away, they fail to send home money for food or rent. To keep from being dispossessed, Lillian and Mary split the living expenses, and because Louise is so young, Lillian assumes the role of mother.

After high school graduation, Lillian takes a job with the Federal Reserve Bank and she begins to enjoy the single life. On Friday nights, she and her best friend, Olga, put on their finest attire and head out to dance halls where everyone is doing the peabody, foxtrot and swing.

They arrive early for a special Veterans Dance and take their place in line. A tall good-looking fellow cuts in front of Lillian—she lets him. Now she can't take her eyes off the price tags hanging from his sleeve.

She chuckles and taps him on the shoulder.

"Excuse me," she says. "You forgot to take the price tags off your suit."

As she helps him remove the tags, her heart flips like a nickel. Her ankle-strapped wedge heels make her appear taller than five-foot-four. She's perfect in every way, so when her dark radiant eyes gaze up at the redhead, he turns into a bowl of *kapusta*.

The ballroom doors open and music spills into the night. Bing Crosby's hit song, "It's Been a Long Long Time," invites Joe Low and Lillian Kartalian onto the dance floor—and their first dance never ends.

PART THREE: THE ARMS THAT MADE ME STRONG

Starting Over Seven Times

The pews in Saint Peter and Paul's Church in Manhattan are filled with Russians, Poles, Greeks and Armenians who witness Joseph Low and Lillian Kartalian exchange vows. Their lines are identical except for two tiny words—the bride must promise "to obey." She does, they kiss, and the crowd follows the newlyweds outside into the freeze-your-butt-off chill of January 1949 to throw raw frozen rice at them, then follow them down to the banquet hall for food, dancing and a whole lot of drinking. Everyone dances the polka, and they drink a lot of booze because those things go together like peanut butter and jelly.

As if it isn't cold enough in the city, they head north to Niagara Falls, where you risk freezing off more than just your *dupah*. Dad teaches Mom how to smoke cigarettes because that's what all the glamorous people do. They eat at the finest restaurants, tour the falls, do what honeymooners do, and when they're broke, they drive back to Staten Island to Grandma and Grandpa Low's house just off Victory Boulevard. Dad turns up a dusty trail, which he calls Tobacco Road, and into a dirt driveway. They grab their suitcases, then Dad carries Mom over the rickety threshold into his mother's kitchen.

Most of Dad's siblings are grown and living on their own, but there are always lots of people in the Low house, lots of noise and commotion. The kitchen has running water and a round tin bucket for bathing. There's an outhouse in the backyard, but if you're a man it's easier to open a window and aim for the great outdoors.

When Dad's hungry he isn't going to eat any "Greek-Armenian shit." He insists Mom learn to cook Grandma Low's Russian-Polish delicacies, so between working at the Federal Reserve and traveling back and forth to Manhattan, Mom begins her schooling in the fine art of Grandma's cuisine. She watches her mother-in-law carefully—it's the only way to learn. There are no formal measurements in Grandma's recipes. It's a pinch of this, a handful of that, two mugs of liquid, but if your mugs are smaller than mine, you might need three. Mom passes the Russian-Polish cooking test.

Now it's time to make a baby. But that's not easy when you have a tiny bedroom with thin walls and nosey people on the other side of them. It's not easy when you have pride and shame, but others don't seem to worry about strange noises that permeate through the house. It's nature. Who cares? You shouldn't be ashamed of nature.

Mom and Dad try repeatedly with no luck—no baby on the way. People around them are making babies as if they're coming off General Motors' assembly line. Fertility abounds in the Low family but not for Joe and Lil. Dad wants a son—in a bad way. It must be Mom's fault there's no baby.

"Go to the doctor," Dad orders Mom. "Get some answers!"

She does, but the doctor says there's nothing wrong with her. They try again, and although they've been trying for only a few months, Dad becomes disenchanted only because it doesn't occur to him that he's having more sex than a gigolo. He sends Mom back to the doctor because the infertility couldn't possibly be coming from the Low family.

The doctor tells her, "Your womb is made for making babies."

Dad tries again, and again.

In the midst of their dilemma Dad's parents buy a piece of property in Old Bridge, New Jersey, right next door to their friends, the Marchucks. Dad's going to help Grandpa Low build three houses on the land. This leaves him with time to decide whether or not he wants to follow them or remain in Staten Island.

His sister, Anna, lives up the road, and although Dad doesn't like the ambiance of the neighborhood, if he stays, he'll still be close to family. So he rents a house on the other end of Tobacco Road. It's really Wild Avenue, but if you call it that, people might think it was named after the Lows.

It isn't much trouble moving their meager belongings half a block. They do it on foot the way Dad did it in the old days. It's a pretty good house; even the pet-sized cockroaches think so. Now Mom and Dad finally have some privacy to try their luck at making the son Dad wants.

Since Mom still isn't pregnant, Dad goes to the doctor even though he thinks this is all Mom's fault.

"Your sperm count is *low,* Joe Low," the doctor chuckles.

Then he tells Dad to stop wearing such tight underwear. He does, and they get pregnant. Now Mom quits her job at the Federal Reserve because that's what women do when they're starting a family. She cleans house, cooks Russian-Polish food, chases cockroaches and waits for Dad to come home from work. Until now, she hadn't noticed how often Dad stops off to have a few too many drinks with Uncle Johnny and Uncle Frankie. *He's just celebrating,* she tells herself. She's pregnant and he's going to have the son he always wanted.

Dad hates his job at the chemical plant. He quits and finds another that offers more opportunities. He gives Mom just enough money to pay for the rent, utilities and food, and he keeps the rest of his cash in his pocket because that's what real men do. Mom sits at home because she's pregnant. She manages to scrape by while Dad continues to come and go as he pleases. Dad, the man's man, spends all his extra cash on booze and fun stuff. He's mostly absent because he's got a full-time job, an "on-the-side" scheme; he goes fishing, hunting, drinking, and any extra time he has now is devoted to building houses on the Low property.

Grandpa Low is low on cash, but that's okay—Dad abounds with ingenuity. In the middle of the night, Dad steals lumber, nails and shingles from a construction site—enough to build three houses on the Low property. But he's not a smart thief; after going through all the trouble of robbing the building materials, he forgets to swipe a level and all three houses end up crooked.

The time is getting closer for Mom. Amid the baby boom she goes into the hospital and delivers a baby girl. If it were a boy, he would've been Dad's namesake.

Mom names her daughter after Queen Elizabeth, but when I come along, I will call her Sis. Sis has Dad's freckles and red hair, and with her cute round face she looks just like a little Russian doll.

Dad isn't very religious but he insists his children be raised in the Russian Orthodox Church. That's where Sis is christened. There's a celebration with lots of food, booze and dancing. The relatives come bearing gifts of cash and bonds to be saved for Sis's future, but Mommy doesn't have enough money to pay the bills, so little by little she spends Sis's gift money and cashes in the bonds.

Dad doesn't have time to help with the baby. He doesn't change her diapers, he never gets up with her in the middle of the night, he doesn't walk the floors with her when she's sick, and he doesn't feed her. Mom does it all because "that's women's work." Dad sticks with working outside the home and fun stuff. Mommy tries to be a really good mother. She makes clothes for Sis, she sings to her, and reads to her. Sis soaks up everything and before she's two she can speak clearly and she's potty trained.

When it's time to go to a family affair, Dad is the proud husband and father. He adores the image his fine family portrays. Sis looks so cute in the pretty dresses Mom makes for her and although she's young, it's clear she's smart. Dad admires intelligence. She's a reflection of him and he feels complimented.

Mommy gets pregnant again. This time Dad will surely have a son. But with another baby on the way, he becomes frustrated with work. He quits his job and looks for a better one. He needs to relieve the stress, so he goes to a bar and gets drunk because that's how men are supposed to relieve tension—and they have every right to—they're the breadwinners. He comes home drunk late at night and pushes Mommy around while accusing her of cheating on him, being a terrible mother, an awful cook. He grabs a tomato from the kitchen table, goes into the bathroom, looks in the mirror, and squishes the tomato all over his reflection. When he runs out of steam, he goes to bed to sleep off the booze.

Tomato juice drips from the bathroom mirror onto the faucet. A giant clump of smashed tomato sits in the middle of the sink. Seeds and bits of tomato are scattered around the sink, the floor, and on the toilet.

Mommy cleans it up while Dad snores.

In no time Dad finds a better paying job, and since he's still earning some "on-the-side" cash, he wants to move to a nicer house. Mommy does the packing, being very careful not to bring along any pet roaches. She anticipates having a fresh start in East Brunswick, while Dad looks forward to being closer to his family.

The weekend drinking expeditions Dad has with his brothers become burdensome. Aunt Lena is able to reel in Uncle Frankie, and Aunt Millie puts a stop to Uncle Johnny's excursions, but Mom isn't so successful with Dad, the rowdy *individual* from the 1st Platoon.

Dad's happiness is intermittent. He has periods when he's fun to be around, interesting to talk with and reasonable. Times like these give Mom hope, but soon Dad becomes frustrated and goes overboard on the booze again. During his bad spurts he tells Mom it's *her* fault he's miserable. Then he accuses her of infidelity—it doesn't seem to matter that she's almost nine months pregnant.

August 1953 rolls in and Dad awaits the arrival of his son. Instead, I burst into the world. Mommy names me after Catherine the Great of Russia. I'm not Russian-Polish looking at all, I'm darker— like Mommy. My christening in the Russian Church is followed by another party with lots of booze. Relatives come bearing cash and bonds for my future, but in short order, Mommy uses the bonds and cash for bills and food, just as she did with Sis's money.

Mommy's busier than before. Although I sleep a lot, she's got diapers to wash by hand and bottles to sterilize. Sis is almost three and needs lots of attention, but I steal away half of her time and the only routine she's ever known changes for good.

While Mommy's busy cleaning and cooking, Dad sticks to manly things—working and drinking. He comes home soused and swears, "You're cheating on me, Lil!"

"You need your head examined," Mommy winces. "What the hell are you, crazy?"

"I'll give you crazy!" he yells. Now he's on another tirade, scaring the hell out of her.

By the next day Dad's sorry for acting like an ass. As always, he'll make up for it. He wants to take Mommy and Sis on vacation to Florida and leave me behind with his mother.

"It wouldn't be fun if we brought along a crying baby," Dad insists.

"But your mother tips the bottle with the Marchucks every day. She gets so shit-faced I'm afraid she might drop Cathy on her head."

"She'll be fine, Lil. Don't worry so goddamned much. Let's just go and have some fun!"

So off they go. A week later they return, all tanned and happy. When Mommy notices the empty vodka bottles she feels compelled to inspect me from head to toe. Obviously Grandma hadn't bothered to wash me, my bottle, or much of anything else, but that's okay because she didn't drop me on my head.

****

It's time to move again. Mommy packs up our belongings, Dad borrows a truck, loads it up, and off we go to an apartment in Newark, New Jersey. Sis is only four years old and will miss the deadline to make it into kindergarten because she won't turn five until December —but she's certainly ready for school. She can read, hop on one foot, skip, and when Mommy and Dad tell others how smart and coordinated she is, they have her doing acrobatics of the mind and body. Come September, they'll start her off in a private school in Newark, and when she turns five, they'll move her into the public school system.

After the move Dad acts like an ass again, so it's time for another fine vacation. Mommy and Dad drop me off in Manhattan with Yaya and the Baron, then they head down to Florida with Sis. By the time they return, I'm squeaky clean, and I learn a new word—Turk. Dad doesn't care about my new word—he's annoyed because he's tapped out, but Mommy's the one who has to become a magician in order to stretch her grocery money.

The minute she gets caught up with the bills, Dad wants to move again, so we head out of Newark about thirty miles south to

Laurence Harbor, where Dad finds a house for six hundred dollars. Not a bad deal in 1955. I don't think it's really a house. It's not much bigger than a garage. I sleep in a tiny space that connects one room to another. It could be a closet, because when I look up, I see a few dresses hanging above my head.

Mommy's pregnant again. This time she's sure to give Dad the son he deserves—but out pops another girl. They name her Jane—clean and pure as the snow on the mountaintops. Jane's coloring favors Mommy's side of the family, but the Low and Kartalian genes blend in such an unusual way that her hair isn't quite brown, and it isn't quite red. It's mahogany and it dances in the sunlight like red wine as it's being poured from an urn.

Two little girls live next door to us in Laurence Harbor: Nancy and Diane. Sis plays with them outside and I stay in the house watching them through the window. I follow Mommy around while she sings, "Bye Bye Blackbird." She belts out the words as though she's telling us how she feels. She croons while she cooks, cleans, when she mends our clothes, and when she bathes my baby sister. Even though Jane never looks dirty, she gets a bath every day. I can't wait for her to start walking, because I'm lonely. I want to play with her.

I'm slower than the average child. It takes a long time to potty train me, but when I finally figure it out, I learn that making cocky in a potty is a cause for celebration. When you make cocky, your Mommy jumps up and down and shouts, "Yay!" I don't talk a lot, but I can yell "Yay" with Mommy. It's so much fun, I run back to the potty several times a day trying to manufacture another reason to rejoice.

I want to hug and kiss everyone all the time. When we're out for the day, I go up to strangers and kiss them—whichever part of them comes level to my mouth. That's dangerous, especially when you kiss a man from the front or the back, which I do, and that causes strange men to yell "Hey!" and "Oh my!" and "What the hell are you doing?"

Mommy's face turns as red as a pomegranate. She tells me I shouldn't be kissing and hugging everyone in the world. I'm trying not to, but it's difficult because I just love everyone.

Mommy says I walk as if I'm dancing. I dance everywhere I go. And now that I know a few words I sing them instead of saying them. I also make loud noises, but that's construed as being slow—as in dumb. I think lots of thoughts, but I don't have enough words to describe the jumble of pictures in my head. I know what I want and how I feel, but everything I know is stuck somewhere between my brain and my mouth, like a dime in the crack of a sidewalk.

I hardly know my dad. He leaves the house before I wake up, and most of the time he doesn't get home until after I'm asleep. Once in a while I get to show him how clean I am after I take my bath.

"Oh, how nice and clean you are," he says. "Now give me a kissie and go to bed."

I kiss him only because he says it's okay. I know not to try to hug or kiss him unless he says I can. Sometimes, throughout the day Dad comes and goes like the wind in an open window. On Sundays he stays home and sits in front of his black and white television while I change the channels for him. Once in a while, if I sit real still without making a peep, I can sit on his lap. I don't know much about him, but I know for sure that he's the king of this castle. It's Mommy's job to take off his shoes and wait on him every time he yells, "Lil, bring me coffee!" He's extra special and so is Sis. I want to play with her, but I'm not big enough yet, so I sit by the window watching her. Jane's not big enough to play with me and I'm not big enough to play with Sis. Every day I ask Mommy if I can go out and play with Sis, and every day she says the same thing.

"Soon, when you're a little bigger."

Finally the day comes when Mommy thinks I'm big enough. I'm so excited, I dance and shout the same way I do after I make cocky in the potty. I run outside toward Sis and the girls next door. I'm so happy that my heart swells up like a cake in the oven, but when Sis sees me getting closer she shrieks.

"Run!" Sis shouts. "Don't play with her. She stinks!"

All three of them run and I run after them, but I can't catch up. It doesn't seem to matter. They keep yelling, "Stay away from us. You stink! You fart!"

I know they don't want to play with me so I stop running and collapse under a big tree. I lean up against the trunk and cry. I've never felt so sad. Within ten minutes I have the best and the worst feelings ever and I'm surprised at how intense they are. I don't have the words to explain what I'm feeling. When I can't cry anymore, I go back in the house and follow Mommy around like I do every other day. I'll just wait for Jane to get bigger. She'll play with me and I won't chase her away even if she smells worse than I do.

Dad is becoming restless again. He tells Mommy he doesn't like Laurence Harbor and he wants to move. He wants a fresh start.

"How the hell many do you need?" Mommy says, "Don't you know that wherever you go you've got to take yourself with you?"

Dad doesn't get it.

He finds a house for rent on Old Bridge Turnpike in South River. It's bigger and it's even closer to Grandma and Grandpa's property on Englishtown Road. Mommy packs us up again and waddles into our new home with Dad, Sis, Jane and me.

Soon Mommy is ready to deliver again. This time she's sure to give Dad a son. Instead, I get another baby sister, a redheaded Russian doll named Anya. I'm thrilled with Anya, because just like Jane, she'll soon be walking, and playing, and the three of us will have so much fun, we won't be able to stop laughing, even if we stink.

Jane and I are like milk and cookies. When we play we don't use too many words, we just look at each other and we know what we're going to do next. Mommy sings while she does her chores and we hold hands and dance to her music. It's a good thing we're tone deaf because Mommy sings off-key. Life is so much fun that we aren't aware of all the things we don't have. Who needs a bunch of toys and books anyway? Mommy recites poems and tells us stories about three dopey pigs and a wolf who can huff and puff and blow your junky house in. Sometimes she says, "The wolf is locked up in the house and he screams, 'Little pig let me come out,' and the little pig says, 'Not by the hair of my big ugly snout.'" When you don't have books, you can change the story as easily as you change your socks. Jane and I play from sunup to bedtime and it's so much fun, I can hardly sleep at night.

I don't want to miss anything. I want to sing, dance and celebrate making cocky. I love my life!

Dad isn't very happy. He goes out, gets drunk, starts a fight and the cops have to break it up. They crack him in the face with a billy club and now his nose is mangled. He makes an appointment with a surgeon to have it fixed, and when the bandages are removed, exposing an even uglier nose, he screams.

"Jeeeeeeeeesus Christ! The goddamned doctor butchered my nose worse than the goddamned cops did."

Every time something bad happens Dad wants a do-over. He thinks it's about time we all have another fresh start in a new house.

Mommy doesn't get to choose where we live, but she tells Dad, "You better think long and hard before you pick the next place, Joe. This is the last time I'm moving. I mean it!"

Dad thinks hard and he chooses a place just a half-mile away from Grandma and Grandpa. The house is a bargain, only ten thousand dollars, and Dad takes a loan under the GI bill so that he could own it and not have to deal with "pain-in-the-ass landlords."

It will be the seventh place Joe and Lillian Low lived in since they were married nine years earlier in 1949, the sixth place Sis lived in and the fifth place for me, and I won't turn five until the end of August.

Number seven is stuck in Dad's head. He thinks his seventh house will be lucky. He kisses Mommy, then rubs his ugly nose on hers like the Eskimos do. Now Dad is smiling as if he woke up with a horseshoe in his mouth and that makes my heart blow up like a penny-balloon and pop right out of my chest.

A Bargain from Gimbel's Basement

Dad says most of our stuff is junk. Mommy thinks it's good enough—
it just needs to be cleaned up—but Dad gets rid of the crap so we don't
have too many things to move. He takes Mommy to the appliance store
and buys her a wringer washing machine. American Express issues
credit cards in 1958, but Mommy and Dad don't have one. No one they
know has one, but if you have a good rapport with retailers, they'll let
you buy now and pay later, so they buy everything "on time" because
Dad wants to keep lots of cash in his pocket.

Next stop is a furniture store in South River. The guy who owns
the store is Jewish and his name is Irving, but Dad calls him "Oyving
the Jew." Dad likes "Oyving the Jew" because you can bargain with
him and get him to throw in some free stuff. Better yet, he'll let Dad
pay "on time" even though they've hardly been acquainted. Mommy
and Dad choose a dining room set, cheap bed frames with concrete
mattresses, and a black couch with silver sparkles. Oyving lets them
pick out some free wall hangings to go with the modern furniture, so
Dad chooses a happy face and a sad one, and he names them "Comedy
and Tragedy." Now he tells everyone he knows to "go see Oyving the
Jew because you can make such a deal with him."

Dad's buying things "on time" like a maniac, but he says not to
worry because each year he earns more money.

"Times are good," Dad exclaims. "Everyone's got a job.
Anyone can get a loan, even a dog or a cat, because nobody verifies
personal information."

Mommy thinks money burns a hole in Dad's pocket, but I
never saw him on fire. She wants to know why Dad never gives her a

raise. She says the only time she gets one is when she climbs to the top of the stairs. So Dad finally gives her a raise, but it isn't even enough to spark a little flame.

We all move into the twelve hundred square-foot mansion on Englishtown Road in Old Bridge, New Jersey. It sits on a cellar and there's nothing down there, so it's a great place for playing Old Mother Witch when it's colder than a well digger's boot outside. A breezeway connects the house to a two-car garage and it all sits on a corner lot with a view of two gas stations and a firehouse. Our backyard is a small forest, with a giant oak that's great for climbing, sitting in, praying in, and a million other things. I'm in love with that tree. Two of the other trees are chuck cherry—perfect for Mommy's homemade wine, which she uses for medicine because she's our primary care doctor. Our property is only a couple of blocks away from Duhernal Lake, so it'll be like living in a resort.

Dad wants the house to look really nice, so he hires a man to pave the front driveway, but the dirt driveway in the back can stay the way it is. Next, he gets a mason to brick the front of the house. The sides and back are left undone so our house looks special from the front, but if you look at it from any other angle, you think you're looking at a different house.

Mommy tells Dad he's spending too much money on stuff we don't need. What we really need is a swing set and a sandbox, so Dad goes out and buys a double swing set with a sliding board and a teeter-totter. He gets some wood from Grandpa for a sandbox, but it lays in the dirt until Mommy hammers it together. After that, she treks down to the lake with an empty bucket and brings it back full of beach sand. She makes so many trips she can't even count how many times she's been back and forth to the lake stealing sand.

From our backdoor you enter a mudroom, which leads into our kitchen. There's a hole in the mudroom floor and if you peek through it, you can see the dirt on the ground. That's no big deal because Dad's going to fix the hole someday. In the meantime, when you drop things like a Cracker Jack toy, it might bounce into the gap and disappear forever. The hole reminds you to watch where you're walking because one of your legs could end up down there with spiders, bugs—and maybe the devil. Next to the kitchen is our dining room and through the archway you enter our living room. A fireplace sits at one end, and on the opposite side a stairway leads up to one bathroom and three bedrooms with teeny closets. It doesn't matter that the closets are so small because we don't have much of anything to fill them. There are holes in the walls behind every door because the house has no doorstops, but Dad's going to fix them someday.

Mommy and Dad claim the largest bedroom. Sis wants a room all to herself—she refuses to sleep with me because I stink and I fart. That's true. I fart. Sometimes hardly at all, and sometimes I do it a lot. If I held in all of my farts I might explode like Mommy's pressure cooker. Once in a while I fart on purpose, especially when I'm not allowed to talk, so it's the most intelligent thing I get to say all day. Sis says she never farts. She doesn't do such disgusting things. Mommy says nothing about that, but whenever someone else tries to claim they never, ever farted in their entire life, she says, "Yeah, sure. You smell like roses."

Dad thinks Sis deserves a room of her own because she's the oldest. So Jane and I are paired as sleeping buddies, which turns out to be a lot of fun because we get to talk and laugh when Mommy sends us to bed too early as she *always* does.

After Jane and I say our prayers, I imitate Dad.

"I don't want to hear a peep out of you, Jane," I murmur in my deepest, meanest voice.

And before I can finish whispering, "Now get the hell to bed!" Jane and I are quivering like jackhammers.

The hilarity tires us out, and just as I'm drifting off, I hear strange scratching sounds, squeaking and fluttering in the walls. Something other than people is living in this house and although I'm not supposed to make a peep, I scream.

"Maaa!"

Mommy and Dad come running up the stairs to see if I got hurt, and I know Dad loves me because he ran just as fast as Mommy. When they see I'm okay, Mommy calms down, but not Dad.

"What the hell's the matter with you?" he yells. "I told you not to make a peep. Now go the hell to sleep. And you better not scream again because you might wake up the dead, goddamn it!"

I know I can't wake up the dead because once I yelled at a dead bird and it didn't even flinch. Even though I'm afraid to open my mouth, I tell Dad to listen to the wall. He's just about to have a fit, but then he hears something, too. Now Mommy and Dad put their ears up against the wall. They hear the fluttering and scratching—and they know something is very wrong.

"It can't be birds," Dad says. "What flutters at night? What the hell is small enough to fit between the sheetrock, goddamn it?"

Dad thinks for a minute.

"Jeeeeeeeesus Christ! Son-of-a-bitchin' bastard! Goddamn it!"

"Oh my God!" Mommy shouts. She runs out of the room and returns with a handful of rags. Now she's running around, stuffing rags into the holes.

Dad tells me not to worry and go to sleep. He turns off the light and goes downstairs with Mommy.

I can't sleep because Dad keeps complaining about the son-of-a-bitchin' liar who sold him the goddamned house.

"There's goddamned bats living here," he says. "If I ever see the son-of-a-bitch who tried to take me as a sucker I'll teach him a lesson he'll never forget!"

"What do you mean, he tried to? You're the sucker who bought the place," Mommy chuckles.

She always laughs when things happen that you can't do anything about.

"Stop being a wise ass, goddamn it," Dad says. "What the hell is so goddamned funny?"

Mommy can't answer because she's still laughing at *Dad's bargain from Gimbel's basement.*

"Jeeeeeeeesus Christ! Enough, already!" Dad yells.

That means there'll be no more laughing.

Mommy goes back into the kitchen—I can hear her moving pots around and putting things away. She's probably laughing silently while her whole body shakes from the inside like her washing machine. That's what she does when Dad tells her to stop laughing. She laughs in secret. I know Dad's watching television because I can hear it. I hear everything and sometimes it's enough to drive me crazy.

Just as I'm dozing off I hear a siren—a loud, piercing, never-ending siren—and it's coming from the firehouse across the street. Bats! Curses! Sirens! Now I have to try to fall asleep all over again.

In the morning I wake up in my new house, hop out of bed, run downstairs, and pause in the doorway of our kitchen. Dad's telling Mommy he's going up in the attic to see things for himself. He knows all about poisons because he works with chemicals. He's going to make a concoction and use it to kill whatever the hell is up there. Mommy runs back and forth pouring Dad's coffee, buttering his toast and cooking his eggs over-easy. Dad rips off a piece of toast, dips it in the egg yolk and says, *"Motzi."* That means *to dip* in Polish. In between bites Dad talks a mile a minute and Mommy pays attention to him as if he's her teacher. She smiles and agrees with him because he asks her questions in a way that require only a yes or no, and I never hear her say no.

Dad looks up and sees me leaning on the doorjamb. I know I'm in trouble by the look on his face, but I don't know why. He growls at me to get the hell upstairs, wash my face, brush my teeth, comb my hair, and get dressed before I come downstairs, goddamn it. He wants to know how many times he has to tell me, but I know he doesn't want an answer. If I could, I'd tell him *"This is the first time you said that, Dad. You didn't holler at me in the other house when you saw me in my pajamas."* I swiftly run and do as I'm told.

I get dressed and head downstairs as Dad is coming up with a flashlight in one hand and a broomstick in the other. He's wearing a baseball cap. This is the first time I see him in a baseball cap. He usually wears a fedora. I ask him how come he's got the cap on and he tells me it's so the bats don't stick to his head. I turn and follow him into the bathroom all the way to the back where the stairs lead to the attic. He tells me to get the hell out of here, so I do. I hear him go up the steps and open the attic trap.

"Jeeeeeeeeesus Christ!"

As he tries to get down the steps and replace the trap door, it sounds like a herd of elephants being dropped from an airplane. He shoots out of the bathroom gasping for air, drenched in sweat, with a look of fright spliced with anger.

Back in the kitchen he informs Mommy there's thousands of bats up there and they're hanging from every inch of available space, overlapping one another like roof shingles, and there are bat droppings all over the floor of the attic.

"It's goddamned disgusting. I've never seen anything like it before in my life."

He wants to try and get his money back for the house because he's been cheated, but then he remembers that he bought the house "as is" and signed legal documents.

When he calms down he says he's going to make the best of this—he'll get rid of the bats even if it kills him. Except for the bats, he thinks he has a nicer house than anyone else in the family.

"Who cares whose house is better than whose?" Mommy says.

"The reason you get nice things is to show them off," Dad argues.

"No, Joe, you get them for yourself."

Now Dad runs out and buys some poison, he mixes it up, pours it into a metal tray, opens the attic trap, slides in the poison and quickly closes the door. He figures he'll have to wait a week or so to see what happens.

When Dad's sisters and brothers come over to see our new house, he takes them on a tour and they all say, "Oh how nice!"

They drag out the words *oh* and *nice* for a long time so I think they're just kidding.

I don't have to kiss or hug the aunts and uncles on Dad's side of the family unless it's Easter or Christmas because his family doesn't do that kind of thing. When Grandma and Grandpa Low come over it's a royal honor! They have a rule that they don't visit with their children because they have too many of them. Their children have to come to them and that's that. The only time they go over to one of their children's homes is on special occasions such as christening parties and nickel-dime poker games. Dad takes them on a tour and asks them how they like this and that, and what do you think of the fireplace? Grandma smiles and Grandpa nods his head. They don't say much, but that's okay—Dad got the royal honor of their visit.

When company comes I don't hear anyone talk about the bats, but when Jane and I go outside to play we sing really loud, "We have bats, thousands and thousands of bats! Bats, bats, bats! Millions and zillions of bats…"

Until Dad pops his head out the window and yells, "Shut the hell up!"

When his head disappears, we sing our song in a whispery giggle.

****

Bright and early on Saturday morning, Dad heads out for the day. Mommy says he's gallivanting. I don't know what that means, but I know that after breakfast he visits his parents, and after that he does his "on-the-side" stuff.

Yaya and the Baron show up at our new house and now there are a million hugs and kisses going on. Mommy speaks with them in Armenian while my sisters and I line up waiting our turn to be kissed by the Baron and smothered in Yaya's boobs. The Baron kisses Mommy on the cheek, then Sis, me, Jane and Anya. Sis wipes off his kisses because she hates being kissed and she doesn't like the Baron. She says when she was two years old he made her carry a dozen eggs and when she tripped and broke them, he hollered at her. I don't know why he hollered. Maybe he never heard that you can't cry over spilled milk. And if you can't cry over that, you shouldn't cry over broken eggs, especially when you can scoop them up with a spoon, scramble them, fry them up and eat them.

Now Yaya kisses Mommy six times, and in between each kiss she says, "I love you. I see your picture on the television every day." She pronounces *television* like Maurice Chevalier. She does the same with the rest of us and adds, "I miss you all my life, and I cry for you." She says this five times and it takes fifteen minutes for the salutations to be completed.

When the hugs and kisses are over, Sis disappears. My other sisters and I follow the grown-ups into the kitchen. I wish Sis would come because she always misses all the fun.

Mommy puts on coffee and we sit around the table. Jane, Anya and I each have a lap to sit on. We have tiny nude babies that we got from the gumball machine. They're half the size of my pinky. We make them dance on the table while Yaya and the Baron sing, "Dee, dee, dee, doo, doo, dee." Yaya says she can make them dance, so we pass her the babies and she drops them into her cleavage. Her boobs always pop out at the top of her dress because they have nowhere else to go. They're bigger than cantaloupes so I have to sing half the alphabet just to reach her bra size. In Armenian we call boobs *dzidzees* and if they're big we say they're *menz*. We're allowed to say *menz dzidzees*. It's not a sin to say it in Armenian, but if you say big boobies in English, you might get into trouble. Yaya moves her shoulders up and down, side to side, and the babies in her *menz dzidzees* dance around. We laugh, but it's more like screaming and it's a good thing Dad isn't here because he would have none of this at the table. But he's not here, and Mommy lets us laugh all we want. Even the Baron cracks a smile and that's a miracle.

The babies begin to slide down and suffocate in Yaya's *menz dzidzees* so she reaches in and pulls them up. If we look away, we calm down, but when we turn to see the babies in Yaya's *dzidzees,* we laugh like a bunch of lunatics. Everyone has their mouths open so wide I can see missing teeth and lots of rotten ones. The Baron must be rich because his teeth are filled with gold. That's a good place to hide your treasure from pirates and bank robbers. Now I know what I'm going to be when I grow up—a tooth fairy.

The Baron laughed enough to last a year. He shuts his treasure chest and goes into our living room to rest. Jane, Anya and I follow him. When we dump our wooden blocks onto the floor the Baron tells us to build him a castle to live in. While we're building, something swoops down the chimney and flies out of the fireplace. It's a bat and it's supposed to be asleep because it's daytime. Uh oh! I don't think Mommy told the Baron we have bats. People wouldn't come here if they knew because they don't like creepy things, and because they don't know that the bats won't bother you if you don't bother them. They just want to sleep all day and eat bugs all night. I guess Dad's poison concoction isn't working.

The Baron flies to his feet, screaming and yelling in Armenian, calling the bat a *shev shoon*. I want to tell him that it's not a *black dog* —dogs can't fly—but I don't. He picks up a throw rug, swings it at the bat and misses. Mommy and Yaya watch him from the other side of our dining room and they're doubled over. Mommy looks like she has to pee because her legs are crossed like when she's waiting in line to use the toilet. She's laughing silently like she does when Dad's angry. Soon Mommy and Yaya are grunting and wheezing, and they just can't stop.

This is the most fun I ever had in my whole life. I hope it takes a long time for the Baron to catch the bat because it's hilarious watching him fling the throw rug at it and curse it when it can't understand a word of Armenian.

The Baron finally knocks the bat out of the air and it plops onto the floor. He kicks it into the rug, rolls it up and shoots out the front door. He throws the rug onto the walkway and jumps up and down on it, cursing at the top of his Armenian lungs. Every car going by on Englishtown Road slows down to look at the tall old man in a frenzy. Mommy says he looks like a nut, that he has rocks in his head, and I wonder how they got in there.

Now that the bat is dead, it's time for lunch. While we're eating the Baron chastises Mommy in Armenian. She just lets him holler and it doesn't bother her a bit. After he flees the kitchen Mommy tells Yaya that the Baron acts as though he's the lord of the farts and general of the toilets. Now the pair of them are giggling and slapping their thighs while the Baron fumes over the bats.

After several attempts at eliminating them, Dad finally calls an exterminator.

"If you kill the bats in their habitat," the man says, "they'll rot out all of the walls and the house will be ruined. Then you'd have to tear out more than half of the house and rebuild it. The only way to get them out is to smoke them out, but the babies might not leave."

The exterminator tries to smoke them out, but most of them hang around and live through it. His second attempt isn't any more successful so every night before we go to sleep, we listen to the scratching, squeaking and fluttering of our freeloading tenants, and the loud, piercing, never-ending siren from the firehouse across the street.

****

The excitement of the move is over and we resume our normal lives. Dad goes back to his routine, working and not coming home most nights until long after my sisters and I are asleep. Mommy has a stack of bills to pay and even I know that she stretches every penny like a rubber band. Mommy says the monthly mortgage and taxes are sixty dollars, and with the utilities and all the "on time" bills, there's nothing left for food and clothes. She doesn't buy herself anything. Dad keeps a wad of cash in his pocket because he's a man's man. He needs it for fishing, hunting and going out, and he's short on cash these days, too. He thinks Mommy gets more than enough money already. So Mommy goes to Englishtown Auction to buy fabric. She makes curtains for our new house and she's going to make school dresses for Sis and me because she's our own private seamstress. Jane and Anya will get some of the hand-me-downs, but she'll make them a few things, too. Mommy's a great bargain hunter. She finds new irregular shoes for Sis for only fifty cents. That's pretty good because the shoe store sells them for about five bucks a pair.

When school starts I'm getting Sis's black and white saddle shoes even though they're way too big for me. Until summer ends, I can keep on running around barefoot. I like being barefoot, except when I see Uncle Al. He's married to Dad's sister, Anna. Aunt Anna teaches me how to avoid bad luck by throwing salt over my shoulder, and Uncle Al always lectures me about my dirty feet. He's got a glass eye that shines like a marble and, although his other eyeball moves back and forth while he's talking, I can't help staring at the giant marble. If I poked him in that eye, he wouldn't know unless his other eyeball saw me do it. He always asks me if I washed my feet, then he tells me how I could pick up all kinds of diseases and worms through my bare feet. When he's done lecturing, he tells me to go and play and make sure that my feet are clean the next time he sees me.

****

Mommy says my birthday is around the corner, so I run to the corner and look, but I don't see it.

"No," she laughs, "soon."

When we're grocery shopping I beg Mommy for coconut cake, but she can't afford it. She's going to make one of her own and she'll make her own icing, too.

Grandpa gives Mommy three carpenter's saw horses, but he calls them Johnny-benches. I don't know why he named them after Uncle Johnny because they look like headless horses, but you can't ride them because you'll end up with splinters in your *dupah*. Grandpa also gives her a piece of plywood, some two-by-fours and cinderblocks, and Mommy turns it all into a picnic table with seats. Now my aunts and cousins come over to celebrate my fifth birthday. Mommy puts her lopsided cake in front of me and pulls out a pack of matches—she couldn't afford to buy any candles. She pulls the cover off the pack of matches, removes one match, sticks the book of matches, staple and all, right in the center of the cake, then she tells everyone to sing really fast because the matches burn down quickly. She strikes the match and lights the book in the middle of the cake, and now everyone takes in a deep breath and sings "Happy Birthday" to me in high speed. I don't have much time to make a wish but it doesn't matter. I know what it is. I blow out the matches and wish to be five years old for the rest of my life. That's my one and only wish. That's how much I love my life, everyone, and everything in it.

****

Mommy puts a kitchen chair outside the back door. She grabs a cup of water, a comb, scissors and a towel because she's our very own personal barber. My sisters and I line up, waiting our turn for a haircut. Sis goes first. Mommy trims the back of her hair, then she cuts her

74

bangs so short, they stick up like porcupine needles. Jane and I get the same haircut as Sis. My dark curly bangs stick out so much I can poke out someone's eye if I get too close to them, so I run after Sis but she doesn't want to play.

After Jane's hair is cut, I chase her, pretending that I'm going to poke her eyes out. She knows I'm kidding so she runs away pretending she's afraid of losing an eyeball. I tell her not to worry because I'll just swipe Uncle Al's glass eye when the other one isn't looking and that's when we fall to the ground and laugh until our guts turn into cream of wheat.

When Mommy's done with our haircuts, she trims her own beautiful locks. Her hair is almost black and it's long and lush, with waves that bounce like my pink rubber ball. She goes barefoot in the summer as do my sisters and I, so her shoes last for years. Mommy saved some of her wardrobe from her working days for special occasions but around the house she wears black shorts in the summer and black slacks in the winter. She has a white blouse and a pink one that she alternates from one day to the next. The only real bauble she owns is the plain gold wedding band she wears on her left hand. She doesn't wear makeup except for red lipstick, but only when she goes out. That's when she kisses me goodbye and her kiss stays on my cheek. She has thick-rimmed glasses that outline her dark brown eyes but in the dim light of the kitchen they shine like black pearls. Her eyebrows are perfectly arched and her skin is smooth and creamy like butterscotch pudding. Her body is perfectly shaped—not like an hourglass because that's not for real, but almost. She has big feet—size ten—and *menz dzidzees.* When I grow up, I probably will, too, because I take after her. She doesn't look like television mothers who wear dresses and pearls to mop their floors. She's plain, but flowers turn their heads to watch her when she passes by.

When I come along, flowers wilt. By the end of the day I'm dirtier than my sisters. Instead of a washcloth, I need a spatula to scrape off the muck.

Sis refuses to take a bath with the rest of us so she gets hers first, then I take mine with Jane and Anya. We don't have shampoo, conditioner or bubble bath, but we've got Ivory soap to wash our hair.

And since Mommy is full of ingenuity, she throws a handful of Tide laundry detergent under the shooting spout, which makes a mass of bubbles fit for a spoiled princess. She quickly washes Anya and removes her from the tub because she's too young to be left alone with Jane and me. We stay in the tub soaking in bubbles till our skin is as wrinkly as Yaya's. Mommy leaves us with a washcloth but we don't need to use it. Soaking in Tide makes dirt just disappear off your skin. It probably kills bugs, diseases, worms and mysterious growths, too, because we hardly ever get sick like the other kids in the neighborhood.

I wish Uncle Al could see my feet now—but I can't show him because he lives all the way over in Staten Island on Tobacco Road.

Jane and I fart in the tub. During our farting episode something mysterious appears. It looks like a meatball, but it's the real thing, so we scream, laugh and splash till there's water spilling all over. I swoosh the floating meatball toward Jane, and she swooshes it back at me. When it comes toward me I scream and when it ricochets, Jane screams. We laugh all we want because Dad's not home, or so we think. Now we hear heavy footsteps ascending the stairs. Our eyeballs bulge and we sit in silence as we hear a dragon breathing on the other side of the door.

"What the hell's going on in there, goddamn it? Get washed and ready for bed and shut the hell up before I give you kids a lickin'."

We're so frightened the odds of another meatball appearing are very good. We open the drain to release the water, but we leave the bubbles in the tub because there are so many you just have to wait and let them pop themselves. By morning they'll be gone.

Jane and I are off to bed, but it's too early to sleep so we look out the window because we hear other children playing in the street. At dusk we see bats shooting out like bullets from the attic grate. They fly off toward the lake to feast on bugs while their babies squeal and scratch, waiting for their mothers to return with food. Jane and I tiptoe back to our beds and lie there stiff with fright because we don't want any of Dad's medicine. We never got a lickin', but the way Dad threatens us, we know it's something to fear.

Mommy is downstairs serving Dad his dinner. He wants it hot the moment he gets home, so she keeps the oven lit and puts his dinner in to warm it, then out to keep it from drying up, then in and out again until he arrives. When Dad's done eating he watches television while Mommy washes dishes and mops her kitchen floor. We hear Dad yell, "Lil, bring me coffee!"   She does, and she takes off his shoes and makes sure he has everything he needs.

In the morning I awaken to a lion roaring.

"Jeeeeeeeeesus Christ! Goddamn it, Lil! Who shit in the tub? You let the kids shit in the tub? What the hell's the matter with you?"

I remember the meatball. I'm frightened until I see Mommy in the hallway inflating with laughter while Dad insists on knowing who shit in the tub. Dad hears Mommy burst and wants to know what's so goddamned funny. He also wants to know what the hell is the matter with her, but she doesn't answer him because what he really wants to know is, "Who shit in the tub?"

"Maybe it's your own," she shouts back.

"I'll give you my own, goddamn it!" he roars.

And that's the last word on that subject.

Mommy makes breakfast and coffee for Dad and off he goes to work. With Dad gone, she dusts the wood floors, starts her laundry, and makes a pot of hot oatmeal. We kids have to eat it whether we like it or not because that's all there'll be till lunchtime. It's never enough for me, so if anyone leaves a few specks of oatmeal behind, I lick their bowls clean.

****

On Sunday morning Dad drives Sis and me to the Russian Orthodox Church for Sunday school. I sit in the backseat with my mouth zipped while Dad sings his song about the person who's never going to be an angel.

At Sunday school, when the priest and his wife come into my class, we all stand and say, "Good morning, Father."   Then we address his wife, "Good morning, *Matushka.*"

After Father blesses us the teacher asks, "Who went to church this morning?"

Everyone raises their hands except me. The teacher marks down who went to church and I'm the only one in her book without a check. I hate her question. I wish I could raise my hand but that would be lying. Now I have to listen to a horrible story about Adam and Eve's rotten son, Cain, who kills his brother, Abel, with a rock.

If God is mad at Cain and puts a mark on his forehead, then sends him out to wander so that all the other people in the world can see the mark and know what he did to his brother—where did all the other people come from if God only made Adam and Eve?

I'm confused, so I don't pay attention to the rest of the story. I just color the picture of Cain smashing a rock on his brother's noggin. I mostly use the red crayon because blood is gushing out of Abel's head and splashing all over the place.

When Sunday school is over, I walk past all the parents who've come in to greet their children. I have to go outside and find where Dad is parked. He's sitting in his car drinking coffee, smoking cigarettes and reading the paper because he doesn't feel like going into church to bless himself "twenty-five goddamned million times!"

"It's too goddamned early in the morning for kneeling, standing and spitting at the devil."

I get in the backseat and Sis gets in the front because she's older than me. Dad starts up the engine and begins singing the angel song, and then he talks with Sis. He always forgets I'm in the back because I'm not making a peep. Children should be seen and not heard and they shouldn't speak unless they're spoken to. I listen to their conversation very carefully because someday I want to be able to talk with Dad. Sis tells Dad how she hates the oatmeal Mommy makes her eat. She's sick and tired of it and she wants something different! She goes on about all the things she hates until Dad says, "Don't you worry, I'll take care of it!"

Now she tells him about all her Girl Scout badges and all the good grades she gets in school. He thinks she's really smart and he's so proud of her.

When I'm older I'll get to go to Girl Scouts and sit in the front seat and Dad will talk with me, too. He always tells me to be patient and wait. He says I'll get my turn when I'm older.

So I wait, and wait, and if I wait any longer, I'll turn into a pumpkin.

Sunday dinner is ready at 2:00 p.m. because that's when Dad wants his meal. It's special because we eat one-pot meals all week long and Sundays are the only time Dad has dinner with us. Mommy is making roast beef with gravy, mashed potatoes, and two kinds of vegetables. She dresses our table with a cloth and sets it, and when it's time to eat, Dad sits at the head of the table because he's the king. He tells us to sit up straight, bow our heads, and clasp our hands, then he gives thanks for our food and our health and I like that he does that.

After we fill our plates Dad demonstrates how to hold the fork in our left hand and the knife in our right one. He doesn't want us looking like a bunch of heathens. He can't stand it when people hold their silverware the same way you hold onto the handlebars of a bicycle. He hates it even more when kids mess around at the table.

Now that all the rules are announced and the prayers are done, we break bread. After every two bites of food Dad marvels over the meal. He's eaten in the finest restaurants and none compares to Mommy's cooking. My sisters and I know we're not supposed to talk with our mouths full, we're not supposed to say anything stupid, nor are we supposed to laugh at the dinner table unless Dad makes a joke. But it's hard not to laugh because Dad loves the food so much he keeps saying, *"Homa, homa."*

He previously told us that *homie* means *eat* in Polish. And now that he said it more than once with a charming grin, we know we're allowed to laugh, but I can't stop laughing because I have thousands of unfinished giggles inside of me.

"That's enough, goddamn it," he tells me. "Don't you know when enough is enough? What the hell's the matter with you?"

I don't know what the hell is the matter with me, and I don't know how much *enough* is except when I pour milk and it gets too close to the rim of the cup. I'm confused. Sometimes he wants me to laugh and sometimes he doesn't. Now I'm supposed to figure out how long I'm allowed to laugh. I'm ashamed of myself for not getting it right.

After dinner Dad plops into his easy chair and tells me to change the channel on his TV, adjust the wire hanger, and after that, take off his shoes. I feel honored even though his huge feet stink up the room.

"Lil, bring me coffee!" Dad shouts like a grizzly bear.

I run into the kitchen where Mommy is humming as she stirs sugar and milk into a cup of coffee. She hands it to me and I bring it to Dad without spilling it.

"Okay," he says, "go outside and play. All you kids, go."

Anya has to stay with Mommy because she's so young, and Sis doesn't want to play, so Jane and I go outside for a long time because Dad will yell if we run in and out. Hours later we take our Tide bath and when we're clean and dressed for bed we show Dad how clean we are.

"Oh how nice and clean you are. Okay, go," he says.

We run into the kitchen because we're hungry again. Mommy's scooping out butter pecan ice cream for Dad. We're not allowed to have that because she can't afford to keep buying it. But Dad insists that she buy it for him and when he wants some, she better have some waiting in freezer because he's the czar and you don't take food from a czar.

Mommy puts her finger over her lips.

"Shhh," she says, then she gives us a teeny spoonful to taste.

We kids get a small bowl of corn flakes to fill our bellies and when we're done we lie on the living room floor and sing along with the Mouseketeers. We get to see Mommy's brother during the commercials. He's the Tarzan for Lucky Cakes.

"Maaaa! Uncle Buck's on TV!" we scream.

Mommy comes running into the living room shouting, "Don't blink!"

Even though I never tasted a Lucky Cake, I'm so excited to see Uncle Buck that Dad has to say, "Enough already."

When the show's over we have to go to bed, no ifs, ands or buts. We run over to Dad to say good night.

"Gimmie kissie," he says. "And I don't want to hear a peep out of you."

Sundays are always like that.

A White Christmas

I hope Santa brings me a pair of leotards for Christmas, and gloves and a scarf or a hat because it's colder than a polar bear's butt outside and I always turn into a cherry Popsicle hiking to and from school. But I can't tell him what I want because Dad says it's not nice to ask for things.

My Sunday school teacher at the Russian church says Christmas is in January, but Dad wants to celebrate it on December 25th like all the Catholics in his family, so I'm not supposed to pay attention to my Sunday school teacher. Dad makes his own rules and those are the ones we follow.

On Christmas Eve, while we're waiting for Dad to bring home a tree, Jane and I sprinkle sesame seeds onto Mommy's Armenian cookies, then Mommy hammers four nails into the mantle so we can hang the red stockings she made for us.

It's dark when Dad finally pulls into the driveway. He drags the tree into the house, leaving a trail of pine needles from the backdoor into the living room, but Mommy will clean them up. Dad sets the tree in its stand and ties it to the pipes that run up from the cellar so that it won't fall over. Mommy pulls out a small box of decorations and Dad tries to untangle the lights. He curses at the light cord as if it has ears.

"Jeeeeeeeeesus Christ! What a pain in the ass!"

After five minutes of curses, Mommy takes over. She quietly untangles the lights and strings them to the tree. When she's done we sing Christmas carols while we decorate and Dad watches from his easy chair. After that, Mommy gives us each a gift of identical pajamas. We need them because the ones we got last year are shredded wheat from being washed too many times. I love my new pajamas and I love that my sisters have the same ones. It's like being in a pajama club and that's the best feeling because when you belong to a club, it makes you feel special. Sis says she hates getting the same pajamas as us, so now I'm afraid to say how much I love our club.

We go up to bed, but I can't sleep because I hear a lion roar, "Lil, bring me coffee!" Mommy's trying to prepare a Christmas ham. She stops what she's doing to wait on Dad.

In the morning I tiptoe downstairs and peek through the banister to see that Santa really did come. There are coloring books sticking out from three of the stockings. I don't see anything in Anya's stocking, but I see a big jumping horse attached to a frame with springs, and I know it's for her.

I'm so excited that I sprint through the hall announcing, "Santa came!"

I wake up the whole house, but not the dead. Jane and I peek into Mommy and Dad's bedroom to ask if we can open presents.

"Go downstairs and wait," Dad says.

Mommy perks the coffee and Dad sips it as he doles out the gifts.

"This one's for Sis," he says.

He passes it to her and when she's done opening it, he does the same for me, Jane and Anya. He helps us open boxes, making sure that we put our wrappings into the garbage, then he hops onto Anya's horse and pretends to ride it. He smacks the horse's butt and yells, "Giddyup," which sends us into fits of laughter. It's Christmas so he doesn't holler if I laugh too much.

We all get new dolls—not the kind you see on television. Our dolls get hurt very easily. If you move them the wrong way, a leg, an arm, or the head falls off, but you can screw them back in. You just have to be very careful with them because they were made in Japan. We get a doll stroller and a little red wagon to share, and a game that's for sharing as well. We get new underwear and socks—sometimes we share those, too. Now we can use our old socks as mittens.

My sisters and I bring our dolls to the breakfast table. Mommy peels a slice of bologna and saves the red peel because Dad uses it to floss his teeth. She dices the bologna and fries it up with scrambled eggs. Dad's eggs are over-easy so he gets to do the *motzi*. After breakfast he sits in his easy chair intermittently roaring, "Lil, bring me coffee!" while Mommy rushes to get our Christmas dinner done because Dad wants to eat early like on Sundays.

Before dinner we get a surprise visit from Dad's brother Johnny, his wife and their kids. Uncle Johnny has a huge sack full of wrapped gifts: crayons, pencils, mittens, and other stuff that Dad calls "a bunch of shit." I reach in and feel around for something soft like a pair of gloves, but it turns out to be socks. Some other cousin who doesn't need mittens will get them. That's the way things go and you just can't cry about it.

After Uncle Johnny and his family leave, Dad says his brother shouldn't bother giving out cheap presents.

"If you can't afford to give something decent, you shouldn't bother to give anything," Dad declares.

I'm afraid to tell him that I like it when Uncle Johnny bursts into our house bellowing, "Ho, ho, ho." I like whatever present I get. It makes me feel special to reach into his bag and choose whichever one I want.

At dinner, when Dad bows his head to pray, he tells God how thankful we are, but a minute ago he wasn't acting so thankful. It's confusing, but I keep my mouth shut. When Dad's done praying we all say, "Amen." He pours himself a shot of scotch because it's Christmas. He raises his shot glass and we lift our Welch's jelly jars up to God so Dad can say cheers in Russian.

"Na Zdorovie!" we repeat after him. Then we break bread together.

After dinner we head over to the Low property. Everyone is in the cellar of the big house—the one Dad built without a level. There's a long open room down there where Grandpa turned some Johnny-benches and plywood into a table. Sheets camouflage the plywood, and whiskey bottles and dirty ashtrays decorate the center.

I try to give all my aunts and uncles the Christmas greeting, but there are so many people it's hard to maneuver my way around. The men sit at the far end of the table with Grandpa and pour shots, which they use to toast everything imaginable: WWII victory, good economic times, having jobs, great families.

"And while you're at it you can toast my ass!" Aunt Edna's husband, Joe, yells.

Glasses rise, clink, and the tenors resound in harmony, "To Joe's hairy ass!"

Aunt Edna hears her husband's toast request and shouts back, "Your ass is toast!"

Mommy throws her head back and laughs as tears seep from her eyes, and she isn't even chopping onions.

The air is thick with laughter, chatter, singing, and cigarette smoke. The singing draws me to the table. I know all the songs. Mommy sings them around the house all the time, so now they're imprinted on my brain. When everyone in the room sings together, joy radiates into every molecule of the smoky air and makes me feel connected to everyone.

Soon laughter and chatter overtake the singing. Because of Dad, the chatter becomes more intense. He's the loudest person in the room. He wants to keep pouring shots and toasting Uncle Joe's hairy ass, but most of the other uncles have had enough. Dad raises his glass and the uncles follow, but they don't drink up. Only Dad does, and that's when I hear someone say that Dad just doesn't know when enough is enough. He doesn't hear that. He just keeps drinking and bragging about his job and all the money he makes and what you should and shouldn't do when raising kids, and it turns into an argument. Dad is acting weirder than I've ever seen him and it makes my stomach ache, especially when he yells and pounds his fist on the wobbly plywood table.

"Jeeeeeeeeesus Christ, Joey, there's more than one way to skin a cat," his sister, Dolores, shouts.

"What the hell do you goddamned know?" Dad belches out.

Grandma leans over to Aunt Dolores and says, "Don't arrrgue. Just let him tingk he's rrright." Then she turns to Dad, "Yuns rrright, Joey."

"Who gives a shit?" Aunt Edna reasons. "Who gives two shits? It's Christmas. Let's be happy. So Joey, what did Santa bring you for Christmas?"

Dad isn't going to change the subject. He's in a fighting mood. Mommy wants to leave, but Dad won't budge.

"Go home, Joey. Da parrrty's overrr," Grandpa insists.

Grandpa finally pulls Dad outside. Dad's slurring a Christmas carol and he wants Grandpa to sing along.

"I'll singk when yuns give me da got-dem keys."

Dad won't hand them over, and when Grandpa tries to seize them, Dad pushes him.

"You think I don't know what the hell I'm doing?" Dad snarls. "You can't tell me what to do anymore; I'm my own boss now."

"Alrrright, Joey. Yuns da boss."

Grandpa throws up his hands and backs away.

Now Mommy tries to get the keys, but he pushes her away and she almost loses her balance because she's holding Anya.

Dad leans on the car and yells, "Goddamn it! Get in the car, Lil!"

Mommy gets in front with Anya on her lap. My sisters are in the back seat and I'm hanging halfway out the door waiting to see what Dad's going to do next. He slides in behind the steering wheel, snorting and breathing heavily, and soon, the odor of secondhand scotch saturates the interior of the car.

"Take it easy, Joe," Mommy pleads.

"I know goddamned *(burp)* well how to *(machinegun-burp)* drive."

He backs out onto Englishtown Road ever so slowly. Snow is just starting to accumulate. When it snows lightly like this I call it falling freckles. White freckles in the sky usually make me happy, but I'm scared. *This is not the kind of white Christmas I've been dreaming of.*

Dad is swerving all over the road.

"The kids are in the car. Be careful, Joe!" Mommy pleads.

But Dad keeps veering into the dirt on the right side of the road and swerving back over the line in the middle. He laughs when

Mommy says he almost hit a pole, and it seems as though he's happy that she's frightened. When Mommy and Dad aren't saying anything I don't even hear the engine or the windshield wipers—all I hear is the echo of my heartbeat.

It's only a half-mile to our house but it feels like forever. Dad swerves all the way home at ten miles an hour, then he skids onto Fourth Street and turns right to go into our dirt driveway. Mommy quickly gets out of the car and my sisters and I follow her. The door to our house is already unlocked because people who live in the country never lock anything. When Mommy brings us up to bed I cry.

"Is Daddy going to sleep in the car? Is he going to freeze?" I ask.

"He's coming in," she says. "Don't worry. Nothing's going to happen to him."

Whatever she tells me always comes true, but I worry anyway.

In the morning I zoom downstairs and stand in the kitchen doorway leaning my cheek up against the doorjamb. Dad looks fine. Mommy's running back and forth waiting on him. I want to talk about what happened last night, but I'm supposed to speak only when spoken to. Worries bounce around my head like pinballs, so I purse my lips to hold them in.

Dad tells Mommy about work and all the things he's going to do and all the money he's going to make.

"Someday," he says, "come hell or high water, I'll be a millionaire and we'll all be happy."

I was already happy and so was Mommy.

Childhood Revelations

Carnival music drifts toward Jane and me, then an ice cream truck appears and kids seep out of the woodwork like a bunch of starving Armenians to buy Popsicles and ice cream. As they slurp up their treats, Jane turns into a frog, leaping around with bulging eyes.

"Maaa! Ice cream!"

I know things she doesn't—we don't get ice cream from the man in the truck. If Mommy has extra money for ice cream and, *if* it's on sale, she'll buy some at the grocery store and we'll get a teeny scoop on top of a wafer cone. Jane runs into the house all excited and I follow her just to see what Mommy says.

Anya is sitting on the potty in the corner of the kitchen with her bloomers down around her ankles. Mommy's telling her to make *cheesh* and cocky. Other mothers say pee and pooh, but Mommy always says those words in Armenian, unless she's in a funny mood— then she tells Anya to make *cheesh* and kookle-berry-kooks.

Jane asks Mommy if she can get ice cream from the man in the truck.

"No. He's too expensive. It's barely noon. No snacks before meals."

That's her rule and I wonder why she made it because there aren't any snacks in our house unless you count the ones she saves for Dad and the Cocoa Puffs she hides for Sis.

Both Jane and I are disappointed until Anya announces that she made *cheesh* and cocky. We forget about our discontent as we dance and sing.

"Anya made *cheesh* and kookle-berry-kooks, kookle-berry-kooks on the old kook kook."

Mommy dresses Anya and sends her out to play with us. We sit on the steps outside the washroom door to watch people as they stroll down to the lake. Everyone going by wears a bathing suit. We don't have bathing suits—we swim in bloomers, holey ones.

Jane spots a large family heading toward the lake and she freezes up. Her arms stiffen at her sides, her fists clench and her eyes pop out of her head.

"Maaa! Chocolate people! Maaa look! Chocolate people!" she screams at the top of her lungs.

The entire chocolate family glares at Jane. The grown-ups smile as she yells up through the kitchen screen. Mommy comes to the window and now Jane is pointing and shrieking.

"Look at the chocolate people, Ma!"

Mommy bursts into silent laughter. Her mouth opens wide, her eyes squint and her body vibrates.

"People come in all different flavors," Mommy says through the screen.

The summer has just begun and Jane already learns that you don't get ice cream from the man in the truck, there are no snacks before meals, and people come in different flavors just like ice cream. Now we have a new word game. People with freckles like Grandma are polka dot. Sunburned people and Indians are strawberries, and yellow people are lemons. Jane and I aren't black or white—we're vanilla, but by the end of the summer Jane will be honey and I'll be chocolate because I'm so Armenian. Now we've got chocolate and vanilla people, and there are hairy people and some who look like animals. As we sit on our stoop people watching, along comes a man with a round face and a tiny nose. We call him a bird. A grouchy-looking man with an angry mug like Mrs. Marchuck goes by so we call him a bulldog, and the girl with a long neck is a giraffe. We laugh uproariously, and the bird, the dog and the giraffe look at us as if *we* have rocks in *our* heads.

Mommy calls us into the house to give us the new flip-flops she bought at the auction for ten cents apiece. I put them on but the button between the toes pops out every two seconds. Although it might be a disappointment to Uncle Al, I take them off and go barefoot. I'm a tomboy. I don't care if I get dirty. Mommy doesn't either. She lets me be a dirt magnet because that's what soap and water are for. I climb trees, dig holes and play Cowboys and Indians with Jane, Anya and the new boy next door. His name is Raymie. The only other place he's allowed to go besides his own yard is ours, so he's stuck playing with three girls all summer long. We use our fingers as a pistol and pretend to shoot one another. We fall dead, then we come back to life. We swing on the swings, taking turns jumping off to see how far we go. Mommy says we'll break our necks if we fall, but we keep jumping anyway.

"Go ahead, keep it up," she says, "but don't come crying to me if you kill yourselves."

Raymie has red hair like Anya, but he says he has something we don't have.

"What?" I ask while he holds himself as if he's got to pee.

I glance down at his cupped hands and I know there's something in there that I don't have, and although I've never seen one, I *do* know what you call that thing: a *jooje.* That's how you say it in Armenian. I don't know how you say it in English because those words are a sin to say in English. Raymie is still holding his *jooje,* so I bribe him.

"I'll pay you a penny if you show it."

He quickly grabs the penny and pulls his pants halfway down. My sisters and I look at his *jooje* and explode into giggles. This encourages Raymie so he moves his hips from side to side, flipping his *jooje* back and forth as if it's a trophy, then he turns around and wiggles his butt, which prompts us to sing.

"We see your heinie all bright and shiny. You better hide it before we bite it."

He twists back around, gyrating his hips, making his *jooje* dance like Fred Astaire. After a while we think the *jooje* is no big deal, only because we have no idea that Ginger Rogers can make it do the real boogie-woogie.

It's kind of boring, so we run away and he pulls up his pants. We go back to the fun stuff, pretending we're monsters or having burping contests, which I win because I can burp better than Dad after he has a long sip of beer.

When we're thirsty we drink from the garden hose, and if we're lucky, Mommy brings us some watered-down Kool-Aid. She makes a whole gallon of it from one nickel-packet because she's got to stretch everything further than the elastic on my old bloomers.

Raymie hears his Mom calling his name and he goes running home. We know it's lunchtime so we spill into the kitchen where Mommy has chicken soup waiting for us. That's what we have for lunch most days because we don't live in a restaurant. I load my soup with crackers until all the broth is soaked up. When my spoon has done its job, I use my tongue until my bowl looks as though it has just been washed. I drink my milk holding up the cup until every drop trickles into my mouth. I'm still hungry so Mommy tells me I can have a carrot. I look in the refrigerator to see if there's something better than a carrot in there. I find milk, eggs, carrots, Oleomargarine, mustard, mayonnaise, onions, potatoes and Mommy's homemade medicine— chuck cherry wine. I grab a carrot, put it up to my nose and imitate Jimmy Durante.

"Ha cha, cha, cha, cha. It ain't a banana, it's me nose."

"You're a silly goose," Mommy chuckles.

I might be silly, but I don't think I'm a goose because when I tried to lay a golden egg all that came out was a fart.

After lunch I check to see if Mommy's laundry is dry. I yell through the screen and she comes out with her laundry basket. Mommy's laundry is cleaner than everyone else's. Other people hang out undershirts with giant yellow armpit stains and underpants with "shit stains." That's what Aunt Edna calls them. Mommy uses bleach and Tide detergent and sometimes she'll scrub a spot until her fingers are raw. I might have dirty feet but at least my bloomers don't have "shit stains."

****

It's Saturday and Mommy's side of the family comes over for a picnic. Dad loves picnics so he doesn't go gallivanting today. He stays home and makes a barbeque pit with cinderblocks and an old oven grate, and he sets up a picnic table that he found somewhere. I heard him say it fell off the back of a truck so I'm surprised that it didn't break into a million pieces.

Mommy's sisters live in the Bronx. They caravan to New Jersey and pull up along the side of our house at the same time. The car doors open and out spills enough people for two baseball teams: Aunt Mary, Uncle Harry and their gang; Aunt Louise, Uncle Joe and their tribe; Aunt Chris, Uncle Bill and their flock, Yaya and the Baron.

Yaya grabs Dad's face and kisses him on both cheeks.

"I love you so much," she says. "You're such a nice man, *very*, very nice man."

"You're a nice lady, *very*, very nice," Dad says with a laugh concealed in his smile.

We all get squished in Yaya's *dzidzees* and kissed for about three minutes. While she's telling Jane she misses her and sees her picture on the *television*, other cousins are standing to the side mimicking her. Dad says Yaya is a broken record.

When Aunt Chris kisses and hugs us she tells us she brought us a bargain from Gimbel's basement.

"What's that?" we ask.

"A bag of herns," she says. But she forgets to give it to us. Too bad she's not an elephant. They never forget anything.

Aunt Mary gets everyone to sing the song about the gang being all here.

"So what the heck should we care…"

I sing the word *heck,* but my brain echoes *hell* because I hear it so much.

My cousin Richie and I are the first ones to join in. Now the whole gang is singing "Heart of My Heart" and "Give My Regards to Broadway." People strolling down Fourth Street headed for the lake sing along as they pass our house. When I do my rendition of "Hello, Dolly" by Louie Armstrong, Richie joins in, clenching his fists, waving his arms in rapture, pulling his brows together like he means every word he sings. I *love* that!

When the sing-a-long is over, Mommy, her sisters and Yaya go into the kitchen to prepare food. Their *dzidzees* take up half of the space in there. When I try to squeeze by, my head bumps into them and bounces around like a dodge ball. They talk to the food as they cook. They say "potatoes, tomatoes" in Greek, and in Armenian, they ask the potatoes and tomatoes "how are you?" just because it rhymes, because it makes them laugh. That's what they do—they laugh.

Outside, Dad and my uncles are having a pretend sword fight with the skewers.

"On Guard!" Dad bellows.

Uncle Bill tries to jab him but he only sideswipes him.

"Nah, nah, ya missed me."

Uncle Harry comes at Dad and gets him right in the chest. Dad falls down and plays dead. Just then Uncle Joe jabs Uncle Bill in the butt as he walks by.

"Ouch, what'd ya do that for?" Uncle Bill shrieks.

In the midst of all this they're firing up the coals. When it quiets down, the Baron tweets his familiar angry song.

"The Turks are a bunch of savages! They're no good!"

Everyone listens—for a split second.

Mommy and her sisters bring out some burgers and hot dogs. We'd rather have the *shish kabob*, but we've got to wait for that. The tomatoes and peppers are on the skewers over the coals. Uncle Harry turns them as they slightly blacken. When they're cooked, they're removed from the skewer, peeled, and thrown into a pot. Later when the lamb's done, we'll spoon the tomatoes and peppers over it alongside our pilaf. There's no better feast.

After we eat, Dad rolls out the alcohol. When Mommy's side of the family is around, he doesn't drink as much as when we're at the Low property, but I keep my eyes and ears open anyway. While Uncle Joe cools off the Baron with a few squirts from the hose, Dad and my other uncles salute to everyone's health, then they talk about all the politicians.

"Ike is an ass! Republicans are self-serving, greedy bastards," Dad insists just as my cousins and sisters run by in their bloomers, being chased by Uncle Joe and the spurting hose.

"You don't like Eisenhower just because he's Republican," Uncle Harry shoots back. "Hell, Joe, the economy is good, and almost everyone is working."

"That's because of F.D.R. and Truman," Dad says. "What the hell does Eisenhower do? If anyone looks at him cockeyed, he thinks they're a goddamned communist!"

While Dad and my uncles are talking politics, I discover a bald spot on Uncle Harry's head. It's perfectly round and I wonder why he's missing so much hair. I *really* want to know, but when I work up the courage to ask, he just tells me it keeps him cool in the summer. That doesn't answer my question, yet I'm afraid to ask again because Dad doesn't want me to be "asking so many goddamned questions."

Before the day is over Mommy and her sisters plan a family trip to Incarnation Camp, the place they spent their summers as children.

When it's time for everyone to leave there are a million hugs and kisses. Dad's family is quick—you just say goodbye and they leave, but it takes forever to say farewell to Armenians.

After everyone's gone Dad plops in front of his television and my sisters go to bed while I follow Mommy in and out of the house helping her clean up.

"Lil, bring me coffee!" the lion roars.

I bring Dad his coffee and place it on his side table.

"What the hell's the matter with you?" he growls.

He jumps up, grabs my arm, turns me around and smacks me on the butt. The bottom half of my body goes flying forward.

"What the hell are you, stupid?"

I don't know what I did, but I know he doesn't want an answer. He smacks me again.

"You have a big goddamned mouth. It isn't nice to make fun of anyone."

Now he's smacking my butt the same way you beat a dusty rug hanging on the clothesline.

Mommy flies into the living room chanting, "Enough, Joe."

Dad wags his finger in my face as he warns me, "The next time I hear you asking anyone about their bald spot, or any other goddamned personal question, I'm going to give it to you double. Think before you talk, goddamn it!"

"I'm sorry, Daddy!"

"That lickin' was just a tiny dose of medicine, just an appetizer. You're lucky you got it from me and not Grandpa Low. Now, get the hell to bed, and don't make a peep!"

I run upstairs crying. I put my feet in the tub and wash them with Ivory soap. *I wish Uncle Al could see my feet.* I head for bed in my bloomers because it's hotter than a jalapeno pepper up here and it makes you "sweat bullets." I thank my lucky stars that Dad isn't Mexican like Uncle Bill. If he was, he'd make me eat hot peppers with refried beans, which Dad says is "nothing but a goddamn fancy name for leftover shit and all that hot tamale crap makes you sweat bullets all day long." I only have to sweat bullets at night because Dad's Russian and Polish and he doesn't make me eat any crap that he won't eat.

While Mommy's washing pans and silverware, Dad's yelling for her to come and take off his shoes, the siren is blaring, and so is Dad's TV, but none of it drowns out the sounds of the bats. I can't sleep so I say my prayers.

I'm sorry for being disrespectful, God. Next time I'll think long and hard before I open my big mouth because I don't want another lickin'. I know I'm not supposed to ask for anything, but this isn't really a thing, God—can you please send me a breeze because I'm sweating bullets? And thanks a million for not making Dad be a Mexican like Uncle Bill because I'd die if I had to sweat bullets all day long. Amen.

A Touch of Class

To prepare for camp, Mommy's taking us to Englishtown Auction for sneakers and bathing suits. Sis doesn't want to go, but Jane and I do. We hop into Mommy's old red sedan along with Anya and head down Englishtown Road toward the auction.

The auction sits on forty acres of land. Farmers buy and trade animals down here and crowds of people surround the auctioneer to bid on stuff that Mommy calls junk.

There are throngs of people here. They come in all different shapes, sizes, and flavors just like jellybeans. You can come down here and buy almost anything that the human mind can imagine. There are meat and fish counters, bakeries, delis and hot peanut stands. There are booths with Polish food, Jewish, Italian, Russian and German food, but no Armenian food. There are no other Armenians around. The Baron says the Turks killed most of them. The only Armenians I know are Mommy, her family and my sisters. That's why you get a good whiff of every country except for Armenia.

I smell sugar and hot delicious oils all at once and it makes my mouth water like a runny faucet.

There are rows of fruit stands run by disheveled old men and women with messy hair, stained aprons, dirty hands and missing teeth, who tell you not to touch the merchandise before you even get close enough to touch it. Mommy knows all of her prices so she won't buy any fruits or veggies down here unless they give her a better deal than the sale price in the supermarket where she gets green stamps, too. She buys bananas and puts them in Anya's carriage.

Piglets roll around in small, muddy pigpens, and live chickens are stuffed into cages like canned sardines. I hear grunting and clucking and when the wind swirls around I get a good whiff of fruit and cocky all at once, so I'm not sure whether to be disgusted or delighted.

Just past the animals is an old man with long gray hair dressed like Jesus. He stands on a wooden crate yelling at everyone who passes by. People stop, listen, and throw coins on the ground for him. If I didn't pay Raymie my penny to see his *jooje,* I could've given it to the Jesus man who proclaims, "The world is coming to an end. Now is the time to repent your sins or you'll end up in hell, burning in the wicked flames."

I might burn in the wicked flames for looking at Raymie's jooje or for asking about Uncle Harry's bald spot. I'm sorry, God.

Mommy tugs on my arm.

"Come on," she says. "He's got rocks in his head."

"He looks hungry, Ma. I can see his ribs. Can we give him a banana?"

"He's a beggar. He could buy all the bananas he wants with the money people throw at him. Look," she points, "he's got more money than me and I've got four kids to feed."

She pulls me over to a table with piles of new summer clothes. The man who runs this stand has something called a sun-suit. It's cotton, it has elastic around the waist and at the legs, and it ties at the shoulders. Mommy realizes it can double as a bathing suit. She asks the man how much and he says a dollar and a quarter.

"A dollar and a quarter? What do you think, they're made of gold?" Mommy shrieks.

"Vell, how many you vant?" the merchant asks.

"A lot."

"How 'bout a dollarrr a piss?" the man suggests.

"A dollar? Go up the roof and holler!"

Mommy's being silly, but the man's lips can't stretch enough to make a smile.

"You want a dollar?" Mommy says. "I'll tell you what—I'll buy ten for five dollars."

"Vhat?" the man says. "I should make no prrrofit? You tingk I do dis forrr my health? You vant ten, lady? I give you ten of dem forrr eight dollarrrs and dat's final."

"I'll take ten of them for six and a half dollars and that's final," Mommy insists.

"Vell," the man replies, "I give you ten of dem forrr six and a half dollarrrs just to get rrrid of you lady."

"You got a deal!" Mommy shouts.

"No, you da von who gotta deal, lady. Vhat you got is a steal! You gotta steal, lady! Dat's vhat you got. God forrrbid I should make prrrofit! God forrrbid!"

Mommy roots through the sun-suits, picking out several patterns in various sizes. She gives the man seven dollars and when he drops the change in her hand, he snarls, "Good rrridden, lady!"

"Same to you, mister!"

We walk up and down all of the aisles searching for bargains. Mommy says most of the stuff is junk and a lot of the prices aren't really bargains if she can make the items for less than what they're charging. We pass a table with rusted out machine parts and heaps of garbage that old men with rotten teeth and greasy fingers rummage through, and another table full of dirty, nude dolls with missing limbs and matted hair that look just like my dolls. Mom cringes at the pile of legs, arms, heads and limbless bodies.

"It looks like a massacre!" she says. "Who in the world would buy that junk?"

At the next booth there's a guy selling records, and he's playing "Lollipop" by the Chordettes. You only need to hear that song once to memorize it. Jane and I stick our fingers in our mouths and pull them out fast to make the popping sound, then we sing, "Ba-boom, boom, boom, boom." Mommy even sings along and so does everyone else who dances by. I know she doesn't have money for fun things but I beg her to buy the record because it's cheap.

"We don't have a record player," she says. "That's like buying dog food just because it's on sale when you don't even have a dog."

The hubcap man has thousands of hubcaps hanging from wire displays, on his table, and scattered on the ground like garbage. I heard

Dad and Uncle Johnny argue over where he gets them. Uncle Johnny thinks he drives along the highways and finds them on the sides of the roads. Dad thinks he goes out in the middle of the night and steals them off cars, hoping the victims will come to his booth to look for a match.

We pass more food stands to get to the shoe man inside the building. I'm starving so Mommy peels a banana and breaks it into pieces for my sisters and me. We look like a bunch of monkeys eating bananas while other people munch on French fries and ice cream. It bothers me a little that I don't get to eat the fun stuff, but I love being at the auction. There's no other place like this in the world.

We pass the Russian food stand and I see Russian rye bread. I want that more than I want ice cream, but I don't ask because Mommy can't afford to buy nice bread.

The fabric man sees Mommy and asks, "Vhat you need today?"

"Nothing today, thanks."

"I got good deals. New prrrints. You should buy sometingk vhile it's a deal."

"Not today," she says and keeps walking. As she gets farther away, he shouts even louder. He's lucky she doesn't want to make a deal because she's the queen of hagglers. Dad says that's because no one can screw an Armenian.

The shoe man recognizes Mommy before she even enters his space.

"The fifty cent ones are down there," he says as he points to the bottom shelf.

All the Buster Browns and Keds are up top and we can't even try them on because they're so expensive, there's no way Mommy can buy them. Aunt Edna won't buy them either because she says the dog shits in the shoes. When other kids ask me if I have "a boy and a dog" in my shoe, I can't tell them about the shit, so I just say that the boy and the dog couldn't fit inside with my foot.

At fifty cents a pair, Mommy saves a bundle on our no-name sneakers. I want to wear them now because having sneakers is a treat, but Mommy's says I have to wait until we go to camp.

"I'm tired of always waiting for things," I say.

"If you keep yourself busy, time will fly, and before you know it, you'll be at camp wearing your sneakers."

All the way home from the auction the horn on Mommy's car beeps. It has a mind of its own and there's nothing she can do about it. But it makes people in other cars stick up their middle fingers and wave at us, so I wave back at them the same way.

We get home and Dad says he wants something to eat now. Mommy drops everything. She strikes a match to light the stove, pulls out her cast-iron frying pan, pours in some oil, and while that's heating up she grates potatoes and onions into a bowl, then she adds eggs, some flour, salt and pepper. She mixes it, spoons in six heaps and it bubbles up. While they're cooking she zooms upstairs with the sneakers and sun-suits, then she flies downstairs, flips the potato pancakes, puts on some water to boil for tea and starts her second batch. Our house smells so delicious I can lick the air and taste the *latkes* while they're frying.

We kids get milk in our tea, but Dad says that's no way to drink it.

"Tea should be served with lemon," he says. He picks up his glass of tea and sticks out his pinky.

"Why do you always stick out your pinky, Daddy?" I ask.

"Because," he says, "I have class."

"What's class?"

"When you have class that means you're refined."

"What does refined mean?"

Dad takes in enough air to blow the dopey little pigs' houses in.

"It means to have some elegance and grace about you."

"What's that mean?" I ask, because in my head, it just doesn't fit with the pinky.

"Stop asking so many goddamned questions," he says. "Just eat. Nobody likes to be asked too many questions. It's annoying. 'Curiosity killed the cat,' you know."

The first three letters of my name are "cat" and I think what he really means is curiosity killed Cathy.

Mommy is on her feet, running back and forth from the stove to the table to the sink. I tell her I can't finish my food.

"Your eyes are bigger than your stomach," she says, but now she can eat what I left on my plate.

When everyone else is gone from the kitchen, Mommy gives me a rag. In Armenian it's called a *totslot*. I wipe the table with the *totslot* while she washes dishes and sings.

"Do a job, big or small, do it right or not at all."

I sing along and when we're done she tells me what a good job I did. I can't wait to tell Dad how I helped her.

He's in his easy chair, and Jane and Anya are untying his shoelaces and pulling off his gigantic shoes. His feet smell like rotten popcorn so we hold our noses and giggle.

I tell Dad about how I helped Mommy.

"That's what you're supposed to do," he snaps. "Don't brag or go around looking for a reward just because you cleaned up a mess *you* helped to make. Now go tell Mommy I want coffee."

Mommy stirs sugar and milk into the cup and I bring it into the living room, but I trip over Dad's shoes. The coffee splashes all over, and some of it lands on Dad's legs.

"Jeeeeeeeesus Christ, watch what the hell you're doing! What the hell's the matter with you? Are you stupid? What the hell am I gonna do with you?"

I cry, but Dad says I better stop or he'll give me a lickin', then I'll really have something to cry about. Mommy shoots into the living room with a *totslot,* and Dad tells me to clean up the goddamned mess and watch where the hell I'm going next time. He grabs the rag, wipes his pants, then throws it back at me. I try to sop up the coffee but my tears keep burning my eyes. I want to say it was just an accident, but I'm afraid because he's still yelling. Mommy brings me a bowl of soapy water and helps me clean up, and all the while Dad is still yelling at me.

"Enough already, Joe," Mommy tells him. "It was just an accident."

"Just an accident?" Dad yelps. "Maybe you need to teach her to watch what the hell she's doing, Lil."

Someday, when I have kids of my own, I'm not going to yell at them the way Dad yells at me. I'm going to help them clean up their mistakes the way Mommy does.

Dad's still angry so I tell him, "I'm sorry!"

"Okay," he says, "just so long as you learned your lesson. From now on, watch where the hell you're going and pay attention!"

I go to bed, say my prayers and fall asleep to squeaky bats, sirens and Dad's TV.

****

No one has to ask Raymie to drop his pants anymore. Right in the middle of cowboys and Indians his *jooje* appears like a rabbit from a hat. The penny I gave him was for just a peek but he thinks it was a lifetime contract. I won't be seeing Raymie's *jooje* for a while. I'm wearing my new sneakers and I'm on my way to Incarnation Camp.

To pass time, we sing in the car. Mommy and Dad know all the words to every song in the world. If we say a word, a name or a color, they sing a whole song to it.

We say *blue* and they sing, "Blue Moon."

We say *heart*, *yellow* and *sunshine*, and they sing songs with those words. Then I try to trip them up with a hard word like *sin* because I don't think there are any songs with that word, but they start singing.

"It's a Sin to Tell a Lie."

We sing all the way to camp and time flies like a bumblebee.

Incarnation Camp has a gigantic lake with a dock and loads of canoes. The main building has a huge dining area, a recreation room and lots of bedrooms. So many trees surround the camp, there's no need for birds to fly—they can just hop from tree to tree. The best part is that Mommy's sisters are here with their families. We kick things off with a sing-a-long. After that, Aunt Chris says she has our bag of herns, but she doesn't give it to us. We all get settled in our rooms, have lunch and now we're ready to swim all afternoon.

In the evening we kids get to play bingo for candy bars, sing around a campfire, and chase Uncle Pilaf. He's an old Armenian friend. His name isn't really Pilaf, but it matches the clown in him. One night while Uncle Pilaf is getting ready for bed, we kids raid his room. He jumps up and bolts out of the room in his boxer shorts, yelling, "Woo boo boo boo. Woo boo boo boo." When he leaps into the air his feet move as though he's riding a bike. We chase him all through the halls, out the door, and all through the campground.

"Uncle Pilaf, we want your *shish kabob!*" my cousin Geraldine shouts.

"You can't have my *shish kabob!*" he shouts back.

Now we tell him we want his *baklava*.

"You can't have my *baklava*! You're already too sweet!"

Later, when Dad hears about me chasing Uncle Pilaf, I shudder.

"What a knucklehead," he says.

I don't know if he means Uncle Pilaf, Curly from *The Three Stooges,* or me, but the tone of his voice untangles my guts.

The best is saved for last. Uncle Buck writes a musical skit for the grown-ups and they act it out. Dad is the baby in the play, but they can't find a diaper big enough for him so they pin a bed sheet to his bottom. In the play he lives on a farm with his family and they're about to be dispossessed for nonpayment of rent. The landlord warns the farmer to pay up or else, then he leaves and a dozen kids appear, including Dad in nothing but his giant diaper and a baby bottle hanging from his mouth. He's crouched down and he has to lean forward to balance himself because of his beer belly. Now the throng of grown-up kids in the play sing, "Hiya Maw, Hiya Paw, Whattsa mattah, Maw, Whattsa mattah, Paw?"

"We ain't got the money for the mortgage on the farm," the farmer and his wife reply.

Instead of crying, everyone on stage sings, "Sob. Sob. Sob, sob, sob."

When they're done, Dad falls backward and all you can see is his big butt and his freckled legs kicking at nothing while he makes gaga sounds.

Dad is so much fun and so is camp—I don't want to leave.

****

It's back to school—to hide under my desk every time the air raid bell rings, just in case the Russians bomb us. I'm more afraid of the other kids finding out that I'm Russian than I am of being bombed. After two terrifying minutes I can come out of hiding with a twisted stomach and a lump in my throat.

There are three reading groups in first grade. If you're in group one you're special because you're smart. The teacher looks at the kids in group one as if they're better, and she listens to what they have to say. Group two is an average bunch of bananas and group three is just a bunch of idiots. My teacher starts me out in group two, but from time to time she puts me in group three. She can't decide if I'm an average banana or a rotten one. When group one is in their circle reading aloud, the teacher can't stop smiling, especially when Becky so eloquently reads, "Come Dick. Come Dick. Dick come. Dick is coming. Watch Dick come!"

The teacher doesn't look at me that way when I read. She makes huffing sounds and gives me only one sentence or she passes me by altogether so I just look at the pictures. Dick, Jane and Sally are wearing Sunday school clothes to play in the yard, there isn't one wrinkle in their clothing, one speck of dirt on them, and not one hair on their heads is out of place. They probably wouldn't be allowed to play with me if they saw what I look like when I play. I get dirty from head to toe and under my fingernails. My hair gets messy and I usually have ropes and things tied to the loops of my pants just in case I need to lasso a horse or an Indian. I climb my tree and melt into my branch while ants crawl past me in the crevices of the bark. I catch bugs, kiss frogs and go bat hunting. I'll bet Alfalfa and his gang would let me play. I'd rather read about Spanky, Buckwheat, Darla and Stymie, and all the *remarkable* things they do instead of only boring words like jump, run, come and go.

Except for music, art and recess, I'm not crazy about school. When the bell finally rings I'm released from prison. There's snow on the ground, but I have plastic bags to cover my shoes. Mommy ran out of the clear ones and gave me a bread bag. I walk home hoping that it snows enough to make a snowman. I look down to see the clear bag on one foot and a bread bag on the other. We're so poor we don't even have matching bags.

An older boy notices the bread bag. He and his friends point at my feet.

"You have a foot sandwich," they laugh.

I think it's pretty funny myself even though I'd rather be wearing galoshes. Sis and I grew out of the red ones so Mommy passed them on to Jane and Anya. I know the bags look stupid on my feet, but I can't hide them and walk at the same time. The boys tell me I must have tasty toes, so I tell them they taste like nuts because that's all I can think of.

Now they're laughing and pointing even more.

"Toenuts! She's got toenuts!" they yell, as if my toes are for sale.

They can't keep up with me anymore because they're folded in half like a piece of paper, and they're slapping themselves. As I get farther away from them I can still hear them laughing at my toenuts and when I realize it rhymes with donuts, I laugh too.

I want to tell Mommy not to give me a bread bag anymore but when I walk into the kitchen she's on the phone. Normally she greets me at the door and asks what I did in school, then she makes me read my sentences to prove I've been paying attention.

I'm supposed to mind my own business, but I can hear her phone conversation with her sister, Louise.

"It wasn't right that Mama never talked with us about Papa's death. I can't understand why Mama sent us to an orphanage. How could she do such a thing? I could never do that to my kids."

I didn't know Mommy grew up in an orphanage. I thought those places were for children who don't have parents. The only thing I know about orphanages is that cruel people take care of the children in those places, and now I feel really bad for Mommy. She sees me standing here and tells me I can go and play with Jane and Anya. But while I'm in the living room building with the blue and red blocks, I hear everything she says. When she hangs up the phone, she comes into the living room and sits on the floor with us.

"What's the matter, Mommy?" I ask.

"Nothing," she says, but then she cries and she hugs all three of us for a really long time. Her face is soaked and she keeps wiping it with her hand until I run and get her a napkin.

"I'm crying because I love you so much," she says, then she hugs us some more.

That's the first time she says that, but I already knew it. When her tears run out she tells us that everything's fine, then she goes back to the phone and calls Yaya. When the conversation's over, she doesn't sing or hum for the rest of the day.

The next time Yaya speaks with Mommy, she tells her it was the Baron's entire fault that she sent them away.

"Well," Mommy says, "life's too short to be mad at the only mother you'll ever have. I'm not even mad at the Baron—how could I stay mad at someone who has rocks in his head?"

Mommy's happy again because she's humming and singing, and when I tell her about the bread bag and the toenuts, she makes sure that I never have tasty feet again.

Lickin's and Lessons I'll Never Forget

"Hello."

"Is Joe Low there?"

"Yes," I say. "Who's calling?"

"Sam Weissenburger."

"Hold on, please." I put down the receiver.

"Dad! Sam Weissenburger is on the phone," I giggle. *Weissenburger sounds like a smart hamburger.*

Dad grabs the receiver, talks for a while, hangs up, then he reaches for his belt buckle. He undoes it, whips it out, and snaps it at me. My instincts tell me to run, so I head for the other side of the dining room table.

"I'll give it to you double if you don't stop running," Dad growls. "And if you get a double lickin' it'll be your own goddamned fault."

I'm so afraid I don't know what to do. As Dad snaps his belt at me, my gut tells me to keep running. I don't even know what I did.

"What the hell's the matter with you, goddamn it?" he yells.

He whips the belt at me and grazes my arm.

"You think you're such a big deal?" he says without waiting for an answer, then he whips his belt and snaps the back of my head.

I fall to the floor, curl up, and cover my face while Dad hits me on my legs, arms and back.

"You're nobody special," he spits. Whack! "What the hell am I supposed to do with you, goddamn it? Are you stupid?" Whack! "Who the hell do you think you are making fun of someone's goddamned name?" Crack!

I'm in trouble because I giggled when I said Weissenburger. I didn't know that was so bad. Dad giggles all the time when he hears funny names and he calls people schmucks, idiots, jerks, assholes, morons and son-of-a-bitchin'-bastards.

"Keep your goddamned mouth shut. Think before you talk or go around laughing at other people." Whack! "You're not so goddamned smart now, are you?" Snap! "I'm tired of you acting like a wise ass." Whack!

Dad's acting like a monster, and now Mommy's upset.

"Enough, Joe!" she demands. "You're seeing red. Stop!"

But Dad doesn't stop. The lion doesn't hear her so I lie here curled up like a caterpillar as he whacks me.

"That one's for crying. Now you have a reason to cry, goddamned-son-of-a-bitch!" Whack! "That one's for making me chase you. I'm tired of your bullshit."

He's breathing like a dragon, his shirttails are hanging out of his pants, his hair's a mess, he's sweating and his neck veins are popping. It looks like someone beat him up. He stomps over to his chair and perches with his belt curled up in his right hand just in case he has to use it again.

Mommy brings me into the kitchen and wipes my face. I can't stop crying so she gives me a glass of water. Chugging a whole glass of water calms you down. She lifts my shirt and sees the red welts on my back, my butt, my shoulders and arms.

"You'll live," she insists.

I tell her I wasn't trying to make fun of anyone. She knows, but it's mandatory to offer an apology so I go into the living room to see the angry dragon.

"I'm sorry, Daddy. I didn't mean to make fun of someone's name."

"That lickin' hurt me more than it hurt you," he says. "You're lucky you didn't get that lickin' from Grandpa. He would've given it to you double, triple, ten times, maybe. I went easy on you. Next time you make me give you a lickin' you won't be so lucky."

"I'll never do it again, Daddy."

"Just so long as you learned your lesson. Now give me a kissie and be a good girl."

I kiss him on the cheek and he pats me on the head. I'm ashamed of myself. I don't know what to do so I go to bed, climb under the covers and pull the blanket over my head. My heart hurts more than my body.

I wish I wasn't so stupid. Dear God, please make me smarter and remind me to think.

I fall asleep before the bats even wake up.

****

Dad changes jobs again and in between, he was out of work so money is even tighter. But he's happy because he thinks John F. Kennedy is going to win the presidential election and change our country for the better. He loves the Kennedys.

"The Kennedys love you, too, Joe," Mommy says. "They make a nickel every time you buy a bottle of scotch."

I wish I had all the nickels that are going to the Kennedys. I'd give them to Mommy so she wouldn't have to work so hard. Mommy took a job at the bank to help pay bills, and now I have to walk all the way to Grandma's house after school. When Mommy picks up my sisters and me after work, she runs through the house like crazy because her laundry is piling up. She even stays up late at night to cook all the foods that Dad loves. She doesn't mind breaking her back in the kitchen because it makes him happy when he's greeted with a giant plate of stuffed cabbage or a dozen pierogi.

****

Now that I'm seven I'm allowed to leave the yard and go off by myself. On Saturdays I walk to the lake, to the ponds and to the store. I leave Jane and Anya and go off to explore the world, but when I come back they always let me in on their games. Besides, they love when I bring home pockets full of teeny tiny frogs. I kiss them, hoping to turn one of them into a prince, but it never happens. My sisters and I dig deep holes for them to live in, but not too deep because we don't want to end up in China where people eat nothing but fish heads and grasshoppers.

Jane and Anya like it when I bring them candy from Ender's store so I decide to take a silver dollar from Mommy's dresser drawer and buy a bunch of it. I know it's wrong but I do it anyway.

When Mommy figures out what I did she takes me by the hand, leads me up to her bedroom, closes the door and sits next to me on her bed. She looks me in the eye and asks if I took her silver dollar. I tell her no, but I can see that her eyes know I'm lying. I'm ashamed of myself because I don't like what the truth is.

"When people lie they lose their integrity," Mommy says.

"What's integrity?"

"It's doing the right thing," she says, "even when the wrong thing is better for you—even when no one is watching you. If you lie to me I won't believe you even when you're telling the truth. Is that what you want?"

"No!" I shout, "I want you to believe me!"

"It's up to you then, whether or not I believe you and trust you. You hold all that power, not me."

"If you lose your integrity, how do you get it back?" I ask.

"Just tell the truth," she says, and she doesn't even call me a liar or a thief. She doesn't yell at me, she doesn't hit me.

"You know," she continues, "when I was a little girl, my Uncle Harry gave me those silver dollars on special occasions. I decided to save them all of my life and give them to my children when they're all grown up.

"Stealing is lying, and lies are a funny thing; when you tell one, you have to tell another to cover up the first one. They start out like little snowflakes, then they become snowballs rolling down a hill and end up so big they knock down everyone in their paths."

Now I'm even more ashamed. I see that stealing the coin was the first lie and that caused me to tell a second, and if I don't confess, it's an automatic third lie.

"I took it, Mommy," I admit, "I just wanted some candy. I'm sorry." *I really am sorry and I'm so mad at myself for disappointing her.*

"Sorry is just a word—you have to back it up. If you're *truly* sorry, you'll never do it again. And remember, when you do things like that, you hurt yourself the most because you change the way other people feel about you. Now, you can't replace the silver dollar, but you'll have to pay me back by doing extra chores around the house."

I like the way Mommy teaches me a lesson—it hits me right in the heart, but so differently than Dad's medicine. Like a couple of weeks ago when he smacked me square in the mouth with the back of his hand for saying the f-word. I didn't know it was so bad. I saw it on a curb, written in chalk, and I was so proud of myself for sounding it out. All I did was ask what it means, but the instant it crossed my lips, Dad rapped me so hard, the insides of my lips bled. My fat lips reminded me about that word for a week. I still don't know what it means. I only know that I shouldn't ever say a word that's written on a curb, or a sidewalk, but I don't know why.

When you know the *why* of things it's so much easier to stay out of trouble. When I grow up and have kids, I'm going to be just like Mommy.

The Low Property

Mommy rushes Sis, Jane and me off to school, drops Anya off by Grandma Low, then dashes off to work. Jane is in kindergarten. When school lets out for her, she treks a mile and a half by herself, all the way to Grandma's house. That's where I'm going right now and the long walk is scary. My feet sink in the sandy dirt and the cars on Englishtown Road whiz by so fast, my dress flies up, exposing my holey bloomers. I'm tired and famished, and I wish I had a penny for candy. As I pass Ender's a bunch of older kids are chomping on licorice. They ask me if I'm a Low. I tell them yes and now they're laughing at me in a way that makes me feel ashamed. They tell me that Grandma and Grandpa Low are Commies and dirty pigs. I don't know what a Commie is, but I know what they mean by dirty pig. I'm so hurt I want to curse at them. I think of that f-word. It must be extra bad because even though Dad and his family probably invented cursing, they never say that word. Well, except for when Grandpa says "Goodnight fulks" to people he's glad to get rid of. I decide not to say it because I don't want another fat lip.

As I near Grandma's house I can hear Mrs. Marchuck's chickens. Her farm is next door to the big house on the Low property. Dad's sister, Edna, lives in the big one with Uncle Joe and their children.

Aunt Edna always fries up leftover spaghetti for me, and it's good. Mommy never makes fried spaghetti. When Uncle Joe says "that's because she isn't Polish," Aunt Edna tells him to shut the hell up, and look who's talking, and before I know it, they're bickering like a mother bird and a squirrel. I never take their arguments seriously because no one ends up getting punched in the face. Aunt Edna just tells Uncle Joe that he must've taken his *schmaht* pills, then she smirks at me and I almost pee my pants because she previously told me that *schmaht* pills are actually rabbit shits.

Behind Aunt Edna's house is a long trellis with grapevines weaved into every inch of it, and no matter where you sit beneath it, you can reach out and grab a handful of giant purple grapes. The grapes are thick-skinned and seeded. It isn't easy separating the seeds from the grape-meat with your tongue, but I think that's God's way of saying that all good things take a little bit of work. Beneath the arch of the trellis is a long table the length of a sheet of plywood. The benches are made of scrap wood and leave splinters on anyone who is stupid enough to slide their butts off.

On warm days when lots of Lows end up at the Low property, the grown-ups gather beneath the trellis to talk and laugh, curse and argue. When it's a special occasion you can be sure that the table is dressed up in old sheets and decorated with functional centerpieces: whiskey bottles and ashtrays. My cousins and I get to run around and do whatever the hell we want while the grown-ups sit around eating and drinking. At the start it's fun because everyone is happy and the booze makes them hug one another and say things they usually don't say, like "I love you."

When all the Lows are present it's like being in the League of Nations. Grandma and Grandpa's kids married into families of several other nationalities, and they embrace each other through the songs they sing. I may be young but I know that Russian and Polish people like to "roll out the barrel," that "Irish eyes" are always smiling, and "Santa Lucia" is far away. And even though none of us has a "barrel of money," we have each other and no matter how bad the situation, all we have to do is "leave our troubles on a doorstep."

Whenever Grandma's brother, Anthony, comes around it's a cause for celebration. Uncle Anthony has a bum arm that hangs at his side like a broken tree limb—polio screwed up his body, but it didn't touch his heart. Whenever I climb onto his knee, I don't feel like part of a litter—I feel special. Before letting me down to run around, he always gives me a dollar, which I have to hand over to Mommy.

"Let me hold that for you so you don't lose it," she always says.

I hand her the dollar and it disappears, because just like Jesus Christ, she turns it into five loaves of bread—two for now and three in the freezer. With a spoonful of Mommy's chuck cherry wine to go along with the bread, Dad can take communion "whenever the hell he wants" without having to bless himself "twenty-five goddamned million times."

Thirty giant steps from the grapevines, you'll pass a bunch of junk before reaching an open cesspool. Whatever starts out in the toilet, ends up there, so I call it cocky heaven.

Twenty giant steps from the cesspool in another direction is Aunt Helen's bungalow. She's the only lady I know who doesn't have a husband. I didn't know why until last weekend when I heard Dad and his siblings tell the story of how Grandpa rescued Aunt Helen from "the drunken, disabled, wounded, son-of-a-bitchin' bastard, war vet who had no money for food because he spent it all on booze. Then the goddamned bastard was caught eating Moinie's and Gerry's baby food right out of the jar, and poor Moinie and Gerry were starving to death."

"Pop would've beat the shit out of the goddamned bum when he went to scoop up Helen and the girls," another shouted, "but the bastard was out getting drunk."

Before long they were all interrupting one another, and for a few moments I couldn't distinguish what was being said because they were all yelling, "Jeeeeeeeeesus Christ!" I heard Jesus Christ above the muddled chatter so many times, I swore that He and His disciples in the picture on Grandma's wall were going to come to life, jump across the table, spoil their last meal, and change the course of Christian history just to settle an argument that didn't need to be argued in the first place.

"The only reason Pop didn't try to beat the shit out of the son-of-a-bitch is because he felt sorry for the bastard because he had a bum leg," Dad insisted.

"Pop ran after the bastard to beat the shit out of him," my aunt argued, "but the bastard fell down and begged Pop to leave him alone.

114

So Pop took pity on the pissy little shit-ass and left him on the ground."

That was just a normal conversation in the Low family, but it turned into a real argument when they began accusing one another of things that had nothing to do with the subject. The next thing I knew, one aunt was telling another to kiss her ass and the other one said she would just as soon as she washes it, and before long they were calling each other bastards, shit-asses, snot-noses and goddamned sons-a-bitches. They yelled across the table until one aunt stood up and shook her finger so furiously, I thought a bullet might fly out and kill someone.

"You stupid son-of-a-bitchin' bastard, you can kiss my smelly ass and go to hell!" another aunt replied.

I thought I was already in hell and I wondered why The Last Supper was hanging on the wall.

"Enough is enough, yuns!" Grandma pleaded.

With all the madness, I don't think anyone heard her.

"Whooooooo gives a shit?" Aunt Edna yelled to her sisters.

Then she saw the worry on my face so she turned to me with a smile and a gleam in her eyes, and whispered, "Who gives two shits? Who gives three shits? Who gives tens shits?"

I was comforted knowing that at least one person in the room was in a laughing mood, but I couldn't help thinking, *I give a shit.*

In the midst of it all, my cousins were running in and out of Grandma's house for a drink of water or a piece of sugar bread. When the door opened, a cloud of smoke would attempt to escape. Save Grandma and Grandpa who quit years earlier, all the adults puff away like choo-choo trains whenever the family gathers together.

Cigarette smoke swirls down so low, the only way to avoid it is to "stop, drop and roll" on Grandma's dirty floor. When conversations grow more intense, more cigarettes are lit. You don't even have to see them lighting up because the bits of tobacco on their lips cause them to spit. Amid the spitting, the yelling and the slamming door, we always smell as though we just escaped a burning building.

With excitement like that, I wonder how my teacher expects me to be interested in Dick, Jane and Sally, who never do anything but come, go, look, jump and run. If Dick and his friends hung around us Lows, their books would be much more interesting, because if Sally didn't feel like running or jumping whenever Dick told her to, she just might tell the bossy little bastard to kiss her smelly ass and go to hell. Then I wouldn't have to read baby words like *run, look* and *go* hundreds of times after I've already learned them.

From Aunt Helen's house, ten frog leaps will get you to a shanty. It's forbidden to children, so I don't go near it unless Grandpa *isn't* around. Inside the shanty is a built-in rowboat—just like an in-ground pool. Grandpa dug out a hole, fit in the old wooden boat and attached a cheap filter. Every morning he dumps in his catch of baby fish, which he calls killees.

There are always dead killees floating belly up, and although Jane and I secretly enter Grandpa's shanty, we have never murdered any of his killees. But that doesn't stop him from pointing his finger at us like a loaded gun.

"Yuns kids killt my killees," he bellows. "How many times do I have to tell yuns sons-a-bitches to stay away frrrom da got-dem killees?"

He never hits us or chases us so Jane and I just find a place far away from him to laugh at the way he says "got-dem." We mimic him and accuse each other of killing the killees. It's so much fun having a fake-Low argument, our sides split open and our guts turn into chicken gravy.

****

Grandpa painted words onto an old rotten piece of plywood, "Killees 4 Sale." The sign is nailed to a tree at the front of the property near Englishtown Road. Even though Grandpa is as scary as a monster, it doesn't prevent fishermen from coming back again and again to purchase killees from his built-in rowboat.

It's about twenty-five giant steps from the killee shed to the two-car garage that never saw a car a day in its life. It, too, is forbidden to kids. But when curiosity gets the best of me, I find myself in Grandpa Low's spook house. Spider webs with dead bugs drape every item like gowns on a wedding procession from beyond the grave. Some webs are barely visible so the bugs appear to be suspended in animation. Others glisten where the sun filters in. The garage is a haven for mice and possibly monsters. Wooden and metal gadgets of every kind, mostly rusted and broken, fill the garage. There are shovels, axes, doorknobs, glass jars filled with rusted screws, nuts and bolts, and best of all—an old spare toilet that someone took a shit in!

As I turn to leave the garage I become entangled in a spider web. I shriek and whimper trying to peel off the sticky threads. Then I exit the spook house shivering in my skin because Grandpa comes by. He pays no mind to me. Instead, he just follows his nose to the spare toilet, takes one look and goes ballistic.

"When I catch da son-of-a-bitch who shit in da got-dem toilet, I'm gonna beat da livin' shit out of 'em and make 'em clean it up with derrre barrre hands!"

Thankfully, he can't blame it on me. That thing is too big to have come from my *dupah,* but I wonder how he's going to beat the shit out of the person who evidently has none left in him. I know not to ask. Grandpa says he's going to leave the "got-dem shit" in the "got-dem toilet" as "got-dem evidence" until he can find the "got-dem bastard" who did it.

I don't know who made the cocky, but I'm glad they did because I got to hear Grandpa say "got-dem son-of-a-bitch" more times than I change my bloomers in a month.

The garage is also storage for window frames, dirty rags, a small table, checkers, and an old chess set—everything you can imagine except for toilet paper and most likely a level because Grandpa doesn't really give a damn if something is crooked. He doesn't "give a got-dem how anytingk looks." He only cares if things work.

He built a giant coop out of wood and chicken wire behind the garage for his homing pigeons. Inside are little compartments separated by plywood. And yup, he built that without a level. He attaches notes to the legs of his pigeons, hoping someone finds them and writes back. He lets them out and watches them fly away until they become dots on a distant blue and white canvas, then disappear as if they never existed.

To bring them home, he raises a twenty-foot pole with multi-colored rags tied to the top. He gently waves the rags about in the sky, and just as I'm thinking, *Grandpa, they're probably in New York City pooping on Yaya's windowsill,* we see a dot in the far-off distance.

"Ahuh, ahuh, ahuh," he utters gently.

I see a hint of glee in his eyes as the dots multiply and emerge into recognizable creatures. The pigeons land and dutifully follow the rag-end of his pole to the entrance of their coop. They file in while Grandpa eyes each one, hoping to find a note. I ask him why they're so obedient.

"Becuz, I'm a magician!"

I know that isn't the right answer, but I don't care because he answered my question without biting off my head.

Another shanty, also forbidden to children, sits behind the chicken coop. Mommy thinks that's funny because there's no gold in there—just a bunch of dirty old clothes and shoes that she wouldn't wear to a dog show. I don't care if Mommy won't wear them. I got a good look at the contents when Grandma opened the door to rummage through her stash looking for a skirt for my cousin Moinie. Since then I've been dying to go in there to play dress-up. There's a dried-up wig in there that looks like a dead animal, but when I got a closer peek, I recognized it as one of my aunt's old hairdos. Hanging from a nail is a white pointed bra big enough to double as two dunce caps. I wonder who it's being saved for because except for Grandma, who breast fed nine children and no longer wears a bra, most of the aunts on Dad's side of the family are not that well endowed. Well, not unless they're wearing their falsies.

Among the treasures is a pair of old bloomers, but if I could play in there, I'd just grab a fallen branch, scoop them up, and carry them over to Grandpa's pile of burning trash. Then I'd shake out the cobwebs and bugs from the giant jumble of clothing the same way Mommy shakes out her tablecloth at the back door after dinner.

Ten ballerina steps from that shanty is Grandma and Grandpa's bungalow, and right behind their house is a ten-foot deep cinderblock foundation for a home that no one ever built. It's a huge hole that kids throw lollipop sticks in, that weeds grow in, that bratty little snot-nosed wise-asses like me can be thrown into by older cousins. Just beyond that hole is a house in the woods. A family with a mess of kids live there and catty-corner to them is another house surrounded by junky cars. A load of kids live there, too. Between those two houses there are several boys, some big enough to have left the present for Grandpa in his spare toilet. Grandpa added those boys to his suspect list, but I don't think he'll narrow it down because I've heard the Lows have intense conversations about shit, so I know a lot about that subject.

"Rrrich and famous people don't shit gold," Grandpa says with his pointer swirling above his head. "Derrr shit stinks like everrryone else's. Everrrbody's shit is da same—yuns can't tell which asshole it came frrrom."

If that's true, he'll never catch the cocky maker.

A wooden stand displaying Grandma's artificial flower arrangements and wedding dolls sits in the front yard at the edge of Englishtown Road. Grandma's sign is an old piece of plywood with painted letters that say, "Rose's Art Shop." Family and potential customers park their cars almost anywhere in the front yard—even on the small patch of grass next to the kitchen chair. I don't know why the chair is there, it just is.

Alongside of Grandma and Grandpa's house is a four-seated wooden swing. Grandpa sits there as if he's guarding his empire of pigeons, killees and preloaded toilets. Sometimes he appears to be sleeping, but Dad says Grandpa sleeps with one eye open, which means he really isn't sleeping and don't try anything because you'll have hell to pay. So even when Grandpa looks as though he's sleeping, I say hi as I pass him by. Sometimes he just barely nods his head, but if he's in a jovial mood, which isn't that often, he calls me Kahtee Schmahgahtee. He can't pronounce Cathy, but I don't care. When he rhymes my name I know it's a form of endearment and one of the most playful things I can expect from him.

Another sign nailed onto his house next to the door says, "Please Ring Bell." It was placed there for those unexpected customers. Below the sign is the famous bell. The wiring for the bell is exposed and stapled to the exterior of the house. Grandpa doesn't give a "got-dem" how it looks as long as it works.

I don't have to "rrringk" the bell because I'm blood and "blood is thicker than water."

I enter and pass Grandma's art room—that's where she keeps her meat grinder. It's screwed onto her worktable. She has shelves with boxes that contain artificial flower petals, green leaves and rolls of green tape that will be wrapped up and down a wire to give the effect of a stem. Grandma twirls the tape around the wire so quickly the flowers become a blur. All this leaves her fingers stained and when her vegetable garden is in full bloom, she lifts her thumb and brags, "I got grrreen thumb!"

Among the contents of Grandma's boxes, I most admire the nude dolls. They resemble Barbie dolls, but *hers* are hollow and stiff because she bought them cheap by the dozens down at Englishtown Auction. She also has yards of white and pastel colored fabric, lace, ribbon and trim, all of which she uses to transform her hollow dolls into beautiful bridal party dolls.

Another box is filled with yucky secondhand sweaters that Grandma bought for next-to-nothing at the auction. She unravels the sweaters to crochet bedspreads for all of her grandkids. My bedspread is orange, blue, brown, purple and red. It matches everything.

While crocheting, Grandma hums as she sways back and forth in her rocker, and each time she leans forward, she taps her heels on the floor twice—without fail.

Grandma is five-foot-two with eyes so blue: one clear, one cloudy. Her red hair is streaked with gray and pulled back with a hair comb on each side of her head. She wears two brightly colored housedresses, one on top of the other, along with an apron. If she has to go somewhere in a hurry, she'll pull off her dirty apron and the outer dress, exposing a slightly cleaner one, and I wonder why she bothers because she still looks the same. After breast-feeding nine hungry babies and yielding to almost sixty years of gravity, her boobs hang down around her waist like water-filled balloons. Her chest appears flat until you look down and see the bumps jiggling around her waist like Jell-O. She wears plastic flip-flops on her dirt-dusted feet and only the area beneath the plastic straps reveals how white her skin is.

As I enter the kitchen Grandma hops out of her rocking chair and smiles even as it continues to rock as if a ghost had taken her place.

"Yuns hungkrrry?"

Before I can answer, she pulls out three pieces of white bread, sticks her green-stained fingers into the sugar bowl and sprinkles sugar over the bread. All the while, I'm eyeing Grandma's Russian rye, which is exclusively for adults.

Jane, Anya and I pick up our snacks as Grandma slides the spilled sugar into a pile. There's a fly on the rye bread and I try to shoo it away.

"Don't worrry, dey only eat a little bit."

I wonder if it's the same fly I saw hovering over Grandpa's evidence. Grandma puts the sugar bowl at the lip of the table and sweeps the excess crystals back into the bowl because it's a sin to waste food. I'm eating recycled sugar, but I don't care. It's sweet and I like the way it crunches on my teeth against the moist white bread.

We take our treats outside and sit on Grandpa's wooden swing because he's fiddling around somewhere else on the property. Grandma plops Jane and Anya on one side and she sits next to me facing them. She's the only one who can reach the slats beneath our feet. She pushes the swing into motion and I move forward to reach with my toes, helping her gain momentum. Now that we're swaying back and forth I lean up against Grandma's plump arm. She has countless freckles all over just like Dad and Sis. I know they're called freckles, but I ask her what they are because the word *freckle* doesn't explain why only a few people in the world have polka dots all over their bodies.

"Derrre birrrd shits."

Jane, Anya and I chuckle, snort, kick our feet and slap our thighs. I tell Grandma they couldn't possibly be bird shits and she doesn't even care that I said shit. She insists they're birrrd shits and says that all shit, any shit, is lucky. She proves it by telling me that

Aunt Edna steps in shit before she goes to the racetrack, which is why she often wins the daily-double.

Grandma lets us play connect-the-dots with her freckles. When she rests her feet on the opposite bench, Jane and Anya count the "birrrd shits" on her legs while I do her arm. We count for a long time, and even though I expect her to say "hurry up," she doesn't.

When we're done eating and counting, Grandma says, "Yuns have *schmotchkies.*" She lifts the corner of her dirty apron and wipes the sugar from our mouths.

Now Grandma wants to start dinner.

"Kahtee, go tell Mrs. Marrrchuck I need chicken."

That means she's making chicken soup. I stroll down the dirt path that leads to the Marchuck house. On the way, I pass the kitchen chair—the one in the front yard. When I reach Mrs. Marchuck's door I have to muster up some courage before I knock. She's shaped like a cinderblock and I'm sure that if she wanted to, she could tie Mr. Marchuck in a knot and make him beg for mercy. I'm certainly not going to mess with her. I take in a deep breath and knock.

"Hello, Mrs. Marchuck," I chime when she appears.

"Watchoo want?"

"Grandma needs a ch, chicken, please."

Without a word she barrels out the door and it slams behind her. She merges into the cackling brood of hens that run for their lives, pissing her off even more because they won't obey her command to "come herrre."

Dirt and feathers mingle, creating a cloud of dust. Between that and the cackling, I feel as though I'm in a nightmare. Mrs. Marchuck looks like King Kong on a mission and within minutes she grabs the unlucky fowl by its legs with one bare hand and the other around its neck.

She slams the chicken onto a tree stump, and holding it by the nape of its neck, she chops off its head in one mighty blow. The head rolls off the stump and lays on the ground—its eyes look up at me as if it didn't know it lost its body. She lets go of the beheaded fowl and it runs in circles as gook squirts from its neck. *I never want to eat another chicken, but if I don't, I'll starve like the kids in Africa.*

122

As life drains from the chicken, it stops running and drops to the ground just like Dad after one too many shots of scotch. Mrs. Marchuck grabs the corpse and sticks it into a machine with pitted bars set up similar to the ones on Mommy's wringer washer. She turns the crank and the chicken emerges featherless. She hands me the nude, headless chicken and I grab its clammy feet.

"Thank you, Mrs. Marchuck."

She doesn't acknowledge my thanks. She just scoops up the chicken's head and stomps off. I think of a word that rhymes with her last name, but I don't say it.

I follow the path back to Grandma's house, leaving a trail of gook. I pass the chair again. I have no clue that the chair will become part of an experience that will stick with me like gum on the sole of my shoe.

I hurry into Grandma's house and step down into her kitchen; its sunken floor is about four inches deeper than the rest of the house. I go over to the sink and drop in the chicken, but now there's a trail of gook leading up to the sink. Grandma throws a rag on the floor and I clean it up the way she taught me—I step on the rag and skate across the kitchen, creating a path that's much cleaner than the rest of the floor. Then I throw the dirt-brown rag into the sink with the chicken because that's what I saw Grandma do.

Later, I ask Mommy why Mrs. Marchuck always saves the chicken's head.

"Because," she says, "two heads are better than one."

Don't Mess with Grandpa Low

Grandpa throws his garbage into a metal drum, starts a fire and pokes it with a rod as he adds more junk. Flames are threatening the clouds in the sky. Without even looking at me, he knows I'm here.

"Yuns behavingk?"

"Yes, Grandpa."

"Bad kids end up in da garrrbage pile," he says.

I fear Grandpa, but I know he'd never throw me into the fire. He speaks this way to all his grandchildren. The word amongst the cousins is, "Don't mess with Grandpa Low."

His demeanor is always fierce. Even when he's in a joking mood, that can change faster than it takes to sneeze. Once when we were in Aunt Edna's house, I tried making him laugh. I grabbed two dinner plates and held them on each side of my head.

"Look," I shouted. "I'm Mickey Mouse!"

Aunt Edna chuckled, but not Grandpa.

"Stop playingk arrround beforrre I give yuns a lickin'," he warned me.

Aunt Edna insisted that I wasn't being disrespectful, but he wasn't buying it. He started ranting and pounding the table.

"Horrrse shit!"

"Donkey shit," Aunt Edna whispered to me.

As Grandpa carried on about my behavior, with a gleam in her eyes, Aunt Edna leaned over to me and whispered, "Elephant shit, people shit, fly shit."

Before then, I never knew that flies shit.

Whenever I play chess with Grandpa, he's so serious about it, I don't think he knows it's just a game. One time I could swear he moved his queen the way a knight moves, so I pointed out his mistake.

Yuns arrre wrrrongk," he insisted. "Yuns werrren't payingk attention. Now play da game."

The word *yuns* tickles my funny bone, so I laughed before he finished his lecture. But that was another mistake, because you're not allowed to have fun—even if you're having fun.

"Are yuns playingk da game or foolingk arrround?" he demanded to know.

"I'm playingk," I said.

And that's when he sneered at me as if I poisoned his pigeons. I thought I'd have to make a run for it until I saw a smile hiding in the twinkle of his eyes.

For every pint of fierceness Grandpa has, Grandma has a quart of gentleness and a gallon of nonchalance.

While Grandpa's poking the fire, he shouts, "Rrrose, come herrre."

Grandma yells back, "I'm comingk, Frrrank."

"I'm hungkrrry, Rrrose. Make some *kielbasa*."

Grandma drops what she's doing and heads toward her house. I follow her to help her season the chunks of meat just the way Grandpa likes it. It's a lot of work so I ask her why she doesn't buy *kielbasa* from the Polish store like everyone else.

"Becuz, what else is derrr to do?" she says with a smile.

While she feeds handfuls of her meat mixture through the mouth of the grinder, my job is to hold the bottom end of the intestines off the floor as the ground-up meat comes through. When it's filled, she twists and ties both ends the same way Mommy ties a bread bag.

While Grandma's boiling up the *kielbasa* I go out to explore the Low property, but there's nothing much going on today, so I meander back into her kitchen where Grandpa sits with a fork in one hand and a knife in the other. On his dinner plate is a whole ring of *kielbasa* curled up tight and hanging off the edge of his dish. There's a glow of anticipation on his face. He's so mesmerized he doesn't even know I'm standing here with a dropped jaw. I can't believe he's going to eat that entire thing himself. *That's more food than Mommy makes for all my sisters and me.* I know not to say what I'm thinking. Dad gave me a special lickin' to create a filter between my brain and my mouth—but another thought pops into my brain like a hot kernel of corn.

"Grandpa! Your *kielbasa* looks just like a snake!"

He drops his knife and fork. They bounce off his *kielbasa* and clank as they hit the Formica table. He pushes himself away from the table, but instead of his chair moving back, the table moves forward and screeches against the floor. He rises and reaches for his belt buckle.

"Yuns makingk fun of food?"

"No, Grandpa. I'm not making fun of it."

I wasn't—I was comparing. I learned that in school. But there's no use in trying to explain. I've never gotten a lickin' from Grandpa before, but as he undoes his buckle I know that's about to change.

My thoughts are coming in flashes and somewhere between Grandpa reaching for his buckle, and pulling the strap from his loops like a pro who'd done it a million times before, I envision my older cousin Joey L. saying, *"Don't mess with Grandpa; he'll get you back ten times, Kahtee Schmahgatee."* Then Dad's words echo in my head, *"You're lucky I'm giving you this lickin' and not my father. This is dessert compared to what you'd get from Grandpa!"*

I dash out the door and Grandpa comes flying out after me. I'm loaded with stamina so I could run forever, but I don't think Grandpa can—he was born long before the Dead Sea died.

I run down the dirt path toward Aunt Edna's house then I turn toward the woods. Now Grandpa's gaining on me so I run to the other side of the cesspool because I know it's like running to the other side of the dining room table when Dad chases me. Grandpa is coming at me so I turn and run in the other direction. He turns, I turn and we keep going back and forth, and now my foot slips and I'm afraid I'll end up rolling around in cocky heaven. That would be worse than a lickin', but I'm not giving up.

"When I catch yuns I'll give it to yuns double, trrriple, ten times maybe!"

I notice that he says "when" not "if" he catches me.

"Who da hell yuns tingk yuns arrre? Makingk fun of food, got-dem-it! Don't make me rrrun, got-dem-it. Yuns'll be sorrry!"

I sprint back toward Aunt Edna's house and through the path toward the Marchucks' yard. I don't even care if Mrs. Marchuck is out there, because at this moment, I'm more afraid of Grandpa. The chickens are in a frenzy, clucking and flapping as I make a path through them with Grandpa on my heels like a pull-toy. I feel like I'm a chicken being chased by Mrs. Marchuck. Realizing I can be easily cornered, I reverse and lead Grandpa around Aunt Edna's house and out toward Englishtown Road, then back toward the woods again. But this time I make a right turn behind the killee shed. I have to jump over debris, fallen branches and a bunch of other stuff I can't identify because I'm moving too fast. I'm running through an obstacle course in my bare feet and Grandpa's gaining on me.

"Yuns little snot-nosed son-of-a-bitch, yuns'll be sorrry!"

As I flash by his pigeon coop he shrieks, "Look what yuns doingk!"

The pigeons have become flustered. They flap around and group into a corner as if a storm is coming. Feathers sail out of the coop and follow me. Now I've got to slow down because I have a corner to make and I need to manage it at a sharp angle otherwise I might end up at the bottom of the open cellar with a bunch of garbage, mice, rats and enough popsicle sticks to build the house that no one ever built.

Amid the drone of cars swishing by on Englishtown Road and Grandpa's sharp warnings I can still hear the chickens' frenzied clucking. The odor of dirt is more intense as I kick up the unsettled ground. Sweat pours down my face like water from a showerhead. My heart is thrashing. My knees are weakening. I don't know how much longer I can run, but there's Grandpa, a sixty-nine-year-old bulldozer, coming at me with his belt folded up and ready to strike. Too bad for me—fortitude is one of his greatest attributes.

I want to cry, but I don't because I'll get an extra lickin'.

As I reach the front corner of his garage he snatches the back of my collar and slows me down. He grabs my arm and leads me over to the old, rusted kitchen chair that sits in the middle of his front yard as if it had been waiting for this moment.

No one else is out in the yard, but cars are whizzing by on Englishtown Road, and frankly, Grandpa doesn't give a damn if anyone catches him giving me a lickin' because that's what you do to smart-ass kids like me. You show us who's the boss.

Grandpa parks himself on the chair and pulls me across his lap.

"Yuns makingk fun of food?" Whack!

The belt comes down with a nice clean, sharp swipe right on the meatiest part of my *dupah*.

"Yuns don't know what it's like to starrrve." Whack! "I know what it feels like to starrrve," he shrieks as if *he's* in pain, then he whacks me again.

He may have been starving at some point in his life but right now the size of his belly is telling me a different story.

"Got-dem-smarrrt-ass!" Crack! "I'll show yuns how to make fun of food!" Whack! "Derrre, yuns like dat?" Whack! "Next time yuns tingk about what yuns say!" Snap! "Yuns tingk yuns arrre so smarrrt?" Whack! "I'll show yuns how smarrrt yuns arrre!" Whack!

My *dupah* stings as though it was attacked by a swarm of bees, but at least Grandpa has a good aim. When Dad whacks me he always sees red and misses the target.

Grandpa lifts me from his lap.

"Yuns arrre lucky. I went easy. Dat was just an appetizerrr."

Just an appetizer? I'm glad I didn't order the whole meal.

"Neverrr make fun of food again!" he demands as his pointer moves back and forth in my face. "Now apologize!"

"I'm sorry, Grandpa. I didn't mean to make fun of food. I won't ever do it again."

"Dat's betterrr," he says. "Okay, go and behave yunself."

I put my arms around Grandpa to hug him, but he just pats me on the back the same way Dad does. That means go away and be good, and being good means keeping my big mouth shut.

All I want is a hug—a real one. I almost cry, but I hold it in. I push back my hair, smooth out my clothing and walk away straight and tall just the way I'm expected to—with my lips sealed like an unopened letter. No crying, no complaining.

If Dad found out about this, he'd give it to me double or triple, but he won't because Grandpa is no stool pigeon. When Grandpa catches you doing something wrong, he takes care of it then and there with a dose of his medicine, so there's no need for him to ever mention it.

I'll never comment on Grandpa's food again, not even when I see him eating pig's feet and I have to sit there envisioning some poor footless pig wobbling back and forth on its belly like a helpless turtle.

The Last Straw

A whole bunch of us Lows are visiting Aunt Anna and Uncle Al in Staten Island. I washed my feet today and although I keep standing in front of Uncle Al's good eye, he doesn't even notice.

I scamper outside to run wild on Wild Avenue with all the cousins, but before long the grown-ups are raising more hell than us kids. Now I have to leave my game of tag. I follow the noise into the house, and it leads me to Dad. He's drunk and he's arguing with Uncle Johnny over some guy named Bob. Uncle Johnny says Bob is a friend to both of them, but Dad insists Bob is *his* friend.

"You can't *own* people," Uncle Johnny says.

Dad replies with a flying fist but he misses the target, and now things are falling all over until the uncles wrap Dad into the middle of a giant group hug.

Uncle Johnny has to take his family and leave the party. When he's gone, Dad curses him and has another drink.

"Yeah, you're right, Joey," everyone says just to humor him.

Mommy drives home while Dad sloshes around in the passenger seat, complaining. She yeses him to death but he doesn't die —he just falls asleep and we have to listen to him snoring all the way from Staten Island to New Jersey.

In the morning Mommy tells Dad she's not going anywhere with him anymore. She's sick and tired of him getting drunk everywhere they go. Because of him, she never enjoys herself. Dad raises his right hand as if he's in court and swears he'll stay sober the next time; and the next Low celebration is always just around the corner.

****

The "Beer Barrel Polka" prompts all the Lows to hop around like a bunch of kangaroos revved up on Mexican jumping beans. In between the singing and dancing there's lots of drinking because those things go together like *kielbasa* and *sauerkraut*. Dad sips his scotch instead of chugging it, then he skates Mommy across the dance floor in a foxtrot. After that, Dad dances with us kids, and I get to stand on his shoes while he swirls me around in circles. I'm so elated, I want another dance, but Dad is thirsty.

Soon, the booze starts talking, and Dad gets so loud you can hear him above the band.

"Are you okay?" I ask.

"Don't worry about what the hell I'm doing," he growls. "Mind your own goddamned business and worry about yourself."

By the end of the night Mommy can't wait to go home because Dad's plastered and itching for another fight. Five of my uncles turn themselves into pallbearers, surround Dad, grab a body part, and carry him out to the car.

Aunt Edna waits by the door with Mommy as the procession passes by.

"You were the life of the party, Lil," Aunt Edna says, "and you were the only one who didn't drink."

"Joe had enough for all of us."

I look up at Mommy and I think she's so beautiful, but I don't say it. *She made everyone laugh, sing and dance without having one drink. When I grow up, I want to be just like her.*

All the way home we smell secondhand scotch oozing from Dad's pores and lungs. As if that isn't bad enough, he falls asleep and snores like a pig with a cold.

We arrive home and go into the house. Dad stays in the car. I want to wake him up, but Mommy wants to let him sleep.

"Is Dad going to be okay?"

"Don't worry," Mommy says, "he'll be okay. He's got an angel on his shoulder."

She always says that, but I think she's the angel.

Dad finds his way into the house in the middle of the night. His snoring awakens me too early. The putrid smell of secondhand scotch seeps out from beneath his bedroom door through the hallway and into my room. I see it, taste it, smell it, and I feel it deep in my gut. My anxiety opens the door for Dad to add more descriptions of me. I'm not just a stupid ass with a goddamned big mouth—I'm also a worrywart and a black sheep. By the tone of his voice, I know that a black sheep is a reject. *Something must be wrong with me.*

Worrying keeps me from falling asleep. I try not to agonize, but it doesn't work. I sit up in bed listening to the bats. I may have enough earwax to grow a potato farm, but I also hear lots of other things at night that are becoming very familiar—banging sounds and muddled arguments. I know something's not right. Most of the commotion happens on Friday nights and sometimes, Saturday nights, so come the weekends, I try to stay awake. I don't want to fall asleep before Dad gets home, but when I do, I dream that I'm falling off a cliff. I'm in a free fall and about to hit bottom and die when a commotion awakens me.

Mommy's downstairs telling Dad to stop it. "You're hurting me," she says.

I tiptoe to the third step from the top landing in view of Dad sitting on Mommy. She's crying and pleading for him to get off of her, but he won't get up. Mommy is skin and bones and Dad, at twice her weight, is a bulldozer.

"You're a terrible mother," Dad slurs. "You don't do a goddamned thing all day long. You must be going out and cheating on me!"

Mommy says nothing during Dad's rant. He mocks everything about her, even her heritage. *Maybe he doesn't like me because I look Armenian.* He says if it weren't for him they'd have nothing because she spends money like it's water and he's tired of working like a dog and going nowhere.

"What the hell do you do with all the goddamned money I give you?" the dog asks as he slaps Mommy in the face.

I know I'm supposed to mind my own beeswax but something comes over me.

"You leave her alone!" I scream as I fly down the stairs. "It's not true! She's a good mother!"

Dad's shirt is full of perspiration and his shirttails are hanging out of his pants. His hair's a mess and he smells like a brewery. He looks like a grizzly bear and I'm frightened but I'm more upset over what he's doing to my mommy.

"You get off her!"

Now flames are erupting from the dragon. He's trying to stand but he's so drunk he can hardly steady himself. When he finally gets to his feet, he darts after me.

"What the hell are you doing up? Get the hell to bed, goddamn it!"

"Leave her alone," Mommy shouts, then she picks up a dining room chair and moves it in front of her. I wish she would pick it up like the lion tamers do. I saw that on a Saturday morning cartoon. Too bad she didn't see that one.

I sprint up the steps two at a time as Dad sways at the bottom, yelling at me to mind my own goddamned business and asking me what the hell's the matter with me. He tells me I have a big mouth and I should get the hell to bed.

My sisters are asleep. I can't tell them what happened because I'm not supposed to open my big mouth. I'm not even supposed to be seeing what's happening, but now that I have, one too many times, I've got to pretend I didn't. I hop into bed, curl up and pull the covers over my head. I cry silently. I won't get a lickin' if no one hears me. The noises and banging sounds coming from downstairs are muddled beneath the pounding of my heart and my sniffling. I don't want to fall asleep. I've got to stay awake just in case it gets really crazy down there. *Mommy might need me. God, please make Dad stop drinking.*

In the morning Dad's secondhand scotch mingles with the perking coffee. I get dressed then hurry downstairs to see what's happening in the kitchen. Like always, I stop at its threshold and rest my cheek on the doorjamb. Dad's bragging about all the fun he had in the bar, and how he bought rounds of drinks for everyone.

Mommy never has enough money for food and bills. Why would he buy drinks for people we never get to meet?

Dad looks up and sees me standing in the doorway.

Mommy always says he forgets what he did when he's drunk and then she puts her finger up to her lips and says shhh. I don't think Dad forgets because he always remembers what I did.

"How the hell many times do you have to be told to mind your own goddamned business?" he says. He doesn't want an answer because he shoots questions at me like they're coming from a machine gun.

"What the hell's the matter with you, goddamn it? Are you stupid? If you don't start minding your own goddamned business, one of these days I'm going to give it to you good and you'll be lucky you got it from me and not Grandpa. What the hell am I going to do with you?"

Mommy isn't saying anything. She just runs back and forth waiting on him like she always does. I wonder if I dreamt what I saw, but I know I didn't because Dad wouldn't have said all those things if it came from my imagination. I'm almost eight years old and I already know that things happen in the night—a lot. When I try talking about it Mommy just says life's too short to make a big deal out of every little thing and I should just forget about it. So I pretend nothing happened, and soon I really do forget. But Friday nights roll around over and over, and the moment *it* happens again, it makes me remember all the other times *it* happened. Mommy sings around the house less and less. She looks the same, but whatever's inside of her is gone or hiding or lost. Now I'm worried about Mommy *and* Dad.

****

Grandpa Low teaches me a new rule each time we play chess. "Rrrule numberrr one: derrre's no foolingk arrround. Numberrr two: pay attention. Numberrr thrrree: yuns are da kingk and da kingk tells all da otherrr pisses what to do."

I become so reckless with the pawns, Grandpa asks what the hell I'm doing.

"Who cares about the pawns?" I say. "The *king* is the most important man."

"Yuns thingk so?" Grandpa says. "Keep thrrrowingk dem pawns away like dat and yuns'll have trrrouble."

When Grandpa seizes all my men, my king is left unprotected, naked as a tree in the winter. He doesn't show me any mercy, but every time we play he lets me in on a little secret.

"Rrrememberrr, da kingk is da boss, but without da otherrr pisses, he's da boss of nothingk. And when da game is overrr, he sleeps in da same box with da pawns."

I always think of Dad when I play chess because he says he's the king of his castle. Pretty soon he's going to be the king of an empty castle because I heard Mommy on the telephone.

"I'm leaving him. I can't take it anymore. It's too hard living with a man who drinks and fights."

She means it too, because when Dad's gone for the day she pulls out the big blue suitcase and packs her work clothes. She's going to look for a job in the city; maybe the Federal Reserve will give her back her old job. She packs my sisters' clothes and mine, then tells us we're going on vacation, but I know better.

We take a bus into the city and we go down into the subway. As we travel Mommy teaches us everything we need to know to keep ourselves safe, especially in the subway. We have to stay behind the yellow line so we don't fall into the big hole and get run over by a train. If we did, we'd turn into a pancake and someone might pour syrup all over us and have us for breakfast.

We reach our stop, march up the steps, hike to 333 Third Avenue right at 25th Street, then we climb the stairs to apartment 19, where Yaya and the Baron are waiting for us.

Soon I'll be hearing all about the Turks.

Writing on the Ice

While Mommy's out job hunting, the Baron asks who wants to play cards. Jane, Anya and I do. The Baron teaches us how to play war and when his card beats ours, he slams it down and laughs as if he just killed a Turk. When we beat his card, we mimic him, and by the time the game is over we pulverize a whole army of Turks.

In the evening Yaya opens up the sofa and turns it into a bed. Her apartment is small so we're all squished together like beans in a can. After everyone falls asleep their farts mingle with the sounds of honking horns and distant sirens, and I lay awake imprisoned in a smelly symphony. If their farts were electric, they'd blow out the fuse box—and *they* have the nerve to tell me I'm the one who does all the farting. Well, they don't actually say fart, they say *jart* because that's how you say it in Armenian. I don't know what everyone's problem is. We're supposed to go around pretending we don't *jart* when we know we do—every day—especially the grown-ups. They've perfected the art of squeezing their cheeks so that it comes out silently. I know about cheek squeezing because Mommy taught me how to do it after I came home from school and told her I *jarted* out loud in the classroom. My teacher said I didn't have any manners, that I needed to learn some. Her disapproval immediately taught me that it isn't mannerly for a kid to make the sound of a *jart,* yet it's perfectly fine for grown-ups to silently fill the air with an odor strong enough to melt the elastic on their bloomers.

In the morning when all the cockroaches are scurrying to find their hiding places, Yaya tries to kill them with a fly swatter. Bugs and dirt nauseate her so much, she can't walk past anything yucky or dirty without uttering, *"Peef, peef, lesh."* She chases away all the cockroaches, then she makes us hot cereal and tells us not to drop any food because it'll attract bugs to her apartment. So now that the roaches are hiding, we pretend they're not here at all.

After breakfast Mommy takes us out on the town. We head down the stairwell and spill out onto the street where people are speaking Spanish.

"Years ago all you heard were the sounds of Greek, Armenian, Italian and English," Mommy says. "Except for Yaya and the Baron, all the old neighbors moved out to the country."

Walking along Broadway is the best. People in every flavor imaginable roam the streets. Some are dressed to the nines, others in rags, and some sport costumes even though it isn't Halloween. On Broadway there's a huge throng screaming, jumping and acting like a bunch of lunatics near one of the theaters. Mommy holds up each of us for a minute and points to a beautiful lady standing in the middle of the crowd.

"How come everyone's screaming, Mommy?"

"That's Julie Andrews. She's famous. They want her autograph. Come on," Mommy insists, "let's go."

"Can't we get her autograph, too?"

"What am I supposed to do with an autograph?" Mommy says. "We don't need to waste her time or ours waiting on line for her signature."

"If Rock Hudson was on Broadway, you'd wait on line."

"If I waited on line for him," she says, "it wouldn't be for an autograph."

Mommy walks us up to the corner of Broadway and Maiden Lane and there in the sidewalk is a clock—right in the middle of the cement. It says "WILLIAM BARTHMAN SINCE 1884." I don't know who William Barthman is, but I'm in awe of his clock. It tells you what time it is and what direction you're going, so I walk over time to the north, I skip over it, and I dance on it. As long as I'm standing on the clock I'll always be on time. The only thing I can't do is stop time. Mommy wants to go, but I don't want to leave the clock

—I love it! *I don't know why,* I tell her, *I just do.* As always, Mommy sings a song from the words I say.

Restaurants, theaters, and stores line the streets, but we can't go into any of them because we don't have any money to spend. Instead, we just read the signs and eat the sandwiches Mommy packed for us. I know there's no way we're getting anything so I don't ask, but Mommy surprises us. She buys a huge warm salted pretzel, breaks it into pieces just like you break a loaf of bread, and we share it. What a *lucky* day for me! It's *so* delicious!

It's such a fun day, but I'm tired, so I don't mind when Mommy says it's time to go.

I don't know how many nights we stayed with Yaya and the Baron, but it must be too many because the Baron is so annoyed with Mommy he's not yelling about the Turks anymore. On the day Mommy is supposed to meet with someone at the Federal Reserve, the Baron says she can't stay at the apartment. Mommy wants to know where she's supposed to go if she can't stay here.

"Go home to your husband! He's a good man! You can't stay here!" the Baron yelps as spit flies from his mouth onto Mommy's cheek.

"I've only asked you for two favors in my entire life," Mommy shrieks as she wipes her face. "You refused to give me money for shoes when I was a kid, and now, all I need is a place to stay for a little while, and you can't even give me that."

"Go home to Joe! That's where you belong!" the Baron insists.

Mommy turns to Yaya.

"What can I do?" Yaya says. "He's the man. He's the boss. Go home to Joe; he's a good man."

Mommy trembles as tears spill from her eyes. She slips into the bathroom and stays there for a long time, even after the Baron starts banging on the door. He wants her to hurry up because he's got to use the *beckarrron.* They only have one *beckarrron* just like us, which means you're supposed to leave the door unlocked so that people can sit on the bathtub side by side waiting for their crack at the toilet. But I know Mommy's not using the toilet; she's crying. Mommy tells the Baron he has to wait, but he can't, so he leaves the apartment. When

138

she emerges from the *beckarrron,* she argues with Yaya in Armenian. Mommy never gets angry, but she *is* now. When they're done bickering Mommy isn't mad anymore, just sad. Now I'm not sure if we're going to leave or stay. I sit in the living room playing war with my sisters because slapping Turks passes good time. I pretend I don't hear a thing.

There's a poem about going to market and buying a fat pig and when you're done shopping you "go home again, home again, jiggety-jig." That's what Mommy says.

"Home again, home again, jiggety-jig."

Sometimes she just says jiggety-jig and we know that means it's time to go.

We head down into the subway, board the train, and begin our journey home. I think about Dad most of the way there.

As we enter the house I smell coffee. Dad's leaning up against the kitchen sink with his back toward the window. As he sips from his mug, his classy little pinky points up toward heaven. I burst out in tears because I realize I missed him so much. My sisters aren't crying —just me, I'm the crybaby. I run to Dad and hug him. My face is in his stomach and my tears and *schmotchkies* are messing up his shirt. I try not to cry, but I can't help it, so I don't even care if he has to give me a lickin'. He asks me why I'm crying and it's a real question because he doesn't say anything else.

"I missed you, Daddy."

"You *missed* me?" he laughs.

"Yes," I say as I try not to cry.

"All right, all right, I missed you too," he says and he pats me on the head.

Now my sisters and I have to disappear for a while because Mommy and Dad need to talk in private. I don't feel like playing on the swings with Anya and Jane so I sit on the stoop next to the milk box to do some people watching. But it's hard to people-watch because Mommy and Daddy's voices are filtering through the kitchen screen. I'll have to pretend I don't have ears, otherwise Dad will call me a busybody, a black sheep, and then he'll ask me if I'm stupid.

Mommy is telling Dad about everything she doesn't like. She *never* talks about things she doesn't like. *Dad's* the one who does *that!* She says she's horrified at how he sees red when he's angry, and she doesn't like how he acts when he drinks. He's got to stop drinking! She can't go anywhere with him because he always ends up three-sheets-to-the-wind and picks a fight with anyone who's standing in his way. He'd even pick a fight with God if he could.

"I can't keep living like this, Joe," she says. "It's all got to change! Even your partiality with the kids! If you have something to give, you shouldn't just do for one and say the hell with the rest of them, Joe."

I hope Dad doesn't turn into a lion because Mommy's not done yet—she's on a hard roll without the bologna.

"You've got to stop spending money in the bars because I never have enough to buy food. I'm tired of scraping and scrounging like a pauper while you go out living the high life, acting like a big shot, buying strangers drinks and giving other people's kids money. Charity begins at home, Joe, and you've got to start acting like a husband and a father instead of a teenager—gallivanting all the time and hopping from job to job. I'm sick and tired of your misery and the way you always point your finger at other people when *you're* the one who does all the screwing up."

"You're right, Lil," Dad agrees. "I'm sorry. I'll never do those things again. Not ever! I'll quit drinking, too."

"Don't write it on the ice again. Words are cheap, Joe. Prove it! If you don't shape up, next time I'm leaving for good."

"You can't leave, Lil. I love you."

"Then do better right now, not tomorrow!"

"I *swear* to God, Lil, I'll try. I *swear* to God I will!"

Now I don't hear anything—they must be kissing!

I'm so happy that I thank God for answering my prayers. Dad's never going to drink again. Everything's perfect! Now, I don't have to be a worrywart anymore.

Storytellers and Troublemakers

Except for the bats, Friday and Saturday nights have been quiet since we came home from Yaya's. I don't have to worry about Mommy anymore, but I have to figure out how to stay out of trouble. I never saw Dad give Sis a lickin' so I figure I can learn a few things by watching her.

"Take a picture, it'll last longer," Sis snarls when she catches me looking at her.

It's hard not to look at her because I think she's beautiful. I don't want to anger her so I wait till I think she won't notice, but she always does.

"You're ugly," she laughs mockingly. "You have the cooties! I wouldn't want to touch you with a ten-foot pole!"

She pinches my arm with her nails and draws blood. When I scream, Dad appears and Sis whines to him that I never leave her alone. Now Dad tells me I'm a troublemaker and he's sick of my big mouth. I try telling him I just looked at her, but he doesn't want any backtalk.

"Goddamn it," he says. "Stay away from her and stop looking for trouble or I'll teach you a lesson you'll never forget."

While he yells at me, Sis quietly slips away with a smirk and a twinkle in her eyes.

Dad says eight years old is the age of reasoning, so there's no cause for me to be getting myself into trouble anymore. But I'm always screwing something up. In school I make a new friend, Sharon. During recess Sharon and I play, and in class she sits next to me and whispers lots of stuff. She asks what nationality I am so I tell her I'm

Russian, Polish, Greek and Armenian. Then she asks if I celebrate Christmas or Hanukkah. I tell her Christmas. She tells me she's Jewish and she doesn't believe in Jesus Christ. Then she says I'm stupid if I believe in Him. I'm not so sure what I believe, but I know I'm supposed to believe in Jesus because my church tells me to. I think I could stick up for myself so I tell her she's stupid because she *doesn't* believe in Him.

Sharon raises her hand and tells the teacher what I said. She doesn't tell her what *she* said, and right then and there I know that telling half of a story is a lie. The teacher asks me if I said that and I tell her yes, but she doesn't let me finish. She grabs a piece of chalk and writes on the blackboard: "I must not discriminate against Jews." She says to write it a hundred times, then she hands me some paper. I raise my hand but she ignores me. I write the sentence once, twice, then I raise my hand again. The teacher doesn't want to hear one word out of me so I shut my mouth and write the sentence again and again.

I'm worried about Dad finding out because he likes the Jews. He always tells me to pass my subjects in school, grow up, and find a man to marry who will take care of me. Then he tells me I'll be lucky if I find a nice Jewish man because they're good to their wives.

When I hand in my punishment assignment the teacher says if she ever hears me talking bad about the Jews again, she'll send me down to the principal's office. She makes me apologize to Sharon. I do, but now we're not friends anymore.

During recess one of the boys calls me a Commie, then he whispers something to my classmates and now they're all calling me a Commie. I still don't know what a Commie is, but it must be bad because the kids are running away from me. They're laughing at me, and now one of the boys calls me a Low-life. My teacher is standing nearby and hears everything. I wait for her to tell those kids they have to write, "I must not discriminate against Commies," but she doesn't because no one likes a Commie. The next time the siren goes off and we have to march into the hallway to protect ourselves from the Russians, that same kid calls it a Commie drill. I figure out that a Commie is a Russian, and that's what I am.

At home Mommy asks me what I did in school. I show her my work, but I don't tell her what happened. I dash outside and climb into God's umbrella—my oak tree. I melt onto my favorite branch like butter in a frying pan while a bat sleeps upside down above my head— and I wonder if Jesus is real. *I'm not so sure because I don't think you can really feed thousands of people with a few loaves of bread unless you just give them each a tiny crumb and how would that keep them from starving?* Just *thinking* a question makes me feel like a sinner.

I pick bark off the tree and use it to scratch the itch on my arm. I hang upside down like a bat. I watch birds and people, and I sing away my unanswered questions. When I'm up here inside my tree, all my troubles pop like bubbles.

****

Now that Dad isn't going to the bars he has lots of extra spending cash. He keeps a big wad in his pocket because he likes to spend money. He buys a doghouse. Not a real one. It's a wooden plaque that hangs on the wall. There's a hook inside the doghouse and below the house are hooks with little dogs hanging on them. Our names are on each of the dogs. We can stay out of the doghouse by staying out of trouble, which means I'm always in the doghouse. Dad put me in there because I looked at Sis again. He's tired of me bothering her so every time I go into the kitchen I see myself in the stupid doghouse. Mommy doesn't care for the doghouse.

"That's a foolish way to spend good money," she tells Dad.

"I'm not spending it in the bars, so what the hell do you want from me?" the lion roars.

He buys a lot of stuff and he gives money to one of his sisters for a bicycle and other items for her children.

"That's not right!" Mommy screeches.

"I'm the one who earns the money. You have no right telling me what to do, goddamn it. *I'm* the king of this castle!"

"Yeah," Mommy says, "and your castle has holes in the walls, empty cupboards and bats in the belfry, but there's plenty of booze for a party."

"Stop making such a big goddamned deal out of this, Lil. There's nothing wrong in being charitable once in a while."

"Once in a while? Since when is it right to buy things for other kids who are old enough to go out and get a job when your own kids need shoes. And *they* could use a new bike. All we have are a couple of old rusted ones that need to be thrown away," Mommy says. "People who have money for junk food, make-up, and falsies don't need charity, they need priority lessons. And so do you, Joe. Get the money back and give it to me!"

"It's too late," Dad says. "Besides, I'm not an Indian giver."

"The next time you have money to burn give it to me for bills. Otherwise you might as well light a match to it."

****

When Dad's wad builds up again he takes us to the Bronx Zoo. The zoo smells worse than a *jart,* but it's so much fun. I love the animals, but the best one of all is the lady orangutan with red hair. We can't stop laughing because she has the same name as Sis, and the same color hair. Even Mommy and Dad giggle as Sis the orangutan sits there scratching her head and heinie. It's hard to contain ourselves until Dad yells, "All right already, enough!"

After the zoo Dad drives us into Chinatown. The streets and traffic are crazy but Dad doesn't get lost because he used to be a cabbie. He tells us about the time when he was driving a beautiful lady over the bridge from New Jersey to New York.

"The traffic stopped on the bridge and the lady kept saying, 'Mister, mister, how long is it going to be? Mister, when are we going to get there?' I'm not sure why she keeps asking until finally she tells me that she has to use a bathroom. I ask her if it's 'number one or number two?' She yells, 'Number two!' And *she can't wait!* I tell her there's nothing I can do, she'll have to wait. She says she can't. She needs something to go in and she needs it *now!* So I dump out my lunch," Dad chuckles, "then I pass her my brown paper bag. She tells me to close my eyes and I tell her, don't worry, lady, I don't want to see what you're doing. I don't need to look because I have a nose and a set of ears. So while she's back there grunting, I have to roll down the window and stick out my head like a puppy dog, otherwise, the odor would've melted my nose off."

Dad's entire body is laughing, so we have to wait five minutes before he can continue.

"Okay," Dad says breathlessly. "So I got my head hanging out the window until the beautiful lady in the suit tells me she's done making cocky. She closes up the bag and drops it on her seat. When the traffic breaks up and I drive across the bridge, the lady shouts, 'Let me out now!' So I kick the brake, we jerk forward, bob and ricochet, then she throws some money at me and jumps out. I hop out after her yelling, 'Hey lady, you forgot something important!' When she reappears, I hand her the bag of cocky and I tell her, 'Here's your lunch, lady.'"

Dad's story is so funny, he lets me laugh as long as I want and I almost pee in my pants.

In Chinatown, we head to one of Dad's favorite restaurants. The maître d' escorts us to our table and pushes our chairs in as we sit. Dad pushes in Mommy's chair and takes off his hat because that's what gentlemen do. He tells us to unfold our napkins and put them on our lap, sit up straight and tall, fold our hands, keep our lips zipped and be patient. He lets us look at the menu but he does the ordering: egg rolls, egg drop soup, fried rice, chicken chow mein and shrimp with lobster sauce. When the soup comes Dad demonstrates how to scoop it up moving the spoon away from our bodies, and he tells us *never* to leave our spoon in the bowl in between. When the main course comes he shows us how to use the chopsticks. I'm determined to eat every last bite with these sticks because when you're in China you're supposed to do as the Chinese do.

Now Dad has an extra surprise for us. We can pick out a souvenir. There are unusual items inside a glass case, but we can only choose from the bottom row.

"The souvenir is not a toy," Dad says. "It's a reminder of the day we spent together. Every time you look at it, you'll remember all the fun we had."

I choose a purple dragon made of paper.

For me, the best part of the day was when Dad tells his funny story. I'm in love with that part. I love the dragon, too. It's my first souvenir, but with or without it, I'll remember this day for the rest of my life.

Life Ain't Fair

Mommy and Dad rearrange the bedrooms. They give Sis, Jane and Anya their old bedroom and they put me in the small one by myself. Sis says no one wants to be with me because I fart. I know I could drag a fart all the way to the mailbox and back, but I'm not the only one who can.

"You fart, too," I tell her.

"You're ugly," Sis laughs.

"So are you."

"I know you are but what am I?" she says, then she slips away whispering, "You stink. You're ugly, ha, ha."

"Stop it!" I yell.

"What the hell's going on?" Dad shouts.

"I'm just sticking up for myself, Daddy."

"I don't care. It takes two to tango, goddamn it! I'm sick and tired of all your bullshit. Jeeeeeeeeesus Christ already!"

He doesn't hit me, but he looks like he's going to.

I go to the bathroom mirror to study my ugly face. My nose is so big I can sail a ship with it. There's a bump on it from the time I ran into my oak tree. I was using it as second base and wasn't watching where I was going. Mommy pressed my nose with her thumbs to push it back into place and then I had to hold an ice pack on it until it froze. I have crooked teeth and hairy eyebrows that connect, so it's really one big, bushy brow. There are black hairs growing above the corners of my mouth and my neck is so long, I look like a giraffe. This is what ugly looks like and there's nothing I can do about it. *Just when I've figured out that cooties is a made up disease I learn that people might not like me because I'm ugly.*

****

Our house is rearranged just in time to celebrate Easter. Like Christmas, the Russian church honors Easter Sunday on a different day than the rest of the world, but Dad wants to be in sync with his family so we celebrate it the same day as Catholics.

Dad bows his head and thanks the Lord for all His blessings. He's on the wagon, but it's a holiday so he pours a shot of scotch, we raise our jelly jars, clink and chime, *"Na Zdorovie!"*

We eat the magnificent meal Mommy made: fresh ham, scalloped potatoes and all kinds of vegetables. When we're done, we can have the candy from our baskets. They tell me the Easter Bunny left the candy, but I don't think there's an Easter Bunny, a Santa Claus, a Sandman or a Tooth Fairy. If they were real, they wouldn't be so unfair. The Easter Bunny leaves other kids giant chocolate bunnies and candy eggs of all kinds. We Low girls get a tiny chocolate bunny, twelve jellybeans, four malted balls, and a marshmallow egg. We're not allowed to eat it until later in the day, so we dump everything out of our baskets, scrutinize and count each piece, then artfully arrange them in our baskets over and again to visually enjoy them.

Mommy's in the kitchen cleaning up while King Farouk sits in his chair yelling, "Lil, bring me coffee!" I bring it to him, very carefully.

With the kitchen done, we head out to Grandma and Grandpa's house. The aunts, uncles and cousins are there. It's the usual Low celebration and I'm happy because I get to see my cousins. Grandma and Grandpa have about two dozen grandkids, so there are enough of us to make our own Easter parade. We march on the muddy ground showing off the pretty dresses Mommy made while the grown-ups drink, laugh and argue.

Dad is bickering with Grandpa.

"You always favored Johnny," Dad complains. "That wasn't fair, Pop."

148

"I trrreated yuns all da same, got-dem it. But yuns werrre nothingk but a got-dem rrrebel, a got-dem trrroublemakerrr."

It's late and it's time to go, but Dad wants to stay. He's not done arguing with Grandpa, so Mommy leaves him there and drives us kids home.

I don't want to go to sleep. I want to make sure Dad comes home safe and goes straight to sleep without making a peep. I pass the time by putting my ears on the wall. The bats were quiet from New Year's Eve until April Fool's Day, but after a long winter's nap, they're becoming restless again. Soon I'm asleep.

****

Yaya and the Baron visit often now. Although the Baron wouldn't even share a grain of salt with Mommy, she treats him with the utmost respect. She doesn't believe in revenge. Two wrongs don't make a right, so she waits on him and Yaya just like she does with Dad.

After we eat, the Baron asks, "Who wants to play walk-the-plank?"

Jane, Anya and I jump up and down.

"We do!"

We follow the Baron outside. He lies down on his belly in a patch of weeds and we line up to walk barefoot along his spine, one at a time, and jump off his shoulders. We can walk the plank as much as we want because it soothes his aching back.

After Jane and Anya have enough of walking the plank, they run off to play on the swings. I sit in the weeds with the Baron because I like hanging out with old people. Everyone says the Baron is a mean, bitter old man, yet beneath his angry haze, I see a light.

He's never been mean to me—well, just once, but that was my own doing. It was the time I spent a short vacation with Yaya and the Baron.

I was bored and asked to go outside. If I promised not to run off, I could sit on their front stoop. But I forgot about my promise when I heard a bunch of boys around the corner joking and screaming in a Latin lilt as they played cards. I was drawn to them.

"You wanna play knucks?"

"Yes!" I exclaimed.

In knucks, the loser puts out a fist and the winner swipes it with the deck of cards. I lost and got my knuckles rapped. They were so raw, they began to bleed, but I didn't care. The boys made me feel wanted.

Suddenly someone snatched me from behind, lifted me off the concrete porch and planted me right onto the sidewalk. It was the Baron. He grabbed my arm and pulled me back to his apartment, all the while spewing Armenian curses. He got me upstairs and nudged me into the kitchen chair, pointing his finger in my face.

"You broke your promise!"

I did, and I know I was wrong. I put my hands up to my face because I was waiting for him to pull off his belt and whack me—but he didn't. He slid me onto his lap.

"I was sick with worry. If you were in trouble, how could I help you if I couldn't find you? Never make a promise you can't keep! Breaking a promise is a lie," he said.

I felt so ashamed of myself I couldn't stop crying. Although he was furious, he tenderly dried my tears. I knew I was important to him, and everything he said sunk deep into my heart and made me think long and hard about the importance of keeping a promise.

My heart knows that I can't count that as meanness. I love the Baron, but I'm afraid to tell anyone that I do. Except for Yaya, I don't know if anyone loves him, and it feels as though I'm not allowed to love him either, so I keep it a secret.

Now that I'm done walking the plank, the Baron leans back on his hands with his eyes closed and his face up to the sun.

"Grandpa," I ask, "how come you're always angry?"

His eyes swipe me from head to toe.

"When I was your size," he says, "I was living in Turkey."

I'm nine so I guess he's going to tell me a story about when he was nine.

"I was playing in the hills with my brother. From a distance we could see a throng of Turks riding up to our village on horseback. They had guns and swords and they were screaming and laughing. They

150

looked like a bunch of dirty, wild savages. My brother and I stayed in the hills, taking cover behind the brush where we could see the Turks rampage. One by one, they killed everyone in the village: men, women, children, and they tossed babies into the air as if they were soccer balls then caught them on their swords. They didn't just kill people, they cut them into pieces like you cut a leg of lamb for *shish kabob*. And they laughed as if it was fun. I couldn't believe my eyes. I had to touch them to be sure they were open, to be sure I wasn't having a nightmare. My entire family was in that village. Everyone except my brother, all of them murdered. I just can't get that out of my head.

"After the slaughter the Turks stole anything they could benefit from and rode off laughing heartily. I watched them disappear into the distance; and my brother and I wept. But we were brave. We walked down into the village and searched for our mother. We found her familiar hands and feet among the scattered limbs."

The Baron's deeply tanned skin turns red and looks funny against his white hair. His neck veins pop as if it's happening now. He waves his hands as he recalls human limbs being scattered on the ground like windblown leaves. Besides the murderous rampage, the Turks did unspeakable things that he cannot repeat, but in years to come I will learn that he watched his sister and mother being brutally raped before they were chopped to bits.

"My brother and I were sickened," the Baron yelps. "The Turks broke us in half. I was just a boy! What kind of monsters would do such a thing?"

I can't answer him. I feel so bad for the Baron. *I can't believe he lost his mommy like that. I can't believe he saw such horror. I, too, want to know what kind of monsters they are.*

"I didn't think I could go on," the Baron continues, "but my brother and I went to see a Turkish friend who took us in and cared for us. To protect ourselves, we had to change our names and adopt Muslim customs. I stayed there for as long as I could, but staying was like lying—I didn't want to be a Muslim. I couldn't live among those Turkish savages, so I made the difficult decision to leave my brother and my childhood in Turkey. I came to America to escape the horror, but it followed me here.

"All I wanted was to make a family, to have children of my own, and to forget. Is that too much to ask?"

I don't know how to answer him. *He did get married, but he never had his own children, just someone else's.*

He puts his hands over his face, but tears seep through his fingers—all because he can't forget. His memory is a curse, a disease.

I want one of his wishes to come true so I hug him and tell him, "You're my *real* Grandpa."

"I know, *Orrreeorrrt.*"

That's what he calls me: *Orrreeorrrt.*

"Don't ever forget it—what I tell you!" the Baron pleads. "Never, *ever* forget it, all your life!"

"I won't forget, Grandpa. I promise," *and I won't break my promise this time.*

Afterwards the Baron shouts, "Who wants to take a ride and buy a candy bar?"

Only Jane, Anya and I want to. Going for a ride in the Baron's Buick for a candy bar is a treat and we're not passing that up. Mommy tells the Baron to be careful driving because he gets mad at other cars on the road and yells when they make one teeny mistake.

"That's because he got his license from the inside of a Cracker Jack box," Yaya chuckles.

We kids don't care if he got his license from a cereal box. We hop into his Buick and off we go.

****

It's a beautiful summer day. We go down to the Low property for a family gathering. Little Anthony is here and I'm glad because I hardly get to see him. He's a relative from another branch of the family, but I love him as if he were my own cousin. We must've been twins in another life because when we play, without a word, we know what we're going to do next.

The plywood picnic table was moved to a clearing in the woods, about fifteen giant steps from the open cesspool. That's where the grown-ups are partying while we cousins run amok. Dad isn't drinking scotch today, just beer, which makes him burp like a truck driver.

As I'm running past the table, Grandma stops me and hands me some dirty dishes to bring to her kitchen. On the way back to the woods, I find a nickel in the dirt so I cross Englishtown Road to buy myself an ice cream. It isn't nice to eat in front of other people if you can't share, so I gobble it up quickly, then head back across the street. As I reach the middle of the road I hear tires screeching. I freeze as a car swerves and sideswipes my dress, making me spin and collapse. Other cars screech to a halt, and when I open my eyes there's a man standing over me.

"Are you okay?"

"I'm okay."

"I don't think I hit you," he declares.

"You didn't hit me," I say, and then I see Dad and the uncles running toward the street. As Dad reaches the edge of Englishtown Road, I race toward him with my arms out. I want a hug because I'm in a fright.

"She ran out into the middle of the street without looking," the driver yells. "She came out of nowhere. I didn't hit her. She's okay!"

Dad reaches for his belt buckle, and as he unfastens it, I curl up like a caterpillar and cover my face.

"What the hell is the matter with you, goddamn it?" Whack! "I'll show you what it feels like to get hit by a car!" Whack! "Don't you know you have to look before you cross the street?" Snap! "What the hell are you, stupid?" Whack!

While I'm taking my licks the uncles are watching. It's humiliating to have people gawk while I'm being whipped. I try to tell Dad that I *did* look both ways and I *didn't* see any cars coming, but he has no ears. I cry, so he gives me a few more whacks for that. When he's done with the lickin' it looks as though a bomb exploded on *him.* He stomps back toward the woods and so does everyone else because the show's over.

I sit on the ground alongside Aunt Edna's house. Little Anthony comes by, sits next to me and leans his shoulder up against mine. He asks me if I'm okay and I don't know what to say. No one else ever asks if I'm okay. They just tell me I'll live. My heart melts just because he cared enough to ask. I'm not sure how to tell him that I'm *not* okay because I'm *not* allowed to feel sad, or cry, or complain. I *can't* tell Anthony that my father doesn't like me, that whenever I need a hug more than anything, he beats me down. I don't want Anthony looking at me because I don't deserve his kindness. *I wish that car ran me over.*

I leave Little Anthony sitting there. (I don't know it's the last time I'll ever see him.) I go into the cellar of the big house where Aunt Edna lives. Except for ants and spiders, no one goes down there in the summer, so it's a good place to hide and think. *If I wasn't so stupid, maybe Dad would love me.*

When I'm dying of thirst, I come out of hiding and scamper toward the commotion. Grandpa is giving Dad hell for pushing Mommy around while she's pregnant. *That's why our bedrooms were rearranged! Mommy's going to have her fifth baby.* Grandpa tells Dad he doesn't know how Mommy puts up with him.

"You've got some goddamned nerve," Dad shouts. "You're no one to talk. All you ever did was sweep the floor with Mama and us kids."

"Is dat so?" Grandpa smirks.

Now Dad loads up his fists, aims and shoots Grandpa right in the jaw. Dad's steel, bear-sized fists continually dart out like a Jack-in-the-box, from the left and the right and if not for Uncle Frankie who slips in between them, Grandpa would probably end up crashing like a dead pigeon. Now Uncle Frankie is taking all the licks meant for their father so Grandma jumps in front of Uncle Frankie, but Dad can't see Grandma because he's seeing red. Dad reloads his giant paw then punches his mother square in the face. Her glasses shatter, she falls back, and everyone starts cursing and screaming in unison.

"Jeeeeeeeeesus Christ! Goddamn asshole! Son-of-a-bitch! What the hell's a matter with you, Joey, are you stupid?"

After five minutes of that, it finally occurs to one of the Lows that maybe someone should fetch some clean rags, water and ice for Grandma's face. When the ice stuns Grandma, she goes into protective mode to stop her other children from hollering at *her* Joey.

"He wasn't trrryingk to hit me. He's drrrunk. He doesn't know what he's doingk," she lectures. Then she turns to Dad and says, "It's okay, Joey."

****

I'm in fourth grade and Harvey Katz is my first male teacher. He loves teaching and I love being his student. So far, this is my best year in school.

Mr. Katz passes out our graded history tests. When he comes to mine he asks me to step out into the hall where he tells me I failed the history test. I put my arms up to cover my face because I'm waiting for a lickin'—but it doesn't come.

"Don't worry, you're going to do much better on the next test," he says.

Then he wipes away my tears with his wrinkled handkerchief, and hugs me, and it's a *real* hug.

Now I really want to do better. I decide I'm going to study because I don't want to disappoint Mr. Katz. I have a bit of trouble studying. I can't seem to remember places and dates, and the things I do remember are never on the tests. We're studying the Civil War and Abraham Lincoln, and I want to know more about him—more than what my history book says. I *love* that he walked miles just to return a borrowed book, and that he *freed* the slaves because *no one* has a right to own another person, and I love that he educated himself even though he was poor.

I take my history book home, plop into the captain's chair in our dining room, then I slide it all the way in until its arms are under the table. Now that I'm cozy I open my book, but it bores me to death. I notice Sis's seventh-grade history book sitting on the table. I'm not supposed to touch anything that doesn't belong to me, but it really belongs to the school, so I open it and search for Abraham Lincoln. I come across the Gettysburg Address and it grabs me just because President Lincoln wrote it. I decide to memorize it—to make Mr. Katz proud. I read it over and again, and now that the first half of the Gettysburg Address is glued to my brain, I go on to the second half.

Without warning I'm being smacked in the head, pinched, and my hair is being pulled.

"You have a lot of nerve touching my book!" Sis snaps. "You got your cooties all over it." Slap, pinch! "You're stupid! You couldn't possibly understand what's in my book." Slap! "You're ugly! I wish you were never born!" Pinch, slap!

I can't escape her flogging because the arms of my chair are under the table and my feet can't reach the floor. She pinches me with her nails until I bleed, and she pulls my hair.

Mommy shoots into the dining room.

"Enough! Let her read the book. She's not hurting anyone. Leave her alone!"

Sis slaps me in the head again and grabs the book. As if *she's* the boss, she chastises Mommy.

"You better not let her touch my things again. I don't want her cooties all over my stuff."

"It's *just* a book," Mommy says.

"It's *my* book and you better make sure she leaves *my* things alone from now on!"

Then she calls me an idiot and stomps up the stairs as if her shoes are filled with concrete.

Without another word, Mommy goes back into the kitchen. She's tired because she has a baby growing in her belly, so I keep my thoughts to myself.

Now I'll never get to memorize the entire Gettysburg Address. It doesn't matter. All men might be created equal, but all men are not treated equal.

❋❋❋❋❋❋❋❋❋❋❋❋❋

I'm in my new bedroom alone and in the next room, Jane and Anya are sharing a bed on the other side of the wall. I can hear them playing a word game, so I join in from my side of the wall. We're all careful about how loud we get because we're not supposed to make a peep, but laughter breaks out and drifts downstairs into the lion's ears. We hear heavy feet ascending the stairs. As he gets closer we hear Dad breathing like a bull.

I'm the only one of his kids who gets a taste of his medicine. *He's coming to get me.*

"What the hell's going on in here, goddamn it!" he roars.

All at once I hear his belt snapping, I hear screaming and crying. I scamper to the doorway of my sisters' bedroom where I have a bird's-eye view of Dad beating Jane. I want to tell her to roll up into a ball and cover her face because she hasn't had any practice at this yet. She's lying on her back, caught under her sheets, and Dad's saying horrible things to her.

"Leave her alone!" I yell, but he doesn't hear me because he's seeing red. He just keeps whacking her with the belt, over and over and his aim isn't very good. His belt is only supposed to land on your *dupah*—that's what a lickin' is supposed to be. But when you see red, you get a kink in your think.

Mommy sprints up the stairs screaming, "Enough Joe!"

But he can't stop. It seems to go on forever.

"Enough!" Mommy yells while Dad curses and whacks Jane.

She cries and the sound of it all is worse than any horror movie, and the sight of it makes me want to yank out my eyeballs.

Finally, it's over.

"Now get the hell to sleep, goddamn it! And I don't want to hear a goddamned peep out of any of you kids!" Then he tromps downstairs to watch television.

Mommy inspects Jane's body and sees giant belt marks on her legs, arms and all over her chest. Her chest is the worst sight of all. It's purple, and in the center is a huge blood-red buckle mark. She has welts all over. Mommy tells me to get her a glass of water, so I run downstairs and as I near the bottom step I tell Dad that Mommy sent me for a glass of water. He doesn't say a word; the bull just fumes and I'm glad my pajamas aren't red. I bring up the water and Mommy gives it to Jane to calm her down.

Dad returns to the scene of the crime and lifts Jane's pajama top to see the damage. At the sight of her chest he says, "She's skin and bones, Lil! Why the hell can't you feed her better?"

If she had more meat on her bones maybe she wouldn't be so bruised? I'm horrified. All she did was laugh. Besides, we're sent to bed too early and we can't sleep, we've got to do *something* to pass the time.

I finally fall asleep until I begin falling off the same old cliff in my dream. Just before I reach bottom, I awaken, touch my eyes to make sure I'm alive, then I silently cry myself to sleep.

In the morning Mommy and Dad try to figure out how to dress Jane. She stands there quietly as they check to see which bruises they need to hide. The red and purple welts enlarged and turned black and blue. I can see Jane's ribs, but I know she's not starving, she's just growing taller much faster than I am. The sight of her bruises makes me sick. Jane stands there like a mannequin with her arms out, trusting whatever decision they make.

All girls have to wear dresses to school, but our dresses are short-sleeved. So they suit Jane up in a long-sleeved shirt and pants, and the dress goes on over the top of the first set of clothes. That'll be Jane's uniform until the bruises on her legs and arms heal.

Dad says he's never going to hit Jane again because she's too frail.

Now that it's all over, Jane pretends it didn't happen. She never utters a word about it, and neither do I. We know that when bad things happen it's better to pretend they didn't because pretending makes you forget. So Jane forgets. She holds up her head and walks tall, drawing strength from within. But even though she forgets what happened to her, and I forget what I saw—something changes.

Jane laughs silently now. She expresses amusement, but you have to be looking at her to know it because her sounds of glee escape only in a whisper.

Questioning these things would be a huge sin. It's a much bigger sin to *talk* about the man with the belt than it is to *be* the man with the belt. After all, Dad is just disciplining us kids. He isn't like that all the time and it's our own goddamned fault for pushing him to the point that he has to use his belt in the first place.

****

Sis always runs out the door to meet up with her friends on her way to school. She doesn't wait for me—I've got the cooties. She doesn't want to be seen with me. But today she's extra nice. She wants me to walk to school with her. I don't understand until I find out her shoes are at the repair shop, which is on the way to school. Mommy gives Sis a pair of slippers to wear to the shop. The tops of the brightly colored slippers are kind of like socks and they're sewn onto flimsy plastic soles. When Sis slips them on her size ten feet, they shout "look at me!"

It doesn't matter to me that the only reason she wants to walk with me today is because she doesn't want her friends seeing her feet. I'd walk to school with her even if she farted all the way there.

We walk slowly, carefully dodging her friends. We think she's safe until we come upon a bus parked in the lot a hundred feet from the repair shop. When the kids on the bus notice Sis's feet, they open the windows, stick out their arms and heads, point at her feet, and explode into laughter. If the bus were a ship, it would have tipped over and sunk. Sis stops and puts her brown valise on the ground in front of her feet. She won't move until the bus leaves. But it isn't going anywhere, and the valise might as well be invisible because the kids already know what's behind it. Their laughter gains momentum as she stands there.

"If we run," I say, "we'll be in the shop in three seconds flat."

"I'm not going anywhere."

"Come on, Sis. We'll be late for school."

"No!" she cries.

"It's no big deal. Just run!"

"But they're laughing at me."

"So, let them laugh," I say, and I can't help thinking that Sis can't take her own medicine.

"Why are they making fun of me?"

"Because from the side you look like a capital L. Just run, Sis, I'll run behind you to hide your feet."

I grab her valise, and as Sis runs in front of me, I try holding it between her feet and the kids' view. It doesn't work, but in three seconds flat we're in the shoe shop. Sis changes into her regular shoes and instantly reverts to her old self—annoyed at having to be near me. Now that the ugly slippers are hidden in her valise, she doesn't need me anymore. I'm catching on, but I can't tell her because that would infuriate her.

I love her anyway and someday I hope she'll love me, too.

Growing Pains

Mommy goes into labor, and to Dad's dismay, she delivers another girl. Because of the one missing accessory they can't name her Joseph, so they settle on Joanne. She's a redhead, and it just so happens that she's born on Sis's twelfth birthday.

"My birthday is ruined forever," Sis cries as she stamps her feet.

But the lion doesn't roar. Instead, he takes pity on Sis. They go out to the store and when they return, Sis carries in two bags of clothes and gleefully announces that Dad spent a hundred dollars on her.

When Mommy comes home from the hospital, Jane, Anya and I gather around to see our new sister. And while we're getting to know Joanne, Dad's out celebrating.

He buys cigars, passes them out in a bar where he buys rounds of drinks and gets an itch to start a fight, which turns into a brawl, and the police have to drive him home. It's a good thing because the last time he drove home that way, he had another fender bender.

Joanne is christened in the Russian Orthodox Church just like the rest of us. After the ceremony we walk over to the Russian Hall to eat, dance and drink, and as always, Dad ends up three-sheets-to-the-wind, and we Low kids fall asleep to the rhythmic snores of a sick pig.

Joanne is gifted with lots of money and bonds, but Mommy's got to do what she's got to do. It all gets thrown at the bills.

Before the school year is over, Mommy's pregnant again. Dad is positive this one will be a boy. Mommy's tired, and since Dad doesn't want to live in a shithouse, I have to help Mommy wash dishes, dry them, put them away, sweep the kitchen floor and make my bed. When Mommy changes a cocky diaper she gives it to me to shake out into the toilet bowl. I hate that job, but I don't complain because you have to get rid of the cocky as soon as possible, otherwise the smell gets into your mouth and you begin to taste it. Mommy is always running the washing machine because she doesn't want any dirty diapers lying around. I take care of Joanne while Mommy collects our wardrobe from the clothesline, and I follow her around just so I can learn what to do because she needs help. She's tired, she's lost her sparkle, and she doesn't sing much anymore.

Dad will be mad if the house is a mess, but he doesn't help with the chores because he's a man's man. Men don't change diapers, they don't wash bottles and they don't feed babies. The only thing Dad does is hold Joanne once in a while, and that's because Mommy is making him something to eat. But if Joanne cries, Dad roars, "Lil, do something with this kid!" Mommy stops cooking and takes the baby because men cannot tolerate a crying baby.

All that crying is enough to make a man fall off the wagon yet again. Dad falls hard, but he doesn't get hurt—just "shit-faced." I try not to get up when the commotion starts, but when I hear Mommy cry, something in my soul kicks me out of bed. That's when I sit on the third step listening to Dad accuse Mommy of things that aren't true. He always wants to know what the hell she does with all the money, why the house isn't clean and what the hell is the matter with her. She doesn't argue because you can't reason with a drunk. As long as he's not pushing or hitting her I remain on my step. But when he draws his right hand, I shoot downstairs.

"You leave her alone!" I yell.

He fumes and reaches for his belt, but when he's beyond the beyonds he doesn't bother trying to unbuckle it. He just uses his giant paws instead. He chases me and tells me what I am. He hardly catches me anymore. But when he does, he smacks me on the side of the head and it burns my ears, and I see stars, and Mommy has to yell at him to leave *me* alone.

In the morning I put my cheek up against the doorjamb between the kitchen and dining room. Dad's telling Mommy about a fistfight he had in the bar and how he beat the hell out of some big son-of-a-bitch. When he tells Mommy about the rounds of drinks he bought, she interrupts him. She could use that money to buy food and clothes for us kids, she tells him. He starts ranting and seeing red so he doesn't know I'm standing in the doorway. He picks up his coffee mug like you pick up a baseball and throws it at Mommy, full force, as if she's up at bat. It misses her and comes toward me. I duck and it hits the doorjamb. Except for the handle, it breaks into a million pieces before it even falls to the floor, and fragments of the mug and warm drops of coffee land on my head.

Dad runs out of the kitchen and Mommy stands there like a blackboard that's just been erased. We hear the car start up and the tires roll out of the driveway. Without a whimper, Mommy picks up the broken pieces of the mug and I get the *totslot* to soak up the spattered coffee. Joanne cries so Mommy hobbles upstairs to take care of her, leaving me to clean the mess. Afterward I ask her three times if I can go down to the lake before she finally nods yes. She's in some sort of a trance—I don't think she sees me leave the house.

I sit at the side of my yard waiting for Mr. Miller to walk by. He's a retired school principal and he works as a lifeguard down at the lake. Here he comes with the whistle around his neck and his off-white moccasins on his feet.

"Good morning, Smiley."

"Hi, Mr. Miller."

I fall in next to him like a soldier and we walk in time. He taught me how to row a boat and he lets me ask him questions. He even told me the truth about Santa Claus—that he's just a representation of the goodness of the human spirit, and our parents are the ones who really buy the presents. I don't tell him about Dad getting drunk because I'm not allowed to talk about that, yet I wish I could because he's my only grown-up friend. I almost blurt it out because I feel safe around Mr. Miller, but then we reach the boathouse and he has to go to work.

****

Dad and Grandpa had the biggest fight yet and now Dad refuses to talk with him ever again. I walk the half-mile down Englishtown Road to the Low property and the first person I see is Uncle Frankie, my godfather. He's lying in the hammock behind Aunt Edna's house and he doesn't look very well. I want to hug him but I'm afraid I might hurt him because he has deep blue blotches on his legs, he's skinny and frail looking. He has a bad liver. The whites of his eyes are yellowish, but they gleam when he sees me.

"How are you, Uncle Frankie?"

"Good," he says.

But I know he isn't *good.* That's just what you're supposed to say when you're a Low because the Low's aren't allowed to cry about anything.

The last time I saw Uncle Frankie he told Dad he's worried about Little Frankie. Instead of going to school, Little Frankie is running around Staten Island with a bunch of hoodlums from the Gambino crime family.

"Don't worry, Frankie. I'll talk to him. But boys do stupid shit all the time," Dad said. "Don't you remember all the crazy-ass things we did when we were kids: jumping trolley cars, running wild in the streets, and cutting school? And look at us now. We turned out just fine."

"Yeah, considering everything. But I'm not gonna be around for long."

"You're not going anywhere, goddamn it!" Dad said.

"Life is short, Joey. You should make up with Pop."

"I have every right to be mad at Pop," Dad said. "He could kiss my ass! I'm not making up with him."

And he didn't. Not then.

Uncle Frankie looks tired today. He says he needs to take a nap, so I walk over to see Grandpa. He's angry with Dad so I think he might be mad at me, too. He's singing the Schaefer beer song as he fiddles around in his garage. When he sees me, he points to the chess game.

I grab the box and set up the pieces.

"Da Smarrrtest countrrry wins da warrr," Grandpa says while his pointer swirls above his head.

He makes the first move with his knight and leaves all his pawns right where they are. He starts his game differently each time we play, and he always wins, but I always learn something new. Today's lesson is: keep your enemies guessing. I don't have any enemies, but I'll remember what he says and what he doesn't say. Even though he's mad at Dad, he treats me exactly the way he always has.

✸✸✸✸✸✸✸✸✸✸✸✸✸

Dad's in the kitchen drinking his morning coffee. I'm glad he didn't leave for work yet because today I turn ten years old, and the only time I got to celebrate my birthday is when I was five, but Dad wasn't there. He's never around on my birthday. Well, there was one time that he sort of honored it days after it passed. *I can't let myself think about that day.*

I fly downstairs, and as always, I stop in the doorway to lean against the doorjamb. Dad's leaning up against the kitchen sink with his coffee mug in hand. Light shines in from the window behind him but his face appears dark.

"It's my birthday, Dad!"

"So what the hell do you want from me?" he growls.

He's eyeballing me as if I did something wrong. Suddenly he reaches into his pocket and pulls out his stash of cash. It's not as fat as usual, but he peels off a dollar and throws it at me from across the kitchen. I watch the dollar sail upward near the light fixture then drop onto the middle of the kitchen floor. I stare at it.

"Ya happy now?" he growls.

I would've been happy if you just sang the birthday song like Mommy or if you gave me a hug and said, I'm glad you were born.

"Well," he bellows, "isn't that good enough?"

I walk toward the dollar, pick it up and thank him. I'd rather have a hug. He doesn't say anything so I just go back to bed. I don't want this dollar. It doesn't feel good to have it. I fall asleep with the dollar in my hand. After a short nap, I awaken to find that the dollar is gone. I search, but I can't find it anywhere.

****

Dad takes lots of people fishing with him—the male cousins and uncles—and he teaches them what to do. I *really* want to go fishing, too. He used to tell me I was too young to go fishing, but now that I'm older he says I can't go because I'm a girl.

I could learn if he'd give me the chance. Each time he brings home his catch of blues in the giant burlap bags, I line the picnic table with newspaper and fill buckets with water. I scale the blues and after Dad chops off their heads and slices them open, without a grimace, I pull out the slimy guts with my bare hands. If I do a really good job, someday he'll take me fishing. But each time I ask he says no. No, I can't go fishing. No, I can't play the piano. No, I can't take dance lessons. I'm too young. Too stupid. There's not enough money. I should appreciate the roof over my head, the food in my mouth and the clothes on my back because where the hell do I think these things come from? Money doesn't grow on trees, you know?

I know I'm not getting anything so I don't ask anymore.

School is starting soon. Mommy does some sewing, but not as much as she used to. Her belly is huge so she holds Joanne on her hip with one hand while she uses the other to cook, clean and do laundry.

I'm bused off to Browntown School on Route 516 in Old Bridge. It's an old, five-room schoolhouse. A lot of the kids there are cooler than Kool-Aid. I'm not. They want to know if I part my hair with a corkscrew and if I stole my clothes from a bum. I pretend I don't hear those questions. Fifth grade doesn't agree with me, but as long as I pass all of my subjects it doesn't matter because all I have to do is learn how to cook and clean, grow up, and find a man to marry and keep me.

I want to join the Girl Scouts but Mommy doesn't have money for a uniform. Then I find out that a club called the Camp Fire Girls have their meetings just a few blocks from my house and all I need to do is show up. I ask Mommy if I can go. She says yes. I join, and I look like the other girls for the first two meetings. By the third one everyone has a uniform, except me. Mommy tells me to ask them if they have any old uniforms I can use. I ask, but the ladies who run the club look at me funny when they tell me no. I never go back there again.

****

Christmas is only a few months away and I want to buy Mommy and Dad a present. There's a manger in Weber's hardware store for $1.99. That's what I want to give them. They can put it under our Christmas tree and the whole family can enjoy looking at the baby Jesus, the tiny animals, the Wise men and Mary and Joseph, who I think might be Jesus' real father. So my eyes are peeled for coke bottles everywhere I go. After collecting enough of them, I bring them to Ender's. They give me two cents for the small bottles and a nickel for the large ones. Instead of buying candy with the money, I'm saving it in an old Band-Aid can.

****

Uncle Frankie is sent to the hospital. I want to see him but I have to stay in the waiting room with my sisters because "no children are allowed in."

Dad's mother and sisters go off to the Catholic Church to pray for Uncle Frankie while Grandpa, Aunt Lena and Dad remain at his bedside.

"I'm not here for long," Uncle Frankie says.

"You can't go, Frankie! You have to get better. We'll go to the ball games. We'll paint the town red together. You can't leave me, Frankie!" Dad pleads. "You're my pal, my buddy! Don't go!"

But Uncle Frankie does go. It's late in October and I don't even care about Halloween. Aunt Lena is very upset because he was such a loving husband; she couldn't have asked for a kinder, gentler man.

Uncle Frankie's smile is gone, and my cousins, Lori and Little Frankie, will never get to see their father again, except when he's laid out at the funeral parlor. That's where they'll say their last goodbye. I never ask Dad for anything anymore, but I ask to go to the funeral. I want to say goodbye to my godfather.

167

"No," Dad says. "No kids allowed."

"I'm ten. I'm not a baby."

"No goddamn it. Jeeeeeeeesus Christ, this is no time for your goddamned bullshit!"

I run into our dark, empty garage to hide in the corner. I feel sorry for myself. I'm not supposed to, because self-pity stinks. I close my eyes to envision Uncle Frankie, and to feel his kindness. I pull my shirt up to my face, dry my tears and blow my nose right into it, then I fall asleep on the dirty concrete floor.

****

It's November 22, 1963. I'm sitting in the front row of my fifth grade class when the door flies open and in comes a teacher, screaming and crying. She tries to speak but her words are stuck between sobs. A few minutes later another teacher rolls in a cart with a black and white TV on top. As she plugs it in she shrieks, "President Kennedy's been shot!"

Instantly everyone's crying—all the teachers, all the students. All I hear is sobbing, sniffling, moaning, and parts of muddled phrases.

"Oh, my God!"

"What are we going to do?"

All the crying and sobbing and sniffling puts an end to whatever else would've been happening at the moment. The world seems to stop turning.

Later, Dad comes home from work and glues himself to the news. Lyndon B. Johnson is sworn in as the thirty-sixth President. Jack Ruby shoots Lee Harvey Oswald. The chain of events is so negative it leaves Dad asking, "What are we going to do now? What's the world coming to?"

I hear that so many times, I begin to wonder about the world I live in. I'm ten—halfway between the kid world and the grown-up world. The kid world is full of frogs, trees, bugs, little sisters who try to out-burp you, and mommies who give you warm chicken soup. The grown-up world bursts with things to worry about.

The stream of bad news ends in December. Mommy goes into the hospital and Dad's all excited because he's about to have a son. Too bad for Dad, child number six doesn't have a *jooje.* But she's the most beautiful baby anyone has ever seen. They name her Hanna. She has a round face, huge blue eyes with a hint of green, and dark brown hair. Her skin is milky white like Grandma's, but without the "birrrd shits."

Joanne is just a year old when Hanna appears. Joanne's crib is moved into my bedroom and it'll be my job to take care of her when she wakes up at night. I change her diapers, make her bottles and I sing her a sweet lullaby as I slip my hands through the slats of the crib to rub her back. She falls asleep, but Hanna cries incessantly. Dr. Allgair finally figures out that Hanna has milk anemia, which is why her skin is too white. So Mommy switches formulas until she finds one that Hanna can tolerate. She walks the floor with Hanna in the middle of the night and eats toast as she paces. Mommy gains some weight.

Joanne gets stomach spasms but Dr. Allgair says she'll outgrow them. In the meantime, we have two crying babies and they're like dueling banjoes, except it's not as easy on Dad's ears.

"Lil, do something about that!"

All day and all night, Mommy tries everything to soothe the babies. When I'm not in school I help her as much as I can because she never gets a break. She zips around with Hanna on her hip, so I pick up the slack with Joanne. She's only a baby. She needs someone to look her in the eye so she doesn't feel unwanted, like I do.

****

Christmas is creeping up and Mommy keeps saying Santa Claus is poor. I know he isn't even real. Rich kids are the only ones who think he is. My classmates brag about the things on their lists and how they always get new clothes, radios, Barbie dolls and Play-Doh. They drag out *Play-Doh* as if it's the best thing in the world.

Big deal! I get pierogi dough! I can play with it *and* eat it, too!

If there really was a Santa, my note to him would say:

Dear Santa, Before you leave, go up to my father's dresser and take his big fat belts, then go to the china cabinet and take his whiskey bottles. Merry Christmas. Ho, ho, ho.

My classmates want to know what's on my Christmas list, so I tell them I don't need one because Santa isn't real.

"If you don't believe, you don't receive," they chime in unison.

So I tell them if there is a Santa, he already knows what I want. Their mothers sewed little jingle bells into the hems of their dresses and they laugh at me as they jingle away. If they knew how lucky they are, maybe they wouldn't be so *joojemental.*

I've got eighty-something cents in my Band-Aid can now. I'm going to wait until Christmas Eve to buy my parents' gift. I still need more money in order to get the manger, but if I can't save that much, I'll just buy them each a coffee mug. Dad could use another.

Christmas Eve finally arrives. I'm just about to count my money when I hear Dad's car rolling into the driveway. The sky outside is freckled with snowflakes, and the headlights on Dad's car make them sparkle. I run downstairs because he'll be dragging in our Christmas tree. You can count on that just like you can count on Grandma's sugar bread.

"Where's the tree, Dad?"

"We're not getting any goddamn tree!"

"How come?"

"I said we're not getting any goddamned tree. Now get the hell outta here!"

I hightail it back to bed, then I pull the covers over my head. I'm trying not to feel sorry for myself, but I do. I use my blanket to dry my tears, then I see the crib in the corner of my room. *It wouldn't be right for my little sisters to wake up in the morning and not have a tree.* I can't bear that thought. I decide to spend my savings on a tree.

As I'm counting my money, Sis peeks into my bedroom and asks what I'm doing. I tell her Dad isn't getting a tree so I'm buying one with my own money.

"No tree?!"

"Nope."

"How much money do you have?"

170

"I think it's close to a dollar."

"That's not enough for a tree," Sis says.

She disappears, then comes back with her change. Altogether we come up with a dollar and a quarter.

To weather the snowstorm, we slide plastic bags over our shoes and secure them with rubber bands. We help each other put socks over our hands. You need two socks for each hand because you have to put one sock with the hole going one way and the other sock with the hole going the other way.

We walk to the First Aid Squad where they're selling trees, but there aren't many left. They've been discounted to two dollars, which is too much for us, but Sis makes a deal with a guy who works there because she knows him. He takes our money in exchange for the ugliest tree on the lot. I don't care—it's a tree. We drag it home through the snow. Our hair and our faces are soaked but I don't care. I'm happy to be dragging this tree home with my big sister! I feel so special that I cry. The snow camouflages my tears and I'm glad because if Sis sees my tears, she'll call me a crybaby. I don't want to ruin this moment. I'm so happy I start singing "Jingle Bells" and she sings along!

At home we drag the tree into the washroom where we leave it to drip dry. The socks on our hands are frozen stiff and when we pull them off, our hands are bright red. Our clothes go over the radiator to dry and Mommy lights the oven and puts our shoes on the oven grate to dry.

We put up the tree and tie it to the pipes. Mommy strings up the lights, and even though Dad's sleeping, she lets us sing Christmas carols while we decorate. She gives us our new pajamas and now my sisters and I are in the pajama club. *I love the pajama club!* I think it, but I wouldn't dare say it.

The next morning I creep downstairs to check things out. I know it was Mommy who did all of the work, who filled all of the stockings, then "turned with a jerk." Hee-hee!

She also put a ham in the oven. The saltiness of the ham and the sweetness of the brown sugar and pineapples make my mouth water. Christmas smells just as delicious as Thanksgiving.

After Dad gets his coffee he doles out the gifts. Whatever was going on last night is over. It's as if there's nothing wrong in the world.

I watch my sisters open their gifts and it's so much fun to see their joy. I'm just as happy with my red wooden stilts—it's the best present I ever got in my entire life. Well, the best *thing,* that is. The best present I *ever* got was walking through the blizzard with Sis, singing "Jingle Bells" as we dragged home our ugly tree. I'll never, *ever* forget last night!

Thanks, Sis. I love you even more than I love my secret pajama club!

An Unforgettable Affair

I'm being groomed for Hanna's christening party because I look like a mangy dog. Mommy cut my messy locks, and to camouflage those few black hairs growing above the corners of my mouth, she dabs on her foamy concoction of peroxide and ammonia. She does the same for Jane, then sends us out to sit with our faces up to the sun because it accelerates the power of her potion. Jane looks like she has a milk-stache.

"Got any cookies to dunk?" I ask.

"I ate 'em all," she says. "And they were the best invisible cookies I ever had."

I cackle like an idiot because Dad's not around, but Jane laughs quietly as her nostrils wiggle in and out.

Mommy's brother, George, is staying with us for a few days. I call him Uncle Peppy because that's his boxing name. Dad says Uncle Peppy is a has-been because he lost so many boxing matches. Even though Uncle Peppy is a bleeder, he made it all the way to Madison Square Garden in New York City. He went up against guys like Bobo Olson, the greatest boxer to ever come out of Hawaii, so he doesn't care if people call him a has-been because he "was honored just to be in the ring with them."

Uncle Peppy rises early every morning and makes the most extraordinary breakfast of sliced bananas smothered in orange juice. Mommy usually doesn't buy orange juice because it's too expensive, but she gets it for him because he helps feed the babies, and he even changes Hanna's diaper.

"You put the diaper on cockeyed," Mommy says.

"Who cares," Uncle Peppy laughs, "pretty soon it will be all cockied."

After breakfast Uncle Peppy takes me for a walk. Dad never does, so there's no way I'm going to miss the chance to walk with Uncle Peppy. He never makes fun of my dirty feet. He says they're perfect, nice high arches—good for running. I take him down to the lake to show him the waterfalls, and the giant scavenger catfish that fishermen go crazy for. Dad doesn't fish for them because they "eat shit." He won't eat anything that eats shit.

I take Uncle Peppy through the woods to show him the ponds and all the turtles and frogs that live there. As we crunch through the forest, Uncle Peppy asks if my feet hurt.

"No. I like being barefooted. I can walk on anything."

"Can you walk on water?" he says.

He always makes me laugh.

On the way home Uncle Peppy teaches me how to stay healthy and fit. He must know what he's talking about because he's built like a steel tower. The only reason he'll never be champion of the world is because his heart is made of milk chocolate.

Uncle Peppy lets me punch him in the stomach and no matter how hard and fast I throw my fist, I can't hurt him because his stomach is like the Great Wall of China.

"Can you teach me how to box, Uncle Peppy?"

"Okay," he says, "hold up your fists. Now dance around like this. Okay, now, bob, weave, and duck your head like this."

We're dancing around the living room pretending to punch one another as we bob, weave and laugh, when suddenly a bull comes charging down the steps.

"All right already!" Dad fumes. "Enough with the acting like a bunch of goddamned wild Indians so early in the goddamn morning!"

"Good morning, Joe," Uncle Peppy chimes. Then he pretends to throw punches at Dad.

Dad's built like a five-story brick building, but he doesn't look so big and strong next to the steel tower. Uncle Peppy dances around him, growling like the cowardly lion, "Put 'em up! Put 'em up!"

174

"Jeeeeeeeeesus Christ!" Dad spits as he heads toward the kitchen.

"Uh oh," Uncle Peppy whispers. "I'm in trouble."

That's the end of my boxing lesson. I'm not sure if Dad was just breaking up the fun or preventing me from learning how to kick his ass when he's mean to Mommy.

No matter what time of day, if you want to talk with Uncle Peppy, jump on his back or have a race around the house, he never gets annoyed like other grown-ups do. He just goes along with it all. He's always happy and I wish he didn't live so far away, but I know that wishes hardly ever come true.

On the morning of the party Uncle Peppy helps Dad set up picnic tables. Dad is bossing Uncle Peppy around, telling him, do this, move that, and get that.

"Yes sir, Okey dokey Joe-key!" Uncle Peppy says as he salutes Dad.

Whenever Dad tells him to do something, he runs real fast to do it until Dad calls him a *schmuck*. That's when Uncle Peppy tells Dad he's in luck because he's got his own private *schmuck*. Dad's belly rumbles like an earthquake as he tries holding back his laughter. No matter how serious you are, Uncle Peppy isn't going to let you stay that way.

After church all the relatives arrive at our house for another fantastic Low party. Aunt Millie brings her accordion and sings "Danny Boy," the song Father Farringer always sang at Incarnation Camp. Aunt Millie gets a sing-a-long going and I don't think there's a better place anywhere on earth than right here. When the relatives sing the "Smile" song, Mommy sings it louder than anyone. She's tone deaf so it's a good thing Nat King Cole isn't here. Mommy's sitting between Aunt Louise, Uncle Peppy, Aunt Mary and Aunt Chris. Aunt Chris still hasn't given me that bag of herns. I'll get it from her someday, but now's not the time. Mommy and her siblings look so funny when they sing together. There's a painting of *The Last Supper,* but none called *The Last Sing-a-Long.* That's because Leonardo Da Vinci never got to meet my mother. If he were alive today, he'd paint Mommy in the center of his masterpiece and he would name it *The*

Last Sing-a-Long. It would be Da Vinci's greatest work of art because anyone lucky enough to get a glimpse of it would end up with an indelible smile.

Except for Little Anthony, all of my favorite people are here today so it's like being at a human smorgasbord.

As the day wears on I have to become more mindful of Dad. He's drinking scotch as if it was free. I'd like to spill it out, but if I ever got caught I don't even want to imagine what he might do. I leave my cousins and sisters to their antics to sit with Yaya and Grandma, in full view of Dad, but I'm momentarily distracted.

Yaya is wincing at Grandma and mouthing, *"Peef lesh."*

It's one thing to say that when someone *jarts,* but to say that about a person because you don't like how they look is just awful. I wonder why Yaya is being so mean to Grandma so I scrutinize and compare them.

Yaya smells like mothballs. Her hair is perfectly combed. She's draped in a crisply ironed dress that buttons up the front with a collar and a V-neck that showcases her cleavage. She's sporting a little pearl necklace and even though it's hot today, she's wearing stockings and shoes. She's sitting up straight and tall like a proper lady, knees slightly tilted to the side, and her hands are folded in her lap. In spite of her nasty expressions, she appears to be posing for a photographer.

Grandma, on the other hand, smells musty. She's wearing a loose-fitting flowered dress, which she most likely wore yesterday, and as usual, no bra. Her *dzidzees* are jiggling around her waistline. Her red hair is a mess, but once in a while she pulls the hair combs from the sides of her head to sweep back her fallen locks. Her fingernails are dirty and her fingertips are stained green from making artificial flowers. She has rubber flip-flops on her dirty feet and her bare freckled legs are spread apart, but the skirt of her dress is pulled in between her legs so you can't see her bloomers. Her flabby, freckled arms rest on the arms of the lawn chair as she hunches forward, and it's as clear as her good eye—the sight of her family makes her happy.

I suddenly realize how different my two grandmas are. I can't explain why I love them both, but I do. I don't care how clean and neat Yaya is or how messy and dirty Grandma is, I love them madly. But I don't like what Yaya's doing, not one bit, and if I had to be one of them right at this moment, I'd be Grandma. I'd rather be dirty and happy than clean and mean.

I want to tell Yaya to stop, that what she's doing isn't nice, but I have to keep my big mouth shut because I'm just a stupid kid that doesn't know her ass from her elbow. Kids should be seen and not heard. I have so much to think about. I'm upset with Yaya and Dad's getting loud. He cracks open another bottle of scotch because he hasn't had enough yet or because the Kennedys need another nickel.

Mommy's side of the family leaves early because they have to drive all the way back to New York City. I'm not happy that they're leaving, but I'm glad that Yaya will stop making faces at Grandma, and because they won't get to see thousands of bats flying out from the grates of our attic at dusk.

Dad's side of the family is still busy talking, laughing, arguing and drinking.

Soon everyone's had enough and they all leave. The party is a huge success because Dad didn't punch anyone in the face, rip anyone's clothes, or break anyone's glasses.

My sisters go off to bed. I'm up because I'm the black sheep, the worrywart, but someone has to look out for Dad because it just ain't over until Joe Low is snoring. I'm helping Mommy clean up while Dad, who's totally cockeyed, three-sheets-to-the-wind, shit-faced and plastered all at once, announces that he's going out to a bar to have a few more drinks.

Mommy thinks ahead. She hides the car keys. She doesn't want anyone getting hurt because of him, nor does she want him hurting himself. But when you're shit-faced you don't understand these things. Dad wants to know where the hell the goddamned keys are. Mommy says she doesn't know. She's lying, but it's necessary, so I don't know if you can really call it a lie. The English language needs more words because fib doesn't fit the situation, either. When Mommy says she's going to bed, Dad curses and yells.

"Please, Joe," Mommy begs, "please don't wake up the kids."

"Where the hell are the goddamned car keys?"

"I don't know. You're the one who had them last," Mommy says as she heads upstairs.

There's still huge mess to clean up so I know Mommy isn't going to sleep. She just needs to get away. I can tell by Dad's expression that he's going to do something. He's seething like a bull. His face and clothes are soaked with perspiration. There's fury in his eyes.

"I'll help you find the keys, Daddy," I lie.

I'll just pretend to look for them, maybe that'll calm the bull. But he doesn't hear me. He just sees Mommy going upstairs and he follows her. I follow ten steps behind. Now Dad grabs Mommy and knocks her against the wall, demanding to know where the goddamned keys are.

"You're going to wake up the kids. Please, Joe, quiet down. I'll help you find..."

Before she can finish, Dad punches her. Mommy starts to cry, but she cries silently because she doesn't want my sisters to wake up and see what's going on. All I hear out of her is a whimper, but she doesn't even mean to do that.

Dad keeps trying to pull Mommy toward the stairs. As they get closer to the landing I back up. *Maybe I could catch Mommy if she falls.* She tries holding onto the door molding, but Dad's too strong. He's pulls her and when they reach the top landing, Mommy falls. Now she's trying to hold onto one of the steps, but you can't get a good grip on a step. I tell Dad to stop and leave her alone, but he has no ears. He punches Mommy in the chest and she tumbles to the middle of the stairwell.

I scoot to the other side of the banister in the living room.

"Stop it, Dad," I yell, but he can't hear because he's seeing red.

He grabs Mommy by her shirt and punches her in the face. Her glasses break in half and crash onto the stairs. Her face is full of blood and it's flowing like a river. Her blouse rips and most of it comes off of her as she plummets to the next landing. Now Mommy is lying there in her bra with her blouse hanging off of her. I hear a few slight whimpers out of her. Her crisp white blouse is full of blood. Her face, her body and her white bra are full of blood.

"Stop, leave her alone," I cry, but Dad goes right on shaking her, hitting her and yelling at her.

I run into the dining room, grab the phone and dial Grandma's house. Before she could say hello my words tumble out, "Dad's drunk! He's beating up Mommy! He won't stop! Come quick! Hurry …"

Before I could spit out the rest of my words, the bull stampedes into the dining room.   He didn't hear me yell "stop," but he hears me on the phone and now he's livid. I drop the receiver, run through the kitchen and out the back door. Dad's on my heels like a piece of toilet paper. As drunk as he is, he doesn't fall, he doesn't waver. He comes at me like a bulldozer. I step it up and run as fast as I can. He's yelling, cursing, and it becomes a verbal blur, but I don't have to hear what he's saying. I already know I'm a goddamned little snot-nosed son-of-a-bitch who doesn't mind her own goddamned business, who doesn't know her ass from her elbow, who's stupid, who should shut the hell up already. I already know I'm going to get my ass broken, my head handed to me, and I'm lucky Grandpa isn't giving me the goddamned lickin' because he'd give it to me double, triple, ten times maybe!

I pretend I'm the gingerbread man, running away from the baker, his wife, and the pig. I gain some ground and look back to see Dad's still coming at me. I run around the house once, then again and I look back but I don't see him. When I turn and look up, there he is charging at me from the other direction, so I turn again. Dad may be drunk, but he's not stupid. He turned around the way he does when he's sober and chasing me around the dining room table. I'm disobeying Dad and I don't care. I'm not supposed to make him run. I'm supposed to stand there and let him hit me. But as long as he keeps running, I will, too, because when he's chasing me, he's leaving Mommy alone.

My legs are giving out. I must've sprinted around the house ten times, maybe more. It only takes a couple of minutes to drive here from the Low property. *Help me, God, where are you? Help me! Grandma, where are you?*

As I'm dashing around the side of the house I look out at Englishtown Road to see if I can spot Grandpa's car. I don't see it so I keep going—around the front to the other side. As I fly around the corner to the backyard a car is pulling into the dirt driveway. It's Dad's sister, Frances, her husband, Joe, Grandma and Grandpa. Faster than a flea can jump on a dog, Dad's demeanor switches from seething anger to overflowing merriment. Now he isn't even aware of my presence. He ran like a jackrabbit, but he can't stand still. He sways like sheets in the wind then he flops onto the hood of the car, smiling and waving into the window at Uncle Joe. Dad's shirttails are hanging out. Mommy's blood is on his shirt. His hair is a mess, and he smells like he took a swim in Grandpa's cesspool then showered in scotch. When Uncle Joe and Grandpa hop out of the car, Dad says he wants to have a drink with them.

"Yeah Joe, we'll have a drink," they say.

They're lying too. My heart knows that that kind of lie just shouldn't be called a lie or a fib. Lies hurt people, but they're here to save us.

Uncle Joe gets on one side of Dad, Grandpa on the other. They put their arms around Dad's back, and Dad flops his giant, freckled limbs around their necks.

"Come on Joe," they say as they strain to hold up the drunken Jolly Green Giant, "Let's go have a drink."

Dad sings "Old Man River" as they lead him into the house and up the stairs. To appease him, they sing too. The trio is smiling and singing and it just might be a perfect sight if you didn't have peripheral vision. They get Dad into the bedroom, onto his bed and the trio stays up there for a long time.

Aunt Frances hugs me. She's not the hugging, kissing type. She's one tough lady so I'm surprised, but I feel comforted to have her arms around me for a moment. I don't know that she could even imagine how I feel. I don't know that when she was little she suffered through the same kind of abuse. I don't know that Grandpa made her haul heavy sacks of sugar for his bathtub gin, or that he swept the floor with her after she watched him sweep it with *her* mother. Nor do I know that she carries a satchel crammed with guilt from the drowning of her baby brother, Andrei. I'm just glad she's here.

Mommy is sitting at the kitchen table cradling Hanna. Her cut up face is swollen, her eyes are drenched, and one by one, tears flow down to her chin. Her expression is blank and she's quiet as she rocks Hanna to and fro.

Grandma tells Mommy she loves her as if she were her own daughter, her own flesh and blood. She puts her arm around Mommy as she dries her eyes and wipes her bloody nose with a napkin.

I notice Mommy's crisp white blouse in the garbage. It isn't crisp or white anymore. It's ripped and bloodstained. That's when Grandma smiles at me.

"Don't worrry, everrrytingks okay."

I don't know that Grandma used to go through this. I don't know that I'm wearing the same cruddy secondhand shoes Dad wore as a kid. I don't know that he was abused and frightened, and that love didn't come in the form of a pat on the shoulder—but from the snap of a belt. I don't know a lot of things. All I know is that Grandma's smile makes me smile back even though my heart is aching.

Mommy can't smile because her heart is broken in pieces just like her glasses, and her spirit is all shredded just like her crisp, white blouse. I feel sad, but you *can* be happy and sad at the same time for different reasons. There are so many things that make me happy I could burst, but tonight it's hard to think of good things. I try to stop the bad stuff, but I can't. Maybe I shouldn't try, but when the next time comes, I'm never able to stop myself and it makes Dad hate me even more. I may not know my ass from my elbow, yet I know it's not supposed to be like this. Dad is like the clouds in the "Smile" song. But sometimes he's like a rainbow, vibrant and fun. The song is true, but I get so tired of the clouds, sometimes I just want Dad to disappear. But I don't really mean it because I love him so much. I just wish he'd stop drinking and stop being so mean. I wish God would hear my prayers.

Grandma and Aunt Frances are still consoling Mommy. They're telling her what a fantastic mother and wife she is, what a great cook she is, and she probably saved someone's life by hiding Dad's keys.

Rhythmic grunts suddenly begin seeping into the kitchen. The grizzly bear is snoring. It's the sound of safety! The only bad things to come are the morning odor of secondhand scotch, and all the names Dad will call me for not minding my own goddamned business.

Now that Grandpa and Uncle Joe completed their mission, they appear in the kitchen. It's time for them to go. I don't want them to leave, but they have to.

I watch them drive away until they disappear.

Joe Low is snoring, and Hanna and Joanne are crying. Mommy tends to Hanna while I make Joanne a bottle and change her diaper. I rub her back through the slats of the crib, and hum the "Smile" song until she falls asleep.

Mommy is perched on the couch, expressionless, but the marks on her face tell a tall tale. If Leonardo Da Vinci painted her portrait now, he'd call it *The Lost Song.* I'm not supposed to be a crybaby, so I look upward to keep my tears from falling only to see the Comedy and Tragedy plaques on the wall, and suddenly they are filled with meaning.

I hop into bed and I tell God I'm starting to wonder about Him. If He already knows what I'm thinking, I can't get away with lying to Him.

When are you going to answer my prayers? Are you listening? Are you deaf, or just a big bad lie?

I end my rude prayer and lie steeped in a serenade of Joe Low snoring, the aroma of secondhand scotch, and the scratching and fluttering of our freeloading tenants as I review the hours of joy I had today, and the minutes of horror that sucked it all away.

Goodnight, God. Goodnight, bats.

Osmosis

"Someday my ship will come in," Dad chimes. "I'll be a millionaire, then we'll all be happy."

"If you're shit-faced," Mommy says, "you might board the wrong ship and end up on a slow boat to China. You can be happy right now, Joe! If you stopped drinking, we'd have a lot more money to pay bills."

"I'll be happy when there are no bills to pay. So what if I have a few drinks once in a while. A man's got a right to do whatever the hell a man wants to."

Dad goes out to the bar for a drink and it turns into a shit-load of trouble. He gets plastered, closes up the bar, gets behind the wheel, heads home on Route 18 in East Brunswick, and crashes into the concrete divider. The cops come and he resists arrest, so they beat him with billy clubs, handcuff him and throw him in jail. The next day Mommy has to bail him out.

He's all beat up but "it's not from the accident," he says. "The cops did it."

He's afraid he's going to lose his license, so he saves his bloody clothes and shows them to the judge when he goes to court. It doesn't work. The judge fines him and takes away his license, sending him up shit's creek without a shovel.

Now there are more bills, car repairs, lost wages, legal fees. It doesn't end, so Mommy has another serious talk with Dad and he promises to quit drinking.

****

Sis is going somewhere special. I think it's the World's Fair, but she won't say because it's none of my business. Wherever she's going, it must be special because she gets spending money to buy herself some cold drinks—she's sure to get thirsty walking around in the hot sun throughout the day. Instead, she decides to give up her refreshment to buy a gift for the Baron—a Turkish flag.

At first sight of the flag the Baron detonates.

Mommy wants to know how Sis could do such a thing. Through her tears, Sis insists she was just trying to be nice. She swears she didn't know it was a Turkish flag. See how mean the Baron is! Sis wants to know how anyone could be so cruel as to think she'd do such a horrific thing, and she's so convincing, the matter is dropped.

Later, when the grown-ups are out of earshot, Sis cackles victoriously.

****

The Beatles make their debut on the Ed Sullivan Show. Most Americans go crazy for them, but not Dad.

"They're goddamned lucky they're not my sons," Dad hollers. "I'd tie 'em to a goddamned kitchen chair and cut their goddamned hair!"

"Stop losing sleep over a bunch of hairy teenagers," Mommy says. "You've got enough of your own worries without *inventing* things to holler about."

After several days of Dad's ranting, Mommy needs to get away. I hop in the car with her and the babies, and we head for the Low property. It's the only other place Mommy goes besides the grocery store. There, she'll have some women to talk with.

Aunt Helen notices Mommy's big belly and asks, "Are you pregnant again, Lily?"

"Yup."

"How'd that happen?"

"By osmosis," Mommy jokes.

"Who the hell is Osmosis? Are you cheating on my brother?" Aunt Helen asks.

Mommy doubles over. She can't speak. She can't tell her that osmosis is the scientific process of how liquid passes through the walls of living cells.

Aunt Helen keeps asking, "Who's Osmosis?" but when she asks if Osmosis is a colored man, Mommy falls off her chair, giggling and sighing. After ten minutes of that, in a sliver of silence, Aunt Helen pipes up again.

"So who's Osmosis?"

"It's your brother, Joey!"

At home she tells Dad that his sister Helen wants to know who Osmosis is and for the rest of the night, every time they look at each other, they burst from the inside out.

****

Sis still doesn't want me looking at her and she doesn't want me coming near her, not unless it's her idea. She's fifteen years old and I'm going to be thirteen soon. I thought my age might change things between us, but some things never change.

"You're ugly," she whispers as she saunters past me.

So I make an ugly face.

"You're a moron," she says.

"So are you."

"I know you are but what am I?" she says, then she slaps me, pulls my hair, and pinches my arm, drawing blood. I can't pinch her back because I don't have long nails.

"I'm sick of you," she gags. "I wish you were never born. Why don't you just drop dead?"

"You hurt me," I cry.

"Martyr!" she says. "Tough tits!"

I try to figure out what's wrong with me, but I can't. I'm just glad Dad's not around, because he would've handed my head to me.

Dad thinks Sis is really smart. She doesn't even have to open a book to get good grades and she's a real go-getter. He loves that. He thinks Jane is refined and graceful, and he's proud of Anya because her teacher says she's a genius in math and science. She'll surely go to college someday.

At two and three, Hanna and Joanne are just a couple of crybabies who irritate Dad. I'm a big mouthed, stupid ass thorn in his side. Dad expects me to clean, wash dishes, help Mommy with the babies, and just get by in school because I'm destined to marry a man who'll need all these services.

****

Mommy goes into labor, and Dad is sure his seventh child will be a boy. But he gets another girl. Mommy names her after her sister, Louise. She's got a cute round face and flaxen hair. I'm so thrilled with my new baby sister, I don't even mind helping Mommy with her.

The summer rolls by so fast, I don't even realize what day it is today.

As I change Louise's diaper Mommy comes by. I look up at her and she smiles.

"It's your birthday today!" she says. "You're a teenager now!"

She makes it sound so special, but there's nothing enchanted about it until she sits me down, looks me square in the eye and sings the birthday song to me. I peer into her gleaming pearls for the duration of her off-key gift and something magical does happen—I'm filled with a knowing that my mother loves me. Other kids get stylish clothes for their thirteenth birthdays. I don't know it, but Mommy's gift to me will last a lifetime.

The Piano

Dad's new job at Foster Grant has him traveling to Chicago. He takes the bus to the plane and he's gone from Monday through Friday. When he's home on weekends, if there's trouble, it's usually my fault. Sometimes it's because I wince when he tells me to wash the dishes. I really want to help Mommy, but the dishes are becoming overwhelming.

"When you're in high school like Sis, I'll pass the job to one of your younger sisters," Dad swears. "If you don't want another lickin', don't give me any of your goddamned stupid looks. Just do what the hell I tell you!"

I could live with a lickin', but Dad's threats and the tone of his voice tell me what he thinks of me, and that hurts worse than any lickin'. Grandpa says that words are cheap, but I've figured out that sometimes they're not. If someone says they're going to build a house, but all they do is sit there waiting for the house to build itself, then yeah, words are cheap. When someone you love calls you a stupid idiot and they treat you accordingly, those words shred your heart and soul, and not even the finest seamstress in the world could mend you.

I still get into trouble for looking at Sis. Every time she says she wishes I wasn't born, I die a little more on the inside. *I wish I was blind.* If I was, I'd never get into trouble for looking at her.

God, please make me blind!

****

Mommy needs a car, so Dad goes out and buys her a brand new Pontiac Bonneville "on time." A used one would have been fine because Mommy can't afford monthly payments on a new car, but Dad insists he'll give her more money. He also promises to buy plane tickets for the whole family and take us somewhere nice.

"Stop making promises you can't keep, Joe," Mommy says.

"I'll keep my promise because I'm going to be a millionaire someday."

Since Dad can't afford plane tickets for the whole family, he buys one just for Sis and sends her out to California to visit with Mommy's brother, Buck, and his family. After all, she's the oldest.

The family pecking order is as clear as Grandma's good eye. We don't put it into words; we just know where we fall in the lineup, and as long as each of us takes the right number, there's no trouble.

The doghouse plaque in the kitchen disappeared, and our living room furniture fell apart, so Mommy and Dad go down to see Oyving again. They make a good deal on a colonial living room set, and as a bonus, Oyving throws in an eagle, The Declaration of Independence and The Constitution of the United States to hang on our wall.

We the people of the United States, in order to form a more perfect union, establish justice, insure domestic tranquility...

These great words of wisdom now replace Comedy and Tragedy.

****

Mommy never asks me about school anymore. Between laundry, cooking, grocery shopping and the babies, she doesn't have time to breathe. More and more it seems as though she's in another world. Her body is here, but her mind has abandoned it.

I'm busy, too. Besides school, I help Mommy, I have a few babysitting jobs and I'm a soda jerk. I earn fifty cents an hour babysitting and the man who owns the deli pays me sixty cents an hour "under the table," plus tips. I don't have to pay any taxes on my earnings because "under the table" means we're cheating the government out of its share. But then I hand almost all of my cash over to Mommy to save for things I need, like clothes, shoes and shampoo.

If I have time, once in a while I hike down to Grandma's house early on Saturday mornings. Sometimes Dad is already there, sitting on the wooden swing with Grandpa. Dad loves to argue with him, so when I say hello as I'm passing by they don't even see me.

I clean up Grandma's kitchen, then we talk while Grandma rocks in her chair. By now I know that she's had a hard childhood, that her mother dumped her off in Poland. Yet despite her misfortunes, she seems quite content, and I'm in awe of her happiness. Before I leave, Grandma usually gives me a dollar, which I give to Mommy to save for my school clothes. It adds up and when I can buy myself a new dress for school, I'm thrilled.

My aunts begin piling into Grandma's house for one of their usual rowdy conversations. But today their exchange is curiously somber.

"He was flying a kite on the roof of his apartment building," Aunt Frances says. "He wasn't watching where he was going. He hit the wall, fell over, and landed on the sidewalk."

All the women gasp.

"He died instantly," Aunt Frances laments. "Little Anthony was so frail."

Little Anthony? I can't believe what I'm hearing. *Little Anthony is dead?* I race down to the woods where my older cousins are hanging out to ask if it's true.

"Yeah, he's dead. Why should you care? You hardly knew him."

Maybe we only played together a few of times, but we were instant friends, I loved him, and I thought he'd always be there, at least once in a while like my other cousins. My heart crumbles like feta cheese. I don't want anyone to see me crying over Little Anthony so I hide in Aunt Edna's cellar.

First Uncle Frankie dies, then Uncle Anthony, and no one bothered to tell me. Now Little Anthony disappears the same way.

I'll never forget Little Anthony, but I put away my sorrow when I meet Ernesto. He moved here from Cuba with his huge family to get away from Fidel Castro. He's the smartest kid in my class and an inspiration to me. When I'm with him I don't feel stupid. We sneak down to the lake and plop ourselves on the sand to talk, then Ernesto sings to me in Spanish, gazing directly into my eyes as he croons every word. He's kind and gentle, and when he asks me questions, he actually listens to my answers. I just love him.

One day, he finally steals a kiss, just one, and it's my first kiss. But a second one will never come.

On the way home from a football game, Ernesto, his brother and their friends are hit by a fire truck. Ernesto is the only survivor. And while his life is spared, his memory is not. Now he has no clue who I am even though I visit him time and again hoping he'll remember me. He stares at me blankly, as if I'm a stranger, and I realize it doesn't matter to him if I never come back. I'm forced to admit that I lost him, and I learn that it's just as hard to lose someone who's still alive as it is to accept a death. I finally say my last good-bye to Ernesto.

****

Foster Grant transfers Dad from Chicago to Massachusetts. Dad rents a summer cottage up there from June through August so that our entire family can be together all summer long. Sis doesn't want to go, and since she's sixteen, Dad lets her have her way.

My younger sisters and I run through the lush Massachusetts forest as if we own it. I climb trees, inspect every leaf and plant, and I pick blueberries. Mommy turns every last one into treats, and I get to eat blueberry pie as if it's my only choice.

After dinner I hang around the table with Dad because he's a different person since he's been on the wagon. He's teaching me how to sketch faces and three-dimensional objects, and I learn more in one sitting with Dad than in all of my art classes.

He also teaches my sisters and me how to water-ski. Dad spends the entire day with us, and it ends with a comedy show when Dad tries to ski because no matter how fast Mommy revs the boat, Dad sinks like a cinderblock.

There's something magical in the Massachusetts air. Even though six of us girls are crammed into the cabin with Mommy and Dad, there isn't one argument. Too bad Sis isn't here. She *always* misses all the fun.

Miraculously, Dad finally decides to take me fishing. There's an old rowboat sitting on the side of the cottage. Dad puts his gear in the boat and I hop in first because I'm going to row. He gets in and almost tips it over. When it finally steadies, he casts his line.

"When am I going to get a turn to fish, Daddy?"

"Just keep rowing. When we get to the middle of the lake you can stop and I'll set up a line for you."

My arms are killing me because the lake is huge, but there's no way I'm going to complain. I'm out here on the lake with *my dad* and I'm not screwing this up. As we near the middle of the lake, water begins to seep into the boat.

"Don't worry," Dad says. "It's only a little bit."

I pull in the oars to free my hands so that I can stuff the hole, but water keeps seeping in.

"Turn the boat around and head for shore," Dad commands.

Good thing Mr. Miller gave me rowing lessons. I turn it around and as I row, the water level increases.

"We're going to sink, Dad."

"Nah, we'll make it back. Just row faster," he says.

So I do—while he's casting his line, reeling it in and recasting it. The water is covering my toes and soon it'll be up around my ankles. We're sinking, but there isn't a bit of worry on Dad's face. He's fishing as if everything around him is perfect. I realize that I won't be doing any fishing, yet I don't even care. I'm thrilled to be with Dad on the lake, just him and me. I want to scream "I'M WITH MY DADDY!" but I don't because he'll think I'm nuts. He hates it when people act screwy. I'm a teenager—way too old to be acting like a baby.

As the water rises well above my ankles Dad's contagious chuckle infects me. I'm rowing and laughing, and Dad's still fishing, and this boat is ready to sink. At about a hundred feet from the dock Dad reels in his line, shuts his tackle box and yells, "Man overboard!" He jumps out, and I fall out.

We're drenched, Dad and me, just the two of us, giggling and splashing each other. When we get the old wooden hunk-of-junk back to shore, Dad tells Mommy all about the screwed up fishing trip and the piece-of-shit rowboat. He can hardly get the words out because he's snorting. The story isn't really funny, but the way he tells it inflates me with joy.

Every minute of this summer is perfect—especially the imperfections! When you least expect it, things change for the better. And when that happens, all your fears melt away like a drop of honey on your tongue.

✷✷✷✷✷✷✷✷✷✷✷✷✷

My summer has been so carefree I haven't given thought to preparing myself for high school. I'm going into the ninth grade and it's scary. I've got only a week to prepare and I don't have anything to wear. I'm allowed to wear make-up and stockings, but I don't have any of that stuff. I couldn't work all summer because we lived deep in the Massachusetts woods and now I don't have a penny to buy a thing, nor does Mommy have any money to spare. There are plenty of hand-me-downs in the alcove upstairs, but the pickings are slim. When you're getting ready to enter high school you've got to give thought to how you look because you're going to be judged. *I wish I could wear a uniform. I'd rather blend than be singled out for being poor or unstylish.* These days, if you want to fit in, you've got to be a sharp dresser. The boys wear leather jackets, high-roll collared shirts and iridescent slacks. The girls tease their hair a mile high and it blocks out the sun if you stand behind them. They pack on make-up, especially blue eye shadow, and it looks as though their little sisters had a field day with Crayola crayons. They have different colored ballerina shoes for each outfit, mohair sweaters, which they wear backwards, and pencil skirts. The easy girls roll up their skirts at the top and wear them so short, when they sit down you almost wonder which end is the hairdo.

My current wardrobe consists of two white cotton B-cup bras that are pointed. My *dzidzees* pop out of the top so it looks like I have four of them—two pointed and two big round mounds. My bloomers are holey and I don't have any slips. I haven't grown much in height; I'm barely five feet tall and my shoe size is nine. Half of what I own is ragged and wasn't in style even when it was newer; the other half is stuff that just doesn't fit anymore.

I pick through the old clothes and find a black skirt. It needs a zipper so I cut one from an old pair of pants and sew it in—thanks to Mommy and Yaya who taught me how to sew. This one skirt is the only thing I have that's appropriate for school, but I'll find a few tops to change the look each day. I need shoes, and luckily, some of Sis's old size tens are in the hand-me-down bag. I'll just stuff toilet paper in the toes and be good to go.

I hit the jackpot when Sis gets new make-up and throws away her old stuff. When she isn't looking, I seize it from the garbage, along with her old runny stockings. If anyone notices the runs, I'll say, "Gee, when did that happen?"

I give myself a haircut and now I'm as ready for school as I'll ever be.

As it turns out, Madison High is so overcrowded they split the sessions. Sis goes to school in the morning and I go in the afternoon. Every morning after she leaves the house, I help Mommy with my three baby sisters. I eat lunch at home because it saves Mommy some money, then I hop on the bus.

I don't blend in at school; not with the cool kids and not with the college-bound kids who wear dimes in their penny loafers just in case they have to make a phone call. They cluster together in groups holding twenty pounds of books, and the cool girls squeeze into the bathroom to fight over the mirrors, and to talk about their friends who live in "Red Bank." They all seem to visit with their Red Bank friends once a month. I've never been to Red Bank, a town in New Jersey that's south of where I live, so I wonder what's so special about it that everyone knows someone from that town.

"Did you get a visit from your friend from Red Bank yet?" one of the cool girls asks.

"I don't know anyone from that town," I say.

The whole group of them bursts into laughter and I know it isn't because I told a funny joke. When I learn that a friend from Red Bank is your menstrual cycle or, as Mommy says, "your period," I feel like a jerk. Being a reject is too much for me to handle. I've got to do something about fitting in, so after Sis leaves for school I peek into her dresser and her closet. I'm afraid to borrow her stuff because if she catches me, I just know she'll kill me. She's got shoes, skirts, blouses, dresses, lacy slips—so many pretty things. Being in her closet is like shopping at Two-Guys department store.

I settle on one of her slips. I'll put it under my skirt so I won't have to itch from the wool all day long, then I'll sneak it back into her dresser tonight.

I put the skirt on over Sis's slip but it's too long for me so I roll it up. I might not look better but at least I don't itch. I hop on the bus and when we reach school the door opens and in comes a group of kids from the morning session. It turns out that my bus in is their late bus home. Sis is taking this late bus today, so when I see her I jump out of my seat to say hi.

She doesn't say hi back.

"You have my slip on!   That's my slip!" she yells. "Take it off now!"

I don't know how she knows, but then I look down to see that it came unrolled and the lace is hanging out from the bottom of my skirt.

"I can't take it off here."

"You're taking it off whether you like it or not!" she fumes, then she reaches down, tugs the lace and the slip falls to my ankles. I step out of the slip, she grabs it, then verbally demeans me in front of all the kids as I'm exiting the bus. *I want to die.*

After a few weeks, the embarrassment of looking like a rag picker overshadows the humiliation of getting caught with Sis's clothes. I decide to wear one of her blouses. It doesn't matter which one; everything she has is better than the few rags I have. I get away with borrowing a few of her things, but then she catches me, smacks me, pulls my hair and pinches my arms.

"Why don't you just drop dead already?" she snaps.

I can hardly fight back because she's a maniac when she's angry. Besides, I know I'm wrong for being sneaky. Because of me there's mayhem in the house. Thankfully Dad's not around that much so I don't have to suffer a double lickin' every time I fight with Sis.

I try everything I can to put together decent outfits from the hand-me-down bag, but it's hardly worth the effort. No matter what I wear Sis mercilessly demeans me.

"You're ugly and your mother dresses you funny. I wish you weren't born! Rag picker! I don't want to be seen with you!"

The proud, blinding gleam in her eyes shoots at me, and it hits the target—my heart. *I'm no good as a rag picker, and I'm no good when I'm in her clothes looking good.*

****

On weekends I set out on foot to find a job. If I earn some money, I could buy my own clothes. After walking miles around Old Bridge today with no luck, I head home. Just as I'm entering the house, Dad and Sis pull into the driveway. Sis got her license and she's driving Mommy's Pontiac. She prances into the kitchen.

"Dad gave me the car!"

"What car?" Mommy asks.

"The Pontiac."

"What?"

"He gave me the Pontiac," she crows and then dances up to her bedroom.

When Dad comes into the kitchen, Mommy asks, "Did you give Sis my car?"

"I had to."

"What do you mean you had to?"

"She needs a car, that's what the hell I mean."

"That's my car, Joe. You can't be giving away my car without even asking me first."

"I'll get you another one."

"We still have payments on that car. How are we going to afford another?"

"I'll figure it out, goddamn it."

"No," Mommy insists, "tell her she can't keep the car."

"She can keep the car, goddamn it! You'll get another!"

With that, Dad storms out of the kitchen.

****

Mommy knows I've been trying to get a job. She tells Sis to bring home an employment application from the donut shop where she works. Sis doesn't want to. She doesn't want me working in the same place she does. Now Mommy and Sis are arguing, which usually ends in victory for Sis. But this time Mommy is so furious, she doesn't give up, which results in me getting a job in the donut shop where Sis works. But we'll barely cross each other's paths because she works in the office, and I'll be behind the counter serving coffee and donuts.

When Mommy informs Sis that she'll have to drive me back and forth to work, there's another argument. *It seems as though every quarrel in the house has something to do with me.*

"You don't do any household chores, Sis. And since you got the car, driving your sister to work isn't any sweat off your back!" Mommy says. "You have no choice."

When Sis drives me to work she reminds me how she wishes I was never born, that I'm a jerk, a rag picker, and worse. My head feels as though it's going to explode until we arrive at the donut shop. In the presence of our coworkers she becomes delightful—even charming.

I get an hourly wage plus tips, but I'm not working enough hours to accumulate money fast enough to buy a wardrobe. After the first week I'm able to buy some personal items, and some licorice for my baby sisters. I'm excited to show them how to bite off the ends and use the licorice as a straw for milk. They're so appreciative, you'd think I gave them a teddy bear.

Mommy's holding the rest of my money because it'll be awhile before I have enough to buy new clothes. I try staying out of Sis's closet but I almost have no choice. My clothes don't even fit me anymore and if they looked ridiculous before, there are no words to describe how they look now. I get caught again with Sis's clothes, and I looked at her a few more times, so it's my fault there's more fighting.

Dad whips out his belt to teach me a lesson, and after a few whacks he says, "Now get the hell up and wash the goddamned dishes."

I grab a dirty dish from the huge pile, and while I'm scrubbing Dad comes up behind me breathing like a dragon.

"Stop what you're doing and sit down."

I shut off the water and grab a chair.

"You've got to stop touching Sis's things and you've got to leave her alone."

He's very calm but I'm afraid to say what I'm thinking. *I leave her alone and I only wear her clothes because I don't have anything decent.*

"I'm trying to save money to buy my own clothes, Dad."

"What the hell are you doing with all the money you're making?"

"I only work ten hours a week or so. I don't make *that* much."

"Why don't you tell your mother when you need something? She's in charge of getting you kids what you need."

"She doesn't have enough money."

"What you mean, she doesn't have enough? I give her whatever money she needs."

"She says she doesn't have enough."

"Well," he roars, "I'm going to see about that!"

Mommy comes into the kitchen and Dad asks her why she doesn't buy us kids what we need.

"I can barely pay the bills with what you give me. You've got that big wad of cash in your pocket. Why don't you spend *that* on the kids?"

"That's *my* goddamned money."

"That's the problem," Mommy says.

"No," Dad interrupts, "maybe it's because you're always in such a rush to pay the bills. You don't always have to pay them right away."

"Do you have rocks in your head? If I did that, we'd really be in a hole. They'd shut off our electric, take back the cars *and* the furniture!" Mommy rolls her eyes and disappears from the kitchen.

Dad turns to me.

"You know, you're not a baby anymore. We shouldn't have to be buying every little thing you need. Maybe you should work a few more hours."

"Dad, I work all the hours they give me and I really don't make that much money. I'm saving what I make. I just need more time."

"Why don't you play the piano?"

My heart pounds like thunder. I can't believe he's changed the subject. I have wanted to play the piano more than anything, but it's been so long—I forgot I had that dream. *Thank You for finally making one of my wishes come true, God.*

"Where are you going to get the money for a piano?" I ask.

"Don't you know anything?" Dad answers.

I gaze through his glasses into his huge blue-gray eyes. He's peering at me in wonderment. I'm confused. I'm missing something.

"What?" I ask.

"I guess I have to teach you everything myself," he says.

While I'm envisioning my fingers moving over an ivory keyboard, Dad tells me to take a little for myself. I don't know what he's talking about.

"Piano players have quick fingers."

"What do you mean, Daddy?"

"Put a little extra money in your tip cup instead of ringing up every donut."

"That's stealing."

"Stealing is when you take from your family," Dad insists. "Companies are the real thieves. If you skim a little extra for yourself, it's no big deal. Everybody does it; just don't get caught."

I search Dad's face and all I see is kindness. He's earnestly trying to help me. Now he tells me to finish up the dinner dishes and get ready for bed. As he exits the kitchen he yells back at me.

"If you don't look out for yourself in this world, no one's gonna do it for you."

My mind sprints back to the time I stole Mommy's silver dollar. *Hey God, are you drinking scotch, too, because you misunderstood my prayers? When I said I wanted to play the piano, I was thinking of ivory keys that jingle, not coins.*

At work I feel sick to my stomach. Every time I think about playing the piano, Mommy's silver dollar skips across my mind. One day, in spite of knowing better, I skim a quarter. It makes me feel worse than when I sneaked my sister's clothes because I know I'm not giving back the quarter. Every second I'm behind the coffee counter that's all I think about. So the next time I work, I don't play the piano but the time after that, I do. An extra dime here and a quarter there add up to an extra dollar or so at the end of the week. I pretend that skimming is no big deal, but the silver dollar voraciously eats at my soul.

****

I arrive at school early today. My class hasn't started yet so I'm leaning up against a locker in the corridor just waiting for the bell to ring. I'm the only one out here except for a few boys further down the corridor who are laughing and running toward the stairwell. Suddenly the locker door explodes open and flings me across the hall into another set of lockers.

I can't see! I can't hear a thing! I blink but I'm not sure if my eyes are open so I touch them—my eyes *are* open, but I can't see. My entire world is dark and silent!

No less than a hundred times I have wished to be blind just so I wouldn't get myself into trouble for looking at Sis. *What is wrong with me? What the hell am I, stupid?*

The floor begins to vibrate as if I'm in a meadow during a buffalo stampede. I'm alive and I can feel, but that's it. *I'll never be allowed to get a driver's license and I'll never get to see Uncle Buck play Julius in Planet of the Apes, but at least I'll never get into trouble again for looking at Sis.*

"Help!" I yell. "I can't see! Help!"

What happened to me?

I wipe my nose and the tears on my cheeks with my bare arm, then at the top of my lungs I scream as if I'm being stabbed. I hear nothing. I blink away a few more tears only to see what looks like the darkest night without the moon and the stars.

I wish I never wished to be blind. Of all my wishes, why did you make this one come true, God?

Mom will probably tell me that I'll live.

I'm sure I will. I always do, even when I would rather die.

PART FOUR: ANOTHER FRESH START

Bikes and Bats for Sale

Our house is finally up for sale, but Dad isn't going to tell prospective buyers about the bats. He's going to leave them in the dark, same as the guy who sold Dad "the goddamned house."

He patches up the holes behind the doors and makes all the little repairs he had intended to do when we moved into the bat cave ten years earlier. As he works he curses at his tools, at the plaster and the paint. When Dad puts his finishing touches on his "goddamned son-of-a-bitchin' repairs," they actually look great, but only for a little while because he forgot the most important detail: doorstoppers.

On a bright note, the bat-house is sold—for the same price he paid a decade earlier: ten grand.

"We're all getting a fresh start in life," Dad announces to everyone in earshot. "Nothing's better than to start over with a clean slate!"

To prepare for the new house Dad takes Mommy to the furniture store to see their old buddy, Oyving the Jew. They buy a new kitchen set, a living room set, a stereo, bureaus and bed frames. The comfy mattresses are way too expensive, but Oyving has a good deal on the super-duper-firm ones that have a half inch of dust on top—half price and the dust is free. Those are the ones Dad chooses. Oyving lets them buy everything "on time" because Mommy was so good about making payments in the past. They strike up such a good deal they can't help but remind everyone they know to "go see Oyving the Jew down in South River."

"He's even gonna deliver da foinature to da new house," Dad says in his finest Jewish accent. "Cud ya believe dat? Vhat a deal! Vhat a steal!"

Dad doesn't care how much money he owes Oyving or anyone else. He's sure he'll have plenty of cash to pay later. He gave up his job at Foster Grant for a better one at a chemical plant nearby. In addition to some innovative plans he's got in the oven, his other "on-the-side" scheme is rising like dough. His goal is to make a million dollars and now he's so sure of himself, he's practically standing on the dock.

"My ship is on its way in!" he announces for the hundredth time.

"Don't fall off the dock, Joe. You'll make a tidal wave that'll wipe out an island on the other side of the world!"

"Don't you worry, Lil, I'm not gonna fall."

"You will if you're shit-faced, Joe!"

"You'll see Lil. My ship is already in the bay."

"Yours and everyone else's!" Mommy shoots back. "Just make sure you're not plastered because you might board a cargo ship loaded with cow manure that's on its way to a farm in the Middle East."

"There ain't no goddamned farms in the Middle East," Dad spits.

"Get the hell out of here," Mommy laughs. "There's farms in every country. How else do you think people survive? They need *food*, Joe!"

"The only thing those people grow is oil!" Dad says emphatically.

Mommy throws back her head, opens her mouth, and squints her eyes as her entire body vibrates. She tries repeating what Dad just said but only parts of her words escape.

****

Today is almost the same as all my other birthdays: no cake, no card, no gift. No one knows I turned fifteen. Mom used to sing the birthday song to me, but maybe she forgot. It's no wonder. She's like the lady who lived in a shoe. She has so many kids she can't *always* remember all of our birthdays.

"It's a special day!" Dad proclaims, but my birthday isn't what makes it special.

I always keep my mental shit-file locked up tight so nothing seeps out and spoils the good stuff. Dad's announcement catches me off guard. For a moment I think he remembers my birthday. When I realize he doesn't, without warning the lock on my shit-file snaps open and out pops the time Dad bought me a special gift in honor of my birthday. He couldn't remember my age. Mommy had to tell him that I had turned nine just a few days earlier. Right then and there he took me to a toy store and told me I could pick out anything I want for my birthday while leading me over to an above ground pool and insisting how nice it is.

The toy store didn't have any pianos. If I could've had anything, a piano would've been my first choice. But when I glanced up from the pool, some shiny objects caught my eyes. I had never even wished for anything like that, but after seeing a whole bunch of them sitting in a row, teasing me like a Popsicle on a hot summer day, I knew I wanted one. *Oh yeah! A brand new bike would do. A shiny red one!*

"Wouldn't it be great in our backyard?" Dad asked, referring to the pool.

He wanted me to say yes, but the red bike kept calling my name. It helped me to muster enough courage to remind Dad that we live only two seconds away from a lake.

"I can swim in the lake anytime I want to Daddy, and the summer is almost over. Can I pretty-please have a bike instead?"

"Is that what you *really* want?"

"Yes, Daddy!"

"Are you *sure?*"

I peered through his glasses into his magnified, blue-gray eyes and nodded yes.

"Okay then, I'll get you a bike."

I didn't expect him to be so agreeable. I got the bike I wanted and I thanked Dad three times till he finally bowed his head in acknowledgment.

He plopped the bike into the trunk of his car, but he didn't have any string to tie it down, so every time we hit a bump in the road, the hood of his trunk bounced off the bike.

I was relieved when we finally got home.

"Can I ride the bike now, Daddy?"

"Okay," he said, and with his pointer in my face, he added, "You better take care of it because you're not getting another one. And make sure you put it in the garage when you're done riding. I don't want the backyard looking like a shithouse."

He pulled the bike out of the trunk, I thanked him again, and off I went. I was so ecstatic I burst into song as I pedaled along. I couldn't help it. I have a singing compulsion disorder. To this day, almost any word I hear or think makes me break out in song. I was feeling so good, and it wasn't just because of the bike, it was because Dad thought enough of me to buy it.

I'm sure I left behind a trail of joy as I rode up and down every street in Old Bridge. I made it home just before dusk and paused at the corner of the yard in time to witness thousands of bats shooting out of our attic. I wheeled my prized possession through the weeds and sticker bushes on the side of my yard, past the stinky, dented, lidless garbage pails swarming in larvae, up the dirt driveway, through more weeds, and into the garage so that the backyard wouldn't become a shithouse like the ones Dad grew up in.

That night I fell asleep with a smile so big you could hang your coat on either corner of it.

The next morning Mommy was going to the grocery store and I had to go with her. I couldn't wait to get home because all I wanted to do was ride my bike. My mind wouldn't let me think of anything else.

At home I hurried to help Mommy bring in the groceries, then I dashed out to the garage, stopped short at the door and swung it open. I saw the sickle, a couple of corroded tools on the work bench, and a rusty, old secondhand bike that never worked in the first place.

My shiny red bike was gone!

I scampered through the yard in search of it, then I leaped up the three back steps and sprinted into the kitchen where Mommy and Dad were sitting.

"My bike is gone! Somebody stole my bike!"

"It's your own goddamned fault for not putting it away!" Dad growled.

"I did. I put it in the garage and shut the door."

"What do you think, I'm stupid?" the lion roared. "Don't tell me you put your goddamned bike away." Then he picked up his coffee mug with his classy pinky pointed upward and took a sip, gaping intently at the blue Formica table as if he never saw it before.

Mommy never looked up. She didn't say a word. There was complete silence as I stood there expecting them to be offended at the notion of someone stealing my bike. I thought they might offer to help me find it, or perhaps call the police. They didn't.

Without a word I hightailed it out the door into the street, dashing up and down the number streets, across on the named ones, then all the way down Englishtown Road to the Low property. I hunted around all three "shithouses" in Grandpa Low's kingdom, the shanties, the cesspool and the open cellar. I searched through heaps and piles of rusted gadgets, all around Grandpa's pigeon coop, and his killee shack. Nothing. But there was one more place to look: Grandpa's junk-filled garage.

I was terrified of what Grandpa would do if he caught me poking around in there. Even to this day, the way he protects the contents of his garage and all his other shanties, you'd think he was hiding his old bathtub gin operation.

He still insists he's "da kingk of da Low prrroperrrty," and he has a crown and scepter to prove it: a dirty old cap and a twenty-foot long pigeon pole with colored rags tied to the top. And *don't* think for one minute that Grandpa Low couldn't find another practical use for that pigeon pole.

If he found me nosing around his kingdom, he'd have no problem beating my ass, and doing it without mercy. I sucked it up and entered the spook house with a stick in hand to swipe away the cobwebs. Once I got past the mingling odors of dirt and mold, I noticed a bicycle in the corner behind a pile of junk. After clearing away some pipes and a worn-out toilet seat—probably the czar's new throne—I reached for the bike. What I found was just an old set of handlebars. Before I could let go, I heard footsteps.

"Hey yuns! Put dat down, got-dem it! Get da hell outta herrre! Who yuns tingk yuns arrre, touchingk my stuff?" Grandpa bellowed.

What the hell did he think I was going to do with a set of handlebars? *Pretend* to ride a bike? People would think I have rocks in my head. Even at nine years old I knew that would be worse than pretending to go horseback riding through the neighborhood when all I had was a stick with a plastic horse head on the top.

"What da hell yuns doingk?"

"I'm looking for my bike, Grandpa. Someone stole it!"

"Ohhhhh! Someone stole yuns bike?" he said in a way that made me think he was empathizing with me. Then he added, "Stop crrryingk like a got-dem crrry baby. If yuns keep crrryingk, I'll give yuns sometingk to crrry forrr. Yuns want a lollipop?"

Lollipop is just another word Grandpa uses in place of lickin'. Just like Dad, he wears his weapon in plain view, a tool that's meant only to hold up his pants, one that is ever present, reminding me to behave, or to run like hell.

I pulled up my shirt to wipe away my tears. I've seen Grandma Low pull her apron up to her face when *she* doesn't have a hanky—which is never.

"Enough crrryingk got-dem-it! Go find some other got-dem bike den. And if yuns find da son-of-a-bitch who took yuns bike, get 'em back double, trrriple, ten times maybe."

That's all Grandpa had to say. He turned and headed toward his killee shack with a slight limp that didn't hinder his speed if he had to chase you to "give yuns a got-dem lickin'."

My clothes were soaked in sweat, salty tears drenched my face, and the toughened soles of my feet were raw and bleeding. I gave up and hobbled home.

I didn't have the words *then* to say how empty I felt. I still don't. Back into the shit-file it goes with all the other feelings I'm not allowed to speak of. And I won't because I don't want to mess up this special day—we're finally moving out of the bat cave!

I'm all packed up and ready to go. It took me only a minute to box up all of my personal belongings. Since I'm so quick, Mommy enlists me to hold my baby sister, Louise, while she gets her clothes packed up.

Sis comes down the stairs and saunters by.

"Stop looking at me. Take a picture, it'll last longer. Ugly!"

All I can think about now is how I went deaf and blind that day in school when the dynamite exploded and flung me across the corridor. I was so angry with myself for wishing to be blind just so I wouldn't get into trouble for looking at Sis.

I laid there on the floor for what seemed to be an eternity. It was a relief when I felt a tugging on my arm. I followed the lead, up the hall, down the stairwell, through another hall, into a room where I was prompted to sit. I began to feel vibrations coming from the floor; I was never quite aware of them before. Even though crying is against the Low Constitution—I cried.

Suddenly I began hearing sounds as if they were coming from far away. Then light began to re-enter my eyes as if layers of curtains were being peeled away one by one.

I heard the nurse dial the phone.

"Is Lillian Low there?"

It sounded as though she had to argue with Mommy in order to convince her to come to school. That's because it isn't easy dragging a baby and two toddlers around. But Mommy relented.

By the time Mommy arrived in the nurse's office with my three baby sisters, I could see and hear again. Since I wasn't covered in blood, she thought I should stay in school. She has this rule: you don't skip school unless your fever is so high, you can't sit up. You can go to school with a cold, a stomachache, headache, or loss of a pint of blood —with just about any ailment you can think of. If Mommy could've gotten away with sending us to school with chicken pox, she would've. When she learned the neighborhood kids were contagious one summer, she sent Jane and me out to play with them just so we'd catch the pox before September.

The nurse emphatically argued with Mommy.

"The dynamite exploded inches from her face with only a metal door as a shield. She went into shock, Mrs. Low. She should be taken to a doctor."

Mommy finally agreed to take me out of school, but she didn't tell the nurse that she would *not* be taking me to see a doctor. She brought me home instead because she's Dr. Lillian. That's what Dr. Allgair calls her. The only time I've seen Dr. Allgair was when one of my siblings or I needed a booster shot. Dr. Lillian has her own cost-free methods for curing illnesses. When I broke my nose the first, second, and third time, she fixed it with a thumb press and a bag of ice. She just can't afford to run up her medical bills. Not that it matters because every year when she complains about how high her bill is, Dr. Allgair cuts it in half and allows her to pay the balance "on time."

Mommy's remedy for shock: drink a tall glass of water and go to bed.

"You'll live," she told me. I knew that's what she'd say.

By the end of my freshman year in high school, I learned to be careful of what I wish for, and as long as I'm not dead, I'll live.

After losing my sight in school that day, it's even more upsetting to me when Sis tells me to stop looking at her, that I'm ugly, and that she wishes I was never born.

It's no fun being ugly, and sometimes, it's no fun being alive.

Sis struts away with a gleam in her eyes.

Now Dad comes bounding downstairs into the living room.

"Stay right there," he demands, "I want to have a talk with you."

I can't go anywhere. I'm holding a sleeping toddler.

Dad rolls a giant barrel over to the front door, then turns back toward me.

"Mommy's going to need all the help she can get in the new house," he says, his finger wagging in my face. "It'll be your job to help her keep it clean. I don't want it turning into a shithouse."

I can't help but remember that I was supposed to be relieved of housework when I got into high school. Dad *swore* to that! Yet I actually don't mind because our new house is so much bigger than this one. I'll have room to breathe free and places to hide. It'll be nice living in a house *without* bats scratching on the walls all night, *without* the relentless siren from the firehouse across the street. Maybe Dad will give up drinking, and perhaps he'll give Mommy a break and quit shooting for a boy. Seven girls are enough!

Maybe things *will* be better. I give Dad my word.

Now I can hardly wait to go.

Movin' On Up

We move into the yellow bi-level in Green Valley. It's a brand new development in Sayreville, a nice working-class town just north of Old Bridge. The new homes being built here in 1968 are much larger than the existing homes, and all this construction causes the population of Sayreville to almost triple since 1950.

Our new home sits on a 100-by-300-foot lot. The front covered porch leads into a landing with wall-to-wall carpeting. Two sets of stairs stretch away from the landing. The right stairway takes you down into a large family room with gold and brown carpeting that matches our gold and brown colonial furniture. Dad puts a TV in the family room along with a six-foot-long wooden utility box that Uncle Mike built. It looks like Abe Lincoln's casket, but we're going to use it for toys. There are two bedrooms off the family room, a large walk-in closet in the hallway, a half bath, and a laundry room that leads into the garage.

The stairs on the left of the landing funnel you up to an open alcove. On the left is a hallway leading to three bedrooms and two bathrooms—no more sitting on the tub with my sisters waiting for a crack at the toilet! To the right of the alcove is a large kitchen with a gold Formica table, gold swivel chairs, and a gold, brown and white linoleum floor.

Our living room is directly in front of the alcove. Mommy made gold satiny drapes to match the gold carpeting. The stereo is put in there for our listening pleasure, along with the new green and gold contemporary furniture, so you think you're sitting inside of a giant musical jewelry box.

Mommy's gold satiny drapes cover an entire wall in the dining room too. Dad likes the gold because it's elegant. Mommy likes it because she thinks the color will camouflage dirt, fingerprints and footprints.

The neat thing about being upstairs is that you can run in circles from the kitchen to the dining room through the living room, and back into the kitchen. That's the first thing the kids discover, but I see it differently. The next time Dad chases me with his belt, I'll give him a good workout.

Jane is the lucky one enlisted to help me clean. We vacuum, dust, scrub toilets, polish furniture, wash walls—you name it, we do it.

Of all the chores, the worst one is washing dishes. They need to be done all day long because Mommy cooks for a kingdom every day. The dinner dishes are divvied out mostly between Jane and me because we're fast—and probably not as clever as some of our other siblings. We don't realize that moving swiftly and efficiently works to our detriment.

The only job required of Sis is driving me to work on the weekends. All the way there she reminds me what a pain in the ass I am.

"Why do you always have to be so mean?"

"I'm not mean!" she insists. Then she tells me I'm an idiot, I'm ugly, and she wishes I was never born.

"Shut up!" I scream. But she doesn't.

She wants to know why the hell she's the one who always has to go out of her way for me, and why can't I get my own damn ride.

"Shut up!" I explode as my eyes bulge and my head spins.

"Look at you!" she calmly says with a smile and a gleam in her eyes. "You're a lunatic! You can't even take a joke. You're such a big baby. Why don't you drop dead already?"

Sometimes I begin to think I am crazy, and by the time I get out of her car I'm so shaken I can't think straight. I'd like to quit my job so I don't have to listen to her, but I can't. I have to earn money for clothes. It's the only way for me to stay out of her closet.

Before the new school year begins, I do some clothes shopping and go through the hand-me-down bag to renew whatever can be salvaged. I buy my own personal items and I cut my own hair.

On the first day of school as I'm walking down the hall I notice a dark-haired girl staring at me.

"Who the hell are you?" she says.

"I'm Cathy. Who the hell are you?"

Doreen bursts out laughing and we're instant friends. We're alike in a lot of ways. We love to eat, to laugh, we love dancing, and we don't mind hanging around each other's houses. She comes to my house to help us make pierogi, and after tasting one, she thinks she died and went to heaven. Now she doesn't care what's going on. If there are pierogi to be made, she's going to help because she wants her share.

Mommy makes us wear bloomers on our heads to keep hair out of the dough. Doreen goes right along, putting my bloomers on *her* head, but first she announces that she's got to check them for shit stains.

"Sure, you're worried about getting hair in the food!" she says. "What's worse, hair or shit?"

"Shut the hell up and roll," Mommy laughs.

"Roll, you want me to roll?" Doreen says. She drops the rolling pin and gyrates her flour-dusted hips. She's a sight with my holey underwear on her head and flour all over her clothes and face. The contrast of the flour against her dark skin leaves Mommy in stitches.

"What's a matter," Doreen says, "don't I look good as a spook?"

By the time we're done, we've made about two hundred pierogi, and thanks to Doreen, we laughed just as many times. She may have a big mouth, but she's got a heart to match. And her visits always bring out the sunshine in Mommy—in me, too.

The one thing Doreen's mom makes that mine doesn't is Italian food. At her house you don't eat in the kitchen, not the real one. Her mom has a second kitchen in the cellar. That's the one that gets all slopped up. At a glance, the upstairs is comparable to Grandma Yaya's house—impeccably clean and orderly. Mama Rose, Doreen's mother,

213

has beautiful guest towels in her bathroom, but you're not allowed to use them. They're just for looking at. And her upstairs kitchen is so clean it looks like no one's home.

Her cellar, on the other hand, is comparable to Grandma Low's house. It's dark down there, and a little dingy. The furniture is old and you don't have to worry about messing anything up because there are scratches and wear and tear on everything. The cellar is where everything happens. It's where you eat, laugh, and cry. It's where you make memories. It's where your heart grows and where it goes when you need comfort.

Mama Rose keeps her black, wavy hair combed back off her face. A flowered housedress drapes her plump figure like a dancing tent as she sways by the stove, stirring sauce in a pot big enough to take a bath in.

"Oooo," I say, "tomato sauce."

She whacks me on the hand with her wooden spoon.

"It's gravy, not sauce!"

She's simmering meatballs and sausages in that pot while water boils in another. The aroma is so thick you can taste the air.

I lick the gravy off my hand and sit at the table with Doreen and her brother, Jerry. Mama Rose puts a huge bowl of macaroni right in front of me. I think it's for the whole table so I push it to the middle. The next thing I know Mama Rose is smacking me on the back of my head.

"What's a matter, you don't wanna eat my food?"

She pushes the bowl back to me—turns out we each get a half-pound of macaroni. If I don't eat it all, I'll insult Mama Rose. If I do, I won't be tap-dancing any time soon. I manage to eat half, and when Mama Rose isn't looking, I scrape the mound of macaroni from my bowl into Jerry's, and he laughs as if he just hit the jackpot.

I love being here in this dingy old cellar with Doreen and her family. Somehow I know that the upstairs of her house is unnecessary. Anyone who needs to be impressed by its perfection wouldn't know the first thing about breaking bread in the cellar.

Hippies, Birth Control and Babies

Richard Nixon is promising to end the Vietnam War. Flower power is hip in 1969. Acid rock, drugs and colorful clothing are becoming all the rage. Slowly the new trend begins to attract more kids. They're into love, peace, and flower power. Save Doreen, many of my new friends become hippies, seemingly overnight. They spend the money their parents give them on booze, pot and acid. At school they come to me to borrow lunch money because they're starving and they don't have a penny.

My parents don't give me a dime. I use my own money for lunch, for clothes and if I want a car when I get my license, Mommy and Dad aren't going to give me one red cent for it. They won't pay for my insurance either. I've struggled for everything—even quiet peaceful moments with no babies crying, no one yelling at me, telling me who and what I am, so there's no way I'm spending a penny on drugs, booze, or acid rock albums that are just as ear-piercing as dueling wailing babies.

At first I feel sorry for my hippie friends, so I lend them money. I don't want them to starve. After handing them my change, they don't say thanks, they say groovy. Now I hate the word groovy. They're supposed to pay me back, but they never do because they've just spent all their money on booze or a drop of acid for a trip. If I could take a trip, you'd find me in France or Spain. I don't want to keep lending them money, but when I tell them no, they beg me and promise to pay me back. I soon realize that I have to tell them I don't have any money. It's the only way to get them off my back. Just as I'm starting to blend, the style changes. I don't want to get high or wear clothes and beads that appear to come equipped with batteries. I don't want to be a walking billboard that advertises getting high is cool. Dad's epic drinking binges are my anti-drug.

****

Now that I'm allowed to date, the rabbit wants to tell me about the birds and the bees.

"I don't want any goddamned shotgun weddings on my hands," Dad says. "Finish high school and find a man who'll marry and keep you. And just so ya know, men don't want a used woman! So if you end up getting yourself pregnant, don't come home!"

I still don't have any friends from Red Bank, and I know that's one prerequisite for getting pregnant. I'm dating, and I've been down the road a little bit, but there isn't the slightest possibility that I'm going "all the way." There's plenty of birth control around me—a Dad who'll break my ass. And since money is limited, I have to pick and choose what I'll buy myself to wear. New underwear is my last priority because you can't see them. There's no way I'm letting anyone get a glimpse of my ugly, holey, old lady style bloomers and bras. They're staying where they belong—under everything! The baby factory I'm living in also prevents me from going "all the way." I adore my little sisters and even though they're not my babies, my workload increases with each one.

Mommy decides to have a woman-to-woman talk with me. She waddles into my room because she's pregnant, due sometime around her forty-second birthday. She hands me a large box of Modess sanitary napkins, a pamphlet, and a smaller box that contains an elastic belt with two metal hooks.

"Pretty soon you're going to have a menstrual cycle. You'll get your period once a month," she says as she points to the pamphlet. "Read this."

I open up the pamphlet to see a picture of a uterus, ovaries and eggs coming down the tubes. The pictures are better than the boring text, so that's the end of Birds and Bees 101.

Mommy's talk isn't quite as extensive as the one my neighbor got from his mother. Mrs. Mac holds up a plug and simultaneously points to an electrical socket. She tells him *he's* the plug and the woman is the socket. If you put them together, you get electricity.

If you asked me, I'd say that sounds exciting.

Years earlier Mommy's sister Chris gave me her woman-to-woman talk.

"Don't let anyone put anything in any places where they don't belong. And make sure you don't sit on any public toilet seats because if there's any of that *stuff* on the seat, you can get pregnant from it.

Her daughter Geraldine, who's around my age, says "that *stuff* is little fishies," so now we warn each other to watch out for the killees.

I was so enthralled with Aunt Chris's lesson I forgot to ask about my bag of herns.

Since Mommy is on her eighth pregnancy, she's not exactly the one who should be offering birth control advice. But when a cousin of mine gets herself pregnant out of wedlock, Mommy offers her best recommendation.

"Next time keep your legs crossed."

Mommy must have a sixth sense because within days of her giving me the Modess, at the age of fifteen, I get a visit from my friend from Redbank. Now I have to wear that nasty, uncomfortable elastic strap with metal hooks that dig into me. When I'm sitting in class all I can think of is how awful it feels. It diverts my usual thoughts of how to save money, what I need to do at home, my younger siblings, and Dad's antics.

Sometimes I get a few cramps, but Mommy says I'll live. My friends get to stay home from school on the first day of their periods. It doesn't matter what my circumstances are: headache, stomachache, loss of a pint of blood; if I want pity, I should look it up in the dictionary.

****

Our house is under construction. Dad hired men to build a patio with an overhang and a shed in the backyard, and a pool company to install an aboveground pool. Between Dad's job and his "on-the-side" stuff, he's got lots of extra cash and he wants to make sure we have a great party house before summer comes.

In the midst of the 1969 March madness Mommy goes into labor, and I'm to take charge of the house while Dad brings her to the hospital. Between family, the neighborhood kids, and relatives, our house is like Grand Central Station. While Mommy's in the hospital, Jane and I attempt to keep up with the cleaning, and I try my hand at cooking. I've helped Mommy cook countless times, but I've never made anything from scratch without her guidance. When you wear someone else's shoes, you learn that your feet are too small. You also appreciate and hold your mother in the highest esteem because you know she's gone through an awful lot of trouble making sure you have delicious, healthy food.

As I wait for my chicken soup to come to a boil, Dad flies through the door and jogs up the steps.

"It's a boy!" he announces breathlessly.

Joseph is Dad's namesake. My new brother is the eighth child, and the eighth Joseph in our extended family. To set him apart I refer to him as Baby Joseph.

Tears stream down Dad's face. It's the first time I've ever seen him cry because there's no crying in the Low house. He finally has the boy he always wanted. Ironically, he's already telling everyone that he finally figured out the secret formula for making a boy. He's going to make another one as soon as possible because Baby Joseph will need a playmate.

Within a couple of days Mommy and Dad bring home Baby Joseph. He's got blonde hair and dazzling eyes that will soon turn brown. He's perfect in every way.

Joseph is wrapped up in a receiving blanket with his arms locked in snug and tight the way Mommy wrapped all of us. He's dry and fed and now it's time for his nap. During the day, his bassinet is kept in the living room next to the stereo. Between Dad's outbursts, the blaring stereo, seven-year-old Joanne who leads Hanna and Louise in circles, screaming and giggling, pots and pans clanking, arguments, laughter, and visitors oooing and ahhing over Baby Joseph, I don't know how he can sleep.

The birth of a son calls for celebration. *Na Zdorovie!* Since the Kennedys get a nickel for every bottle of scotch that's sold, I think they ought to give Dad a kickback. Cigars are passed out, a christening is planned, and Sis is the chosen godmother. Joseph receives gifts of money and bonds like his seven sisters before him. But his gifts are put away for his bright future because he's special—it's the *jooje*.

Dad's been floating on a cloud of glee, which causes him to do some surprisingly nice things. He's taking me to the movies, just him and me. I can't wipe the smile off my face. We're going to see *They Shoot Horses, Don't They?* It doesn't sound like something I'd pick, but I don't care. I'm with my dad.

"Why would anyone shoot a horse, Daddy?"

"When a horse is injured, if he can't be healed, you shoot him to put him out of his misery. Although it seems harsh, putting it to rest is the most humane thing you can do."

I'm impressed with Dad, touched by his kindness, and comforted by the tone of his voice. Even though I often feel distanced from him, this one beautiful moment rekindles everything. Of course I have to get back to the reality of going to school, cleaning house and washing dishes, but the sentiment stays with me, making every step I take a little easier.

****

I'm at the kitchen sink washing dishes. As Mommy scoots back and forth from the stove to the sink, bringing me more dirty pots, I notice that she look like a capital D from the side.

"Are you pregnant, Mommy?"

She nods yes.

"How could you let yourself get pregnant again?"

My tone is scornful, as if I'm the parent and she's the child.

"It isn't fair, Mommy. There's already too much work to do."

She stands there quietly.

I finish the dishes, then go down to my room to think. I'm ashamed of how I talked to her. She doesn't deserve to be picked on. She's had more than ten lifetimes' worth of torment and abuse—with all of Dad's drinking and anger, and his gallivanting, not to mention a bunch of other crap. I don't know how Mommy could take it. I feel guilty for being so mean to her and I'm *really* sorry, but I don't want to apologize because I'm exhausted from cleaning up other people's messes. Another baby means there's more work to come.

Playing the Piano

I got a new job as a cashier in a grocery store. It's about two miles from my house and if I have to, I can walk there during daylight hours. Walking two miles in peace is far better than riding for ten minutes with Sis.

Dad sees my new job as an opportunity for me to "play the piano" again; he wants me to give Mommy discounts when she does her food shopping.

"I can't do that, Dad."

"What do ya think, they're not robbing us with their high prices? It's no big deal. If a piece of meat is $5.52, just ring up the cents," Dad explains. "That way if anyone sees you do it, you can just say it was a mistake."

So that's what I do. When Mommy comes grocery shopping I give her a few discounts, but I feel sick to my stomach every time.

It's all so baffling, because Dad keeps announcing that his ship is on its way to the Low house. He's come up with an innovative method of replacing broken windshields in cars, and it looks as though it's going to be a huge success.

Before Dad's ship gets a chance to sail into port, Mommy goes into labor and it's turning out to be long and difficult. I'm concerned because she hasn't been feeling well at all. She recently found out that her blood pressure is through the roof and she's double the size she used to be.

As I worry, the phone rings. It's Dad calling to report that child number nine has a dangling participle, or as an Armenian would bluntly say, a *jooje*. He's named after Dad's baby brother, Andrei—the one who fell into the well and drowned. Andrei has huge eyes that are sure to turn brown and just a bit of red fuzz on his head.

Now Dad reminds everyone that Andrei was the result of his secret. He knew all along this one would be a boy. He can't wait to teach his two sons everything he knows. In the meantime, he's celebrating with a few shots of scotch, cigars, and some bragging on the side.

Andrei is brought home and replaces Joseph in the bassinet by the stereo. Grandma Low comes to see Andrei and pins a tiny red ribbon onto his undershirt just like she did for her twenty-nine grandchildren who came before him. The red ribbon will keep him healthy, safe, and bring him good luck.

Andrei is christened in the Russian church, and afterward, the party begins. Dad gets drunk and Andrei receives gifts of cash and bonds, which are put away for his bright future.

In the midst of all that excitement, Jane's knees and elbows swell up two or three times their normal size, and that gets the attention of Mommy and Dad. She's in pain and no one can figure out how this happened, and seemingly overnight. Mommy and Dad take Jane to a specialist, who says she has rheumatoid arthritis. They go back and forth to the doctor with Jane looking for answers, but she continues to suffer.

I help Jane with her arm exercises, stretching them open a little at a time, but her joints are so swollen and stiff, any movement is excruciating for her. Unless she has to go to the doctor, she doesn't get to stay home from school. She never gets a break, not even from housework.

The rheumatologist suggests that Mommy and Dad go to a psychiatrist with Jane. They loathe shrinks, but against their better judgment, they follow doctor's orders. When they get home we hear all about it.

"The goddamned shrink had the nerve to tell us that Jane's arthritis is a result of all the stress she's under," Dad complains.

"What stress?" he asks the shrink.

"Besides going to school and working," the doctor says, "you've got her cleaning house, scrubbing floors, dishes, bathrooms, and taking care of babies. How much do you expect of her? If you can't take care of the kids yourselves, why do you keep having more?"

Dad is furious. He thinks the shrink has some nerve criticizing his parenting skills. For days he goes on about "the goddamned shrink." He beats the horse to death, buries it, then brings it back to life just so he can beat it to death again.

When Dad's shit-faced he doesn't curse the shrink, he blames Mommy. It's all her fault our family has so many goddamned problems. He accuses her of being a bad mother, and when he says Mommy must be cheating on him I don't know whether to laugh or cry. She doesn't argue because she can't win, and she can't escape, so she says nothing just to keep the peace.

When he finally stops complaining, he and Mommy make arrangements to ease up on Jane. Under doctor's orders, Jane is to take aspirin, hot relaxing baths, and continue her exercises. She is supposed to be given breaks for relaxation, but I don't think she gets more than ten minutes at a clip.

As always, I'm under orders to come directly home from school to clean the house and help with the children. I'm allowed out a couple nights each week if I'm not working, but that's about it. When my friends ask me to meet them after school I have to tell them no. Somewhere along the line I've earned a nickname: Cinderella. But I'm not the one in the beautiful white dress kissing Prince Charming. I have baby spit-up on my shoulders and sometimes you'll find me with my hands in the toilet shaking out a diaper full of cocky.

****

Mommy does her grocery shopping every week. I feel sick when I see her walk through the glass doors because I know what I have to do. My stomach aches, my knees go weak, and my entire body trembles as I ring up her order. I give her a few discounts, but I decide that this will be the very last time. I'm *not* "playing the piano" anymore.

I finally tell Mommy that I can't give her discounts. It makes me feel completely ill. She agrees. Somehow I knew she would, but because of Dad, I need to be more emphatic.

"I mean what I'm saying, Mommy. I can't keep doing this. You need to tell Dad."

"Don't worry," she says. "No one's going to make you do it anymore."

I'm relieved because Mommy's word has always been good.

I think I'm safe, but within days Sis walks into the grocery store. She's smiling at me, which she never does, not unless she wants something. The glint in her eyes tells me what she's up to. Her presence is also revealing because I've *never* known her to willingly step foot into a grocery store—not even when we were little. Throughout her shopping trip we lock eyes several times, and each time I mouth the word *no* to make sure she knows what I'm *not* going to do. When she places everything onto the conveyor belt I'm shocked to see that her selections are nothing like Mommy's. Even when I gave Mommy discounts, she wasn't greedy about it. She stuck to her basic shopping list. But Sis loaded up her cart with stuff Mommy would never buy. I panic just knowing her expectations of me. Despite my enormous fear, I squeeze every ounce of courage I can from the pit of my soul just so I can stick to my guns and put an end to the unspoken game I'm constantly being forced to play. I ring up everything. Sis is shocked when she sees the total—incensed because she's got to add some of her own money. As she pays the bill, her fury thickens the air, so I'm relieved when she takes her angry self out of the store and goes home.

It's late when my shift ends. At home, I enter the kitchen where Dad and Sis are sitting. Dad yells at me for putting Sis in the position of having to spend so much money and for humiliating her.

"I didn't put her in that position, Dad."

"Don't backtalk me," he says. Then he tells me what a goddamned troublemaker I am and he wants to know what's so goddamned hard about doing something for the good of the family. Amid Dad's bellowing I catch a glimpse of Sis grinning victoriously just before she runs off. That gleam in her eyes has become all too familiar to me. She knows that in Dad's hierarchy, she's royalty—always right, and I'm always wrong. That's just the way it is. The czar wants to know if I was *trying* to humiliate Sis, then he tells me who and what I am as his belt meets my flesh like a whip on a slave's back.

All men are created equal, but they're not treated equally.

I can't defend myself with words because Dad has no ears. I can't protect myself physically, so I just go fetal to shield my stomach, chest, and face while gathering up the shattered bits of my spirit to hide in a place so remote, it will take half my life to find them. Dad is madder than a psychopath, and his aim still sucks. He's hitting everything except my butt, and it burns as if I've been set on fire.

"You're a goddamned rebel just like my father!" Whack!

"You're lucky *I'm* giving you this lickin' and not Grandpa!" Snap! "He'd give it to you double, triple, ten times maybe!" Crack!

"What the hell are you, stupid?" Snap! Whack!

It goes on forever and when Dad's finally done, he commands me to quit my job and the time I don't have to spend working must be spent cleaning the house.

"Now get the hell up off the floor, goddamn it, and get the hell to bed!"

Dad's shirttails are hanging out, his hair is a mess, and he's full of sweat—he looks as though he hatched in the street. The sound of his breathing makes an irritated dragon seem like a kitty cat. Eyeing his belt, I peel myself up and run.

Early in the morning, Dad goes to the trouble of driving me to the grocery store so I can tell my boss I quit. She wants to know why, but how can I tell her the truth? I tell her I have another job. She hates to see me go, she says, and that's the last I see of her.

In a few days Dad and Sis will have forgotten all about my indiscretion. They'll never mention it again because they're so forgiving, because they don't believe in bringing up the past. I shouldn't mention it either, because the past is dead and gone. Here's a shovel—bury it.

I do.

Soon I forget.

And I live—even though I really don't want to.

The Letter

You never know what Dad's going to do when he comes home shit-faced in the middle of the afternoon. Sometimes he chases my younger siblings, terrorizing them as they scatter like cockroaches. If I annoy Dad, he'll chase me instead, and if we run fast enough, there's time to hide little children under beds, in closets, or in Lincoln's casket.

We don't realize that we are all wearing Dad's secondhand shoes—the same ones he wore as a kid, the ones his father wore in Russia, shoes that never fit, shoes they both hated. Yet here they are, passed onto us as if they were precious family heirlooms.

While in hiding, Dad rummages through the house, searching for us, grunting like wild boar hunting for mushrooms. Sooner or later he runs out of steam and falls asleep. When we hear him snore, we can emerge.

Whenever Dad comes home shit-faced at three in the morning, he pulls out the cast-iron pan and throws in incompatible leftovers, resulting in a stew that resembles puke. I hear him moving about and remain on full alert just in case he decides to do anything other than cook.

In the morning, the remaining concoction in the pan smells worse than the odor wafting out of his bedroom. I gag while scraping his vestiges into the garbage and cleaning up his spills. If it's not me erasing Dad's mess, it might be Jane because Mommy deals with diapers and bottles each morning. I work fast because if Dad awakens to a shithouse, he'll fume.

****

Dad has dreams of going to faraway lands, places of adventure where he can make a million dollars or go on safari: South America, Australia, Africa.

It's late and the kids are asleep when Dad bursts through the door with fury in his eyes and scotch on his breath. He announces he's going to Africa to do some big-game hunting and he'll try to make it big while he's there.

"If I make it big, I'll be back," he slurs.

"What if you don't?" Mommy asks.

"Either way, I'll be back."

Now Dad wants *all* the money in the house. Mommy runs to the bedroom to hide her purse, but he goes after her. I'm on his tail. I'm always on his tail when he's drunk because if he lays a hand on her, I'll jump between them. *I don't want to, but if I have to grab something and crack him on the head, I just might.* Luckily, he's just hollering and searching through dresser drawers. He grabs every dollar, then he finds Mommy's purse and seizes her checkbook and all her cash.

Mommy sits on the bed with her head in her hands. I sit beside her. We hear Dad open and slam the front door as he leaves for Africa.

"Maybe he'll get eaten by a hippopotamus," I joke.

It's quiet for a minute, then Mommy says, "Maybe he'll be mauled by a ferocious lion."

"Maybe an alligator will eat him."

"Maybe he'll pick a fight with a hairy ape and the ape will kick the living shit out of him."

"Maybe a swarm of giant mosquitoes will infect him with malaria," I tease.

"Maybe he'll be charged by a rhinoceros," Mommy says.

"A rhinoceros?"

"Yes," Mommy declares, "a giant, nasty rhinoceros!"

"That's Imposserous!" I exclaim.

Mommy erupts like a volcano. In the depths of our despair, we lie on her bed, laughing until every ounce of energy evaporates into stillness and silence. I look up at the ceiling, then I turn toward

Mommy. Except for the tears seeping from the outer corners of her eyes into her hair, she is still. I don't want her to be sad. I want to tell her I love her, but it feels awkward because no one ever says that except for Yaya and drunks. I go into the bathroom, pull some toilet paper into a bunch and bring it to her. She dries her tears and lights a cigarette. The more Dad drinks, the more Mommy smokes.

"I'm going to bed, Mommy. I love you," I say, then I kiss her on the cheek.

Her mixed expression of surprise and appreciation grips my heart, and brands itself into my memory.

In the morning I'm at the kitchen sink. Suddenly I hear snoring. I peer out the window only to see an enormous set of feet. As I move closer to the window I see Dad sleeping on a lawn chair. He's come back from Africa the same way he returned from South America, Mexico and wherever the hell else he's been.

Mommy comes into the kitchen and now we're both peering through the window, laughing silently, yet fervently. Dad's taken off his shoes and his huge toes are wiggling around inside his socks. His mouth is wide open and his arms are hanging off the sides of the chair. A little boy going by nudges his mother and points at the sleeping dragon as his scotch-fired snores echo through the valley we live in. We laugh even though it isn't funny. Then comes the silence. I glare at Mommy because I'm about to ask a question that's long overdue.

"Why don't you leave him, Mommy?"

As she peers directly into my eyes, I see years of anguish embedded in her black pearls, and I remember her unsuccessful attempt at leaving him. Other visions sprint across my brain, but the one with Mommy at the bottom of the stairs, all bloody—that's an indelible image, one that I cannot hide from my mind's eye.

"Where am I going to go?" she says. "Who's going to take me in with nine kids? How am I going to care for all my children and support them, too?"

I know she's never going to leave us, nor will she send us away like Yaya did to her. She's right. She has nowhere to go.

****

228

Dad turned his bedroom into a private television room. Not everyone is welcome in there so the family is split in half much of the time. The two boys are welcome in there sometimes, but if Joanne, Hanna or Louise meander in, Dad yells, "Get the hell outta here, goddamn it!"

Unless he's giving someone a lickin', Dad's time at home is down time. Sadly, even if Mommy *had* time to spare, she'd be too tired to enjoy it. When bedtime rolls around, Mommy enlists the help of Jane or Anya to get the boys settled and off to sleep. The girls are sent off to dreamland by the czar, whose veins pop as he bellows, "Get the hell to bed, goddamn it, and don't make a goddamned peep!"

At least we older kids got to give Mommy and Dad a kissie before we went to bed. It sickens me to see my little sisters being sent to bed this way. I'm working again, but when I'm home at night, I take them to bed and show them how to say their prayers the way Mommy showed me when I was little. I look them in the eye and tell them I love them. I don't want them thinking they're unloved—it's pathetic to have to go through life feeling that way. I tuck them in, tell them stories, and I create songs and poems *just* for them. I kiss them on the forehead, turn out the lights and hope that whatever little I do will be enough.

Dad saves most of his positive energy for people outside our home and for company. If I ask him for a ride to Doreen's house or to a dance, he tells me to find my own way. Yet when the phone rings and it's one of his friends, he grabs his keys and he's gone for the rest of the night. He's in tune with himself and with people outside our home who love him for his charm and generosity, but he fails to see the longing in the eyes of his own children.

The neglect of my younger siblings weighs heavy on my heart. No one in our family ever speaks of our complicated pecking order, but even the youngest Low kids know who among us are the peasants. We're like the little piggies: "One has roast beef and the other has none."

Then there's the czar's big leather belt and his drunkenness. It breeds a fear that thrives within our home. On the outside, our oyster-yellow house looks happy and inviting with the front porch, and the pool, surrounded by lush trees and grass. Deep inside, however, the *pearls* of common sense, justice, empathy, emotional support, and the expression of love are often missing.

Dad's eyes are on his personal goals. More money than ever before is rolling in, but it's not enough. It's never enough. In the meantime, he's got plenty of cash to drink away, and although we peasant Low kids live by a code of silence, Jane and I do the unthinkable. We secretly talk about what's going on with Dad. Ironically, our fears and hopelessness gift us with courage and faith, enough to rise up and take the risk of getting a lickin' by constructing a letter to Dad. We tell him that we believe he's an alcoholic, that for the sake of our younger siblings he needs to stop drinking. We slip the letter into an envelope and drop it on his bed pillow.

In the morning Dad orders me to take a seat in the kitchen with him. He knows the letter is in my handwriting, so I'm waiting for him to start swinging at me, but he doesn't.

"I'm not an alcoholic," Dad calmly states. "I'm just a drunk."

"What's the difference?"

"An alcoholic has to have a drink. A drunk doesn't have to have one. A drunk can stop drinking anytime he wants to stop."

Now I summon all the courage inside me. "So why don't you stop?"

"I'll stop when I want to stop, not when *you* tell me to stop."

"What about the kids, Dad?"

"What about them?"

"Drunk or sober, they're afraid of you. They feel neglected. You're always hollering at them and…"

"You don't know what the hell you're talking about. It's your mother's job to take care of the kids. If they feel neglected, it's *her* fault. You have no clue what life is all about! You don't know what it's like to work like a dog and have so many people to take care of. You don't know how good you've got it. If I had what you have when I was a kid, I'd thank my goddamned lucky stars," he roars. "My father was a mean son-of-a-bitch. If I just looked at Pop the wrong way, he'd beat the shit out of me. After you walk a mile in my shoes, then maybe you'll have a right to say something. You don't know shit from shine-ola! Until you're grown, you have to do things my way. And if you don't like the way I do things, you can pack your goddamned bags and leave."

I don't say word. I wonder if I was wrong for writing the letter.

After a few weeks I realize Dad hasn't come home drunk and I'm glad that Jane and I wrote the letter. But drunk or sober, Dad's a time bomb—the tiniest thing can easily set him off, and when someone tells Dad that I'm a drug addict, he detonates.

I burst into laughter, because initially, I think it's a joke.

"What the hell's so goddamned funny?" Dad asks.

"It's not true."

"Don't tell me, goddamn it."

"I'm not a drug addict. Who told you that?"

"Never mind who told me. It's none of your goddamned business," he says.

He unbuckles his belt and slides it off like a pro.

"What are you, stupid?" Whack! "I'm sick of your bullshit." Crack!

When he's done beating me and telling me who and what I am, I unpeel myself from the kitchen floor.

"It's not true!" I shout as I run away.

"It better not be true, goddamn son-of-a-bitch," he screams as I escape. "The next time I hear anything like that you'll get it double or triple and I won't have any mercy on you."

Later I lock eyes with Mommy.

"I don't take drugs."

"You better not."

"Who told you I do?"

"Don't worry about who told me."

"I am worried, Ma, because it's not true. I just got another beating for something I didn't do. How does that make you feel?"

Mommy puts her head down and doesn't say a word. Now I feel awful for taking this out on her. *She's not the one who beat me. Maybe I should just shut my big mouth.*

In order to move on, I grab a shovel and bury it—deep inside my shit-file.

****

There's nothing better than going down to the Jersey shore. Grandma, Grandpa and some of Dad's siblings rented cottages in Wildwood along with Mommy and Dad. Sis doesn't want to go, but the rest of us have already packed our bags. Jane brings her best friend along and we all get a much-needed break from our household chores.

To melt away the jumble of junk in my head, I lie on the beach listening to the waves. My eyes wander over to where Dad is surf fishing. He's sober and content, which also helps to unravel my insides.

When he calls it a day, we Lows get dressed for dinner. He takes us to a smorgasbord where kids under twelve are half price, and under five, they're free, which means a couple of my siblings grow younger as we enter the restaurant. Dad can't get away with saying Jane, her friend or I are under twelve because the size of our *dzidzees* would expose him as a liar. I'm embarrassed but the feeling diminishes when we reach our table. We overfill our plates because our eyes are bigger than our bellies. The food can't compare to Mommy's but it's fun because we're all together and Dad's in a great mood.

It's been a long day and I'm tired from strolling the boardwalk and body surfing in the waves. Without a drunk to worry about, I fall asleep quickly.

Hours later I awaken to a commotion. When my ears tune in I realize Dad is in a drunken rage. I jump out of bed and shoot toward the noise. Grandma and Grandpa along with some of the other aunts and uncles are pulling Dad away from Mommy. I don't have to yell "stop." I missed all the action. All I see is Mommy crying in one corner of the yard while Dad's yelling in another corner. Jane and her friend are awakened by the noise. They don't see anything, but hearing it is just as bad. It's horrible knowing your father hits your mother, even if it is only when he's drunk. Just knowing it, you can almost feel every slap and punch, every push, every tug. Jane's embarrassed because her friend hears the commotion, too. That's not the kind of thing you want anyone else knowing.

"It's all rrright, Joey," Grandma says before bringing Mommy into the kitchen.

"Don't worrry, Lily. He'll be all rrright in da morrringk. I love yuns like a daughterrr, Lily. It's all rrright."

When morning comes, everything is all right because no one says a word about the night before. The past is dead and buried.

Mommy makes coffee, toast and eggs, and we Lows get to do the *motzi!*

I Wish I Was Born with a Jooje

Being a senior scares me. I don't know who or what I am, where I belong in the world, or what life has in store for me when the school year ends. All the dreams I once had are in a pipe somewhere. My passion for singing coupled with my frog voice begs me to realize that God was drinking scotch the day I was born. I'll never have dance lessons or piano lessons because "who the hell is going to pay for that?" College isn't a possibility. All I'm good for is cleaning, cooking and taking care of kids so I'll do what I have to do to get by. I'll walk down the aisle twice—once for my diploma and once to get married. Dad'll be proud of me for that.

I've got my driver's license and I'm able to buy a car. With that, another chore is added to my list: drive Jane to work. I do, and I don't yell at her just because she has to be at work so early in the morning. I'm glad Jane was born.

Driving equals freedom. The one thing I look forward to is going out to dance on Friday nights. My friends and I have to go to Staten Island for that. Dad says I'm not allowed over there, but I go anyway. After spending so many hours working, taking care of kids and cleaning, I think I deserve to go out dancing. It's my only diversion, but when Dad finds out about my trips to Staten Island, he puts a stop to my Friday nights out.

No matter what else was going on, dancing cleared my mind and filled me with joy, at least for a while.

In no time at all another rumor reaches my doorstep. I don't know how it got here, but Mommy and Dad are blasting me for whoring around. I want to know who's telling them this stuff but they won't say. Dad smacks me on the side of the head and tells me who and what I am and now, in addition to being stupid and all that other stuff, he says I'm a tramp, and if I bring home any surprises, he'll shoot first and ask questions later. In the midst of his rage he tells me to stop going around with my boobs hanging out.

"When? Where? Who says they saw my boobs?"

"Your beige shirt is shameful," Mommy says. "I don't want you wearing that anymore."

"Oh, the knitted one?"

"Yes," she points out, "that one."

"So, I'm a tramp because of that shirt?"

"If you go around looking like a goddamned tramp, you might as well be one," Dad insists. "What's the goddamned difference?"

Now I can't hold back. I lock eyes with Dad.

"Would you like it better if I was a hippie? If I went braless and wore battery-operated clothes?"

"You have a goddamned big mouth," Dad says.

I attempt to defend myself, but Dad only hears the words in *his* head. When I keep my mouth shut he tells me I have a big mouth, so I might as well be guilty of his accusations.

"Go ahead, hit me," I say as he reaches for his belt.

And he does—again and again. Then he makes me throw away my V-neck shirt.

As I drop it into the garbage, I feel dirty.

My senior year in high school is turning out to be the worst year of my life. Dad won't let up on me. A day doesn't go by without him reminding me who and what I am, and not even a month can pass by without him whacking me with his huge hand or beating me with his belt. The lickin's I get are over and done within minutes, but they add glue to Dad's words, and often, my own brain reminds me of how stupid and useless I am.

****

I've washed the dinner dishes every night this week. Jane's been busy and her arthritis is acting up, but there are other people with two hands in this house besides Jane and me. As I'm clearing the dinner table Dad tells me to wash the dishes. He says I shouldn't have to be told.

"Why do I have to do them again?"

"Just do what the hell I tell you to do, goddamn it!"

In my next life I'm coming back with an Armenian trifecta—a jooje, *and two gigantic hairy balls. Maybe then I won't have to put up with so much crap.*

I don't realize my thoughts are causing me to make some funny expressions. Dad sees me, even though my back is toward him. *Stupid me! It's dark outside and he sees my reflection in the window.*

The dish I'm washing falls out of my hand as the belt whips across my back. Dad cracks it and whips me as though I'm a horse pulling his wagon. I run, but he's on my tail. He snaps the belt at me all through the kitchen and the hallway. I hit the floor like a sack of potatoes and before I get the chance to go fetal, he kicks me in the ribs with his size ten shoe.

"Now get the hell up and finish washing the goddamned dishes. And I don't want to see anymore of your goddamned ugly faces. I'm *sick* of the looks on your face," he spits.

The soreness in my ribs is worse than my back and it isn't going away, but I've got to finish the dishes. I don't feel like moving as swiftly as I usually do. I'm suffocating. I don't really care if I live or die. When Jane comes home and sees the mess I have my hands in, she grabs a dishtowel and digs in. Without any spoken words she resuscitates my spirit.

The Tramp and the Millionaire

Dad's "on-the-side" business is doing well. He pulls a wad of money out of his pocket and gives some to Mommy, but he keeps most of it for himself.

"Here," he says, "it's about time you bought some fancy china."

"What the hell do I need fancy dishes for?" she asks.

"They're impressive."

"Who are we going to impress, the King of England?"

"Maybe I want to impress my family," Dad says.

"Will new dishes make them like us more?" Mommy wants to know.

"What's so wrong about wanting to impress my family?"

"How in the world are you going to impress people who came from the same shithouse as you? If you want nice things, you should want them for yourself," Mommy says. "Flashing your success in front of people who have less than you just makes them feel bad."

"Okay, if you don't want nice dishes, then I'll buy myself a gold toilet."

"What the hell are you going to do with a gold toilet?"

"I'm going to piss and shit in it, okay!"

"That's what I thought," Mommy says.

"What the hell do you mean by that?"

"You're going to piss and shit on your own money," Mommy says when she finally stops laughing. "Isn't that nice!"

"If I want to piss and shit on my money, I'll piss and shit on it. Why the hell should you care? I'm the one who earned it."

Dad puts his big wad back in his pocket. He'll need it for buying rounds of drinks in the bars. Mommy, on the other hand, hides her share like a squirrel hides his nuts.

****

Because of my car insurance payments, I can hardly save a penny now. The only thing I splurge on is a tie-dyed shirt. That's about as hippie as I'll get, but at least I don't look like an eyesore among my hip friends. I'm trying to fit in somewhere and it's not easy.

When I agree to go out with a couple of classmates, I find myself in a Volkswagen Bug with a bag of marijuana. I never smoked pot before. This is the first time I actually get to see what it looks like. They light a joint and pass it to me, so I put it up to my lips and take a puff. I hold the horrid thick smoke in my mouth for two seconds, then let it out quickly. It's the most disgusting thing I ever tasted. As they pass it around I tell them I had enough.

When the joint burns down, they put it on a roach clip and smoke it till there's nothing left. Now they're acting weird, and I don't like it.

"This is groovy, man," they brag.

The word *groovy* smacks my ears like a wet towel on flesh. One of them tears open a bag of potato chips that goes flying all over the car. They grab the chips and shove them down their throats like scavengers. It's all so surreal I wonder if I'm in a dream. I finally tell them I have to go—my dad wants me home early.

"Bummer, man," one of the guys says.

I hate the word *bummer,* but not as much as I hate the word *groovy.*

On the way home they want to play Chinese fire drill. I've never played that game and I don't know how it goes until we stop at a red light and the car doors fly open. They hop out of the car and scamper around the VW like a bunch of Indians doing a rain dance. The big hairy guy I just met yells into the car at me.

"Hey man, don't ya wanna play?"

I'm not a man! I can't help but remember something I found in a *Highlights* magazine. I *think* it was "What's Wrong with This Picture?" Me! I don't belong here! I don't know where I belong, but I know it's not here.

The VW pulls up in front of my house and I'm relieved. I escape that scenario unscathed and it frightens me enough to never go out with them again.

****

Sis and I are now sharing a bedroom downstairs. We don't cross paths all that often anymore because our routines are so different, but several nights a week we find ourselves going to bed at the same time. These are the nights she whispers to me when the lights are turned out.

"You're ugly. No one likes you. You're stupid."

I can't see her, but I can *hear* the smile in her voice. I can even *hear* the gleam in her eyes. More than anything else, I want us to be friends. I tell her to stop, but that only eggs her on more.

"You're too sensitive," she mutters. "There must be something wrong with you if you can't even take a joke."

I try ignoring her, but she's relentless. I feel tortured so tonight I'm using a new approach. As she whispers in her dark corner, I quietly slither out of bed, I take one big step to reach hers, and then I jump on her.

She fights back with a vengeance. We're slapping each other and pulling each other's hair. Our arms are flailing, our *dzidzees* are bouncing around, kind of getting in the way, but I'm not giving up. I grab her hair and pull and I do it just the way she always did it to me.

"You're hurting me!" she cries.

"Tough tits!" I scream because it's about time she tasted her own medicine.

In response, she whacks me so hard, I go flying off her bed.

"I wish you were never born!" she spits. "I hate you!"

Before I can get up to go back at her, she darts out of the room and up the stairs.

"Daddy, Daddy!" she cries.

239

Dad comes down the stairs to the landing where Sis is crying.

"Look what Cathy did to me, Daddy. She never leaves me alone. She beat me up for no reason!"

Sis doesn't tell him how she serenades me every night. She completely excludes the first half of the story!

As I attempt to explain the rest of the story, Dad pulls off his belt and whips me. *It wouldn't matter if he heard my side. He wouldn't believe me.*

I lie still, taking as much cover as I can up against a step, fetal again. I can't escape so I allow the grizzly bear to whip me and curse me until he's done. *I wish I was never born. I want to die, but I have so many reasons not to—my younger siblings, and Mommy. They need me.*

****

Every Sunday Mommy is sure to be in the kitchen preparing a special meal. There's a pork roast in the oven and potatoes that will soon be mashed, spooned onto our plates and pressed in the center to hold the most delicious gravy in the world. Dad is always home and sober on Sundays, and his mood is usually mellow. Oh, he'll give you a lickin' if he has to, but for the most part, Sundays have magical powers that other days of the week often lack.

As Mommy is cooking, the kids are scampering through the house. Dad's in his bedroom watching television, and as long as the kids don't scoot in and out of his room, he'll stay calm. When dinner's ready, he'll be the first one at the table and we'll all be together to enjoy Mommy's wonderful meal.

Her roast makes my mouth water, but I'm saving my appetite, and passing time with the newspaper. I can't say I'm an avid reader. I've never read a book from cover to cover and I don't plan to. Aside from our dictionary, the Bible, and our partial volume of the encyclopedia, I don't own a book. Thanks to Jiminy Cricket I can spell encyclopedia and thanks to overhearing my parents' arguments, I'm familiar with words like audacity, instigator, egotistical, conniver, inebriated, osmosis and asshole. My vocabulary is pretty extensive, so reading is just a big waste of my time. I'm so busy anyway, and when I'm not, my head just needs a break so I mostly look at the pictures. The only thing I actually read is the horoscope. Leo's prediction says I'm coming into a bundle of money and the love of my life is going to sweep me off my feet. Once it said that I'm going to travel the seven seas, but the closest I came to the seven seas is when I transported a bottle of salad dressing from the table to the refrigerator.

In the Sunday paper, I go straight to the funny pages because they don't require much thought. The funnies are relaxing, except for when your little sisters and brothers hop around and step on the paper. My two-year-old brother, Joseph, lies down next to me. He crosses his legs and places his chin in his left hand, mimicking me. Louise comes along with her curly hair and fat little cheeks and plops herself on my back. The next thing I know, Hanna is sitting on my feet. They're all asking me to sing a song because they're still tone deaf. While I'm crooning "Heart of My Heart," along comes Andrei who plops his butt on the newspaper, and the little surprise in his diaper releases an odor strong enough to land me in a body bag. But my brothers and sisters aren't gagging. They're laughing and singing.

"Cocky maker see, cocky maker do, cocky maker, cocky maker, pooh, pooh, pooh!"

I give in to the hilarity because the little cocky maker is happily clapping to the cocky song. Joanne, the leader of the pack, jumps me from behind. It's a creative assault, and Andrei's cocky diaper was their seed of inspiration. Now all five of them are tickling me and laughing hysterically because they think they've got me trapped. I could knock all of them over in a second, but I let them have their fun. I pretend I can't escape from Andrei's new cologne, and the more disgust I express, the more they laugh until we hear the lion roar.

"Goddamn it! What the hell is going on out there? Shut the hell up already, goddamn it!"

"Okay, kids," I say, "the cocky factory is closed."

I grab a clean diaper for Andrei and tiptoe down the stairs with the other kids behind me, stifling their giggles until we're beyond the scope of the lion's ears. Then we explode.

I'm seventeen. This is my life. What else can I do besides laugh?

We finally sit down to dinner, but the little ones have unfinished giggles.

"What the hell's so goddamned funny? Stop *futzing* around at the goddamned table! Jeeeeeeeeesus Christ!"

Silence follows.

I waited all afternoon for this meal and now I can't even eat. I've got awful cramps so I leave the table. My only relief is when I bring my knees up to my chest, but the pain is persistent. I'm sure it'll pass, but Dad says he's taking me to the emergency room. I've never been to a doctor or to a hospital for an illness, so I'm shocked and touched that Dad is concerned enough about my health to get me checked out.

In the emergency room I lie on a bed surrounded by a curtain. A nurse appears with a paper gown and tells me to undress from the waist down. As I'm changing, I hear Dad ask the doctor to check me for something.

The doctor appears and informs me he's going to do a gynecological exam. I never had one of those, so when he tells me to lift my knees and spread my legs, I hesitate. Now he's practically doing it for me. I'm not sure I need him to examine me now because the pain is subsiding, yet he insists. The bright overhead lights are shining on a place that's never seen the light of day, and this doctor has a bird's eye view of the pimple on my butt. He slips on a rubber glove and without warning, he stuffs his finger in a place that's never been touched. When the exam is finally over, he tells me that I have a tilted uterus, that it'll straighten itself out over time.

"You're fine. Get dressed," he says, and he disappears on the other side of the curtain where Dad is waiting for him.

"Don't worry, Mr. Low," the doctor says. "Your daughter is still a virgin."

I was brought into the emergency room because of Dad's curiosity, not my cramps.

During the ride home Dad sings the song about the person who's never going to be an angel. He has never apologized to me for anything, but I wish that he'd at least show some remorse for calling me a tramp. I decide to keep that to myself because he only sings his little ditty when he's happy. If I say something, it will ignite his anger, and I don't want to do that. His fury always steals away every bit of joy and happiness.

✳✳✳✳✳✳✳✳✳✳✳✳✳

Mommy is tired, worn out, and sometimes she gets nauseated for no reason at all. She thinks her high blood pressure is causing her headaches, and although she takes her medication, her pressure is still too high. I know she's worried about herself because every once in a while she leads me to her secret hiding place. She's been saving all the extra money Dad's been giving her and she wants *me* to know where it is just in case something happens to her. When she says "just in case" I know it means *if she dies.* She tells me that I'm to use the money to care for my little sisters and brothers.

"Promise me you'll take care of them," she says emphatically.

The Baron's voice skips across my brain, *"Always keep your promise."*

I love my siblings with all I have to love. To reassure Mommy I look her in the eye so she can see straight through to my heart, and I tell her, "I promise."

Mommy just isn't what she used to be. My little sisters and brothers don't have the same mother I had. I can't help but feel their sadness and it concerns me. Dad doesn't seem to notice. He's still busy becoming a millionaire.

My First Hundred Dollar Bill

Today the sky is as clear as Grandma's good eye. I'm sitting here on the beach watching the waves come roaring at me, then recede as though they didn't mean it. My feet are buried in the warm sand and I wish I had changed into shorts before I headed down here. But when you make the decision to run away, you don't stop to think of appropriate attire. Besides, I wasn't even sure if I was really going to run away. My head is filled with noise and my soul is having a fit, but I don't have the words to express my deepest feelings.

My gut knows that Dad needs to pay attention to what's going on with his kids. *Maybe my running away will get his attention.*

When I listen to the waves and I feel the sun on my face and the warm sand between my toes, the noise in my brain evaporates, and I'm at peace. Suddenly I get an old familiar feeling, the same one I'd get when I climbed into my childhood tree, God's umbrella, and melted into its branches. I rest my head on my knees and merge with the rhythm of the waves. I don't know it, but hours pass and the sun is going down.

"Are you okay?" a woman asks.

I look up to see her standing here with her husband and children. They're staring at me in wonderment.

"What's wrong?" the woman asks.

"I ran away."

"Then you need to go home."

"I'm not going home."

"Then come home with us."

"I can't do that." *I'm supposed to stay away from strangers. But they seem so nice.*

"If you don't come home with us, we're calling the police."

"Please don't."

"Okay then, why don't you come and have dinner with us. If you want to leave after dinner, you can," she says.

I realize I'm more frightened of sleeping on the beach than I am of going to a stranger's house, so I follow them home. As Mrs. G. prepares dinner, I offer my help, but she chases me out of her kitchen.

Her husband and children ask me to tell them all about myself. I have to stop and think because I'm not sure who or what *I, me,* or, *my* is. All I do is scrub bathrooms, vacuum, wash dishes, play with little children, work and go to school.

At dinner I'm treated like an honored guest and it feels awkward to receive such attention. Afterward Mrs. G. tells me I can sleep on her couch. She won't call the police. She'll give me a day or so to think about things. As I thank her, tears escape from my eyes. I can't understand why she and her family would go out of their way to be so kind to me.

I sleep on their couch Friday and Saturday nights, but deep down I want to go home. I *never* wanted to run away in the first place. I just want Dad to wake up! I don't want my siblings to feel the way I do—like a nothing!

I call a friend who tells me that the police are looking for me, and my parents are worried, so I decide to go home.

As I park my car in front of our cheery yellow house, my little sisters come running toward me. When I kneel down to hug them I see pain in their eyes. They wondered where I'd gone, and if I was ever coming back. They missed me. I may have been trying to open Dad's eyes, but what I really did was hurt my siblings. I *hate* myself for doing that to them. I go into the house and Dad is downstairs parked in a chair, staring into space the way I stared into the ocean. He doesn't see me walk past him. As I wait in my bedroom I hear my little sisters shouting.

"Cathy's home! Yay!"

Mommy and Dad come into my room. They both want to know what the hell is the matter with me.

"Jeeeeeeeeesus Christ!" Dad says. "All you ever do is cause trouble. Can't you do anything right? You have no clue how the world works. You don't know shit from shine-ola."

He's probably right because I don't even know what the hell shine-ola is.

"Dad, I..."

"Shut the hell up and listen to me, goddamn it. That's your problem. You never listen. You're nothing but a goddamned rebel!"

Now I get to choose my own punishment. The first choice Dad offers is reform school. The alternative is to quit my job, come straight home after school, clean the house and help with the kids. Either way, the punishment stays in effect until I graduate.

I laugh to myself when I hear the second choice. That's the one I pick.

I quit my job, clean house, and help with the kids. When the car insurance bill comes in I'm asked to pay my share, but I don't have any money because Dad made me quit my job! So Mommy keeps a running tab, and when I get a job after graduation, I'll have to pay them back.

The month passes by quickly and it's graduation day for the class of 1971. I smile when I receive my diploma because I'm supposed to look as though I'm proud. I don't know how you're supposed to feel when you graduate, but I'm frightened. I don't have a boyfriend, I don't have a job, and when I try to imagine what *my* tomorrow is, I can't see a thing.

After all the caps are tossed in the air, I manage to find Mommy and Dad in the crowd. This is the very first time in my life that Dad has set foot onto school property on my behalf. Mommy and Dad kiss me on the cheek, congratulate me and hand me an envelope. Then they leave. I open up the card to find a hundred-dollar bill and a handwritten note. They're proud and prouder still of my accomplishments. This is the first time in my life I have a hundred-dollar bill, and the first time I have ever received a handwritten note from my parents. I choke up. The note warms my heart.

There's nothing going on at home tonight, and Doreen and my other friends have plans with their boyfriends and families, so I hook up with a couple of classmates who are in the same boat as me. They suggest buying some booze and finding a place to drink it.

At the liquor store I grab a bottle of Boones Farm apple wine, and with much trepidation, I approach the cashier who doesn't even bother to ask me for ID.

We drive over to the clay pits, park, crack open our spirits, toast our future, and take a swig. My wine tastes like rotten apples. I don't like it, but I swallow it anyway.

"Here's to changing the world!" Mary says.

"Here's to owning my own company someday!" Ed says.

"Here's to fighting for women's rights," Mary shouts.

"Here's to sending Nixon to Vietnam with a BB gun and putting him on the front lines!"

"Here, here!" they reply.

In between inspirations they chug and I sip. Now that I've forced down half the bottle, I roll down the car window and pour out the rest. I drive home feeling sick to my stomach and cursing myself for not buying a bottle of soda instead. *What the hell was I thinking?*

I sneak into the house and hop into bed, but it starts to spin and I end up hugging the toilet. I climb back into bed and it still feels as though it's spinning. I roll onto the floor, but that spins, too. *I'm never going to drink again.*

Early in the morning I lie in bed wondering what to do next. A tiny voice whispers, *"Move away, go to California, enroll in a school of arts and take up acting classes, dance, piano, anything creative."*

A more predominant voice says, *"You're broke and no one's going to pay your way in the world. You're stupid and ugly. What about your little sisters and brothers? If you go away, who's going to be there for them? What about your promise to Mommy? You've got to stay close to home. If you're lucky, you'll find a man who'll take care of you and you'll set up house close by. That way you can keep your promise to Mommy and make Dad proud all at once."*

The aroma of coffee finds its way downstairs to my hangover, and so does Mommy's voice.

"Cathy, get up and give me a hand!"

I answer the familiar morning chant by running up to the kitchen. I pour myself some coffee and as I take a sip Mommy tells me to get the house cleaned up. Dad tells me to find a job because I've got to start paying room and board—twenty dollars a week, the same as Sis.

It sounds the same, but my deal doesn't include a car.

"One more thing," Mr. Parity chimes with his finger wagging at me. "Don't forget about the money you owe for your car insurance. Now that you're grown up, you've got to pay your own way in this world."

I open up my graduation card, take out the hundred-dollar bill and I hand it back to my parents for my share of the car insurance.

The Dye is Cast

Dad's innovative idea for removing broken automobile windshields has been catching on. He says it's already replacing the older method, which is far more laborious. He put together a kit containing a three-foot-long piece of heavy piano wire and special epoxy glue—strong enough to secure a new windshield. He got the idea years ago while watching men in a body shop hack away at a broken windshield. The glass was then removed by hand. Dad's idea cuts out most of the time and danger. You simply poke a hole into the rubber, stick in the piano wire, wrap both ends around a block of wood. With one man inside the car and another on the outside, they slide the wire through the rubber, cutting out the old windshield in no time.

Dad commissioned a local factory to produce his kits, which he's been selling to small retailers. He also presented his idea to the car-manufacturing giants as an easier, less expensive method of replacing windshields. Suddenly orders come flying in. General Motors wants thousands of these kits and they want them yesterday. To increase his profits, Dad decides that Mommy and we Low kids should do the labor. He brings home giant spools of piano wire, which Mommy and I have to cut into perfect three-foot lengths. Dad won't pay Mommy and me for cutting the wires—we have to do that for the good of the family. Besides, that's just prep work. But he'll pay us a penny for every wire we roll into a one-inch coil, each of which must be artfully slipped into a tiny manila envelope. He expects every capable family member to pitch in, but when Sis complains, she's excused from the chore. In between all the housework, Mommy, my younger siblings and I wrap piano wires into coils. It leaves our fingers dry and bloody, so we're forced to bind our fingers with masking tape to protect them in order to continue working. Under the best conditions, we older ones can wrap and pack about eighty coils an hour. At a penny apiece, eighty cents an hour is half of the federal minimum wage in 1971.

"All for one and one for all, that's the way it should be," Dad chants. "Families should stick together, do for each other, and share whatever they have with one another. Family is more important than anything else in the world!"

Between Mommy, my younger sisters, and me, we're putting out thousands of coils a week, but we can't always meet Dad's quota so he hires extended family members to produce them. He pays them in cash—double what he pays us, but we're doing our part for the good of the family. Producing coils becomes a must-do chore like the laundry because Dad's idea spreads like measles in a Third World country. Dad doesn't do any of the labor—he's the "brain of the operation."

"Okay Bugsy," I want to say, but I just keep that comment to myself.

Besides this company and his job at the chemical plant, Dad has another scheme brewing. It's picked up steam and it's bringing in a bundle of money, so he needs all the help he can get. An old buddy of Dad's runs deliveries for him, which helps to free up some of his time.

Evidently the more time and money Dad has, the more he drinks. I arrive home from my new job only to find the house unusually empty.

"Hello, hello, anybody home?"

No one answers. I walk over to the dining room window and as I peer outside, I see Dad floating belly-down in the pool. I scream like a madwoman. He doesn't flinch. I sprint out to the pool and grab for Dad's lifeless body.

"Daddy! Daddy!"

As I tug on the dead man I hate myself, because I silently wished he'd die every time he came home drunk and caused a ruckus. *Don't die, Daddy! Please don't die!*

Suddenly Dad lifts his head out of the water and chuckles.

"I thought you were dead!"

"I wush jush sheeing how long I could hold my breath," he laughs. "I yoosht to hold it for five minutes. I shtill got it, don't I?"

I punch him in the arm so hard, my knuckles crack.

"I thought you were dead!"

He laughs heartily as I run away crying. I sulk in the corner of my bedroom far too long. I need to shake it off, but I just can't. Suddenly I remember something an old Armenian man taught me a long time ago.

"The dye has been cast," he had said, as if it was the most important statement in the world. "Caesar spoke these words as he led his army into northern Italy!"

"What does that mean?" I had asked.

"You can't undo what's done," he testified. "You must accept what is and march on."

That's what I need to do. Dad's never going to stop drinking. I have to accept that and pick up the pieces as best I can. To pull myself out of this state of false mourning I write myself a note as if it's Dad's last letter to me, and then I hide it. I can't let anyone see this or any of my other poems because they'll make fun of me for being too sensitive and I'll feel even more ashamed of myself than I do now.

I splash cold water on my face and go up into the kitchen to help with dinner. By this time Dad's in bed snoring. The sound of safety causes me to ponder Dad's wisdoms: *Money will solve all our problems. Money is power. It buys everything, even respect and admiration. Anyone can be bought. Everyone has a price. When you have money, the world is at your mercy.*

That's probably true, because throughout the summer almost everyone in Dad's world has been at *his* mercy. And as we head into fall, the only things that change are the colors of the leaves.

****

Mommy calls me into the kitchen to tell me Dad's so plastered she has to pick him up from a bar in South Amboy because they've taken away his keys.

South Amboy made the Guinness Book of World Records for most bars per square mile. If you get kicked out of one bar in South Amboy, all you have to do is stumble to the next corner, and it doesn't matter which direction. It's a wonderland for drunks—and Dad must've gone on every ride.

Mom tells me to get the kids out of the house for a while.

"Where should I bring them?"

"Just take them for a ride for an hour or so and by that time, Dad will be home and asleep."

I pack my five youngest siblings into my car and tell them we're going on an adventure.

"Where?" they ask.

"You'll see when we get there."

I have no clue where I'm going—but I'm on my way. I drive through East Brunswick toward farm country. It's a beautiful autumn day, and the kids and I sing "Old MacDonald" in between counting cows and horses. They're all so happy and well behaved because their little minds are busy, and because they have no clue Dad's plastered again.

On a whim I turn up a long narrow dirt road that leads me into a beautiful apple orchard. It reminds me of how Mommy used to bring us older ones to the orchards for apples and peaches, and how we used to can them and make pies. The recollection is irresistibly sweet. Why shouldn't my sisters and brothers have the same kinds of memories to draw on someday? Although I'm trespassing, I park the car in between a row of trees.

"We're going apple picking!"

"Yay! Apple picking!" the kids cheer.

I'm not prepared for this adventure. I don't have money to pay for the apples, nor do I have any bags, but how can I disappoint them? I promised them a fun adventure and I plan to deliver. I show them how to use their shirts as pockets the way Mommy showed me. Many of the tree limbs are low to the ground, allowing the youngest ones to pick their own apples. When their shirts are full, they dump the apples into the trunk of my car. Andrei picks one apple, puts it in his shirt, runs to the car, throws in his apple, then runs back for another. Joseph, on the other hand, fills his shirt with enough apples for a pie. They're having so much fun I let them pick apples until there's no room left in the trunk.

On the way home they ask me to take them apple picking again. I vow to take them next year when the apples are ready to be picked. As I make my promise, I hear the Baron's voice. *Always keep your promise.*

My brain opens up a new file and makes a note: *Next autumn, bring your sisters and brothers to the apple orchard and don't forget the bags.*

When we pull up to the house Mommy is at the kitchen window. The kids hop out of the car and yell up to her.

"We've got apples!"

We all go into the house to get some bags. Dad is snoring and it sounds as though we're in a hospital full of pigs with colds. These are the sounds that spell safety.

"Did he fall asleep right away?"

Mommy puts her finger up to her lips to quiet me as she hands me a couple of grocery bags.

"Two is not enough, Mommy."

"Why not?" she asks.

"Come see."

She follows us out to the car and when I open the trunk, her face lights up as if she hit the jackpot. As we fill the bags, I tell Mommy how we ended up in the orchard and that I stole the apples.

"Don't worry so much," she says. "More apples than this end up rotting on the ground."

Over the next couple of weeks Mommy makes applesauce, apple pies, and with her leftover dough, cinnamon rolls. When aunts come to visit, they leave with enough apples to make their own pies. When trick-or-treaters come knocking on our door, they leave with an apple and probably curse us because they'd rather have a candy bar. If Mommy is acquainted with the child's mother, she gives them five or six large apples and instructs them to have their mothers make an apple pie. As they drag their heavy pillowcases on the sidewalk, the poor kids turn their heads back at us to get another peek, and it's a good thing they're wearing masks.

Everyone in our house eats so many apples that we do the green-apple-quick-step for weeks. In all likelihood every family on our street is doing the same dance, creating a flushing frenzy—all because Joe Low was three-sheets-to-the-wind on that beautiful autumn day.

Dirty Money

Three-year-old Andrei has been waking up in the middle of the night and running into Mom and Dad's bedroom, crying about bugs and spiders crawling all over his body.

"I used to live a long time ago, but I fell into a deep hole in the ground and died, then I came to this house. And you're my brother," Andrei tells Dad.

Dad thinks he's just having a bad dream. He asks Andrei to name his siblings, but instead of naming us, he names Dad's brothers and sisters.

Dad realizes that the kids must've overheard the conversation he had with his sisters about reincarnation. Aunt Anna insisted that my brother, Andrei, is identical to *her* brother, Andrei, the one who fell into the well and drowned. She's sure he's been reincarnated, and when Dad learns that Joanne's the one who repeated the story to Andrei, he erupts.

"You're almost ten years old, you should know better, goddamn it! Are you stupid or something?"

Off comes his belt. Joanne is no stranger to the leather whip. He's going to teach her a lesson she'll never forget and she's lucky she's getting the lickin' from Dad, not Grandpa.

For days afterward I hear chatter of how mean and cruel Joanne is and that she deserved the goddamned lickin'. Joanne has ears. She hears it too.

As one of the few Low children who are extremely intimate with Dad's leather belt, his fury, his dreadful words, I ache for Joanne. Just like Dad said, she's barely ten! Isn't it the adults who we children

255

are ordered to respect? Aren't they the ones who first presented the reincarnation theory—a theory that is now a misdemeanor?

I can't help but think back to the lesson I received from Aunt Anna, the reincarnation expert. She taught me about black cats and ladders, and curses that brooms cause when you swoosh them past someone's feet. I swept her kitchen floor once and as the broom glided past her, she wagged her finger in my face. With the intensity of a mad scientist she revealed her cure for the broom-curse: she threw salt over my shoulder and hers. The salt bounced all over and then I had to sweep her entire floor again. I was only about ten myself. Old enough to know better? Yes and no. I half-believed her theories enough to test them out. While I roamed my neighborhood, I intentionally walked under ladders and crossed the paths of black cats to see what consequences were in store for me. Time taught me that throwing salt over her shoulder and mine changed nothing for either of us. You can test *those* things, but how do you test the theory of reincarnation when you're only ten? *Why couldn't Dad just have a talk with Joanne?*

I have no choice but to take a sip from my big old cup of shut-the-hell-up.

Dad's fierceness is rubbing off on each of us Low kids in different ways. Unless you're on Dad's priority list, it's better not to come home crying about anything. If the world outside our home *eats* us alive, it's our own goddamned fault! If we get *eaten* alive at home—that's our own goddamned fault, too.

✳✳✳✳✳✳✳✳✳✳✳✳✳

Dad is happy to know I've been dating someone for a while. He wants to know when I'm getting married, but I can't say for sure. I know that's what I'm supposed to do, but I'm a bit confused. I fear leaving Mommy and my siblings. They need me.

Mommy's ill today, but she refuses to let me call the doctor. She says she'll be fine if she can rest a while. I'm minding Joseph and Andrei, and the girls are out playing in the neighborhood. It's relatively quiet in the house, yet Mommy can't seem to sleep. The pain is keeping her awake. She steps into the kitchen, then passes out on the floor. She's still breathing and she has a pulse, but she doesn't answer me when I try to wake her.

I call for an ambulance and for Dad, and as I sit on the floor with Mommy, Joseph and Andrei hang on my back.

"What's the matter with Mommy?"

"She's sick but the doctor's going to make her better." I'm not sure if I believe what I'm saying, but I don't want to alarm them.

Dad comes flying through the door with an expression that says if anything happens to Mommy, his world will end. He needs her like a farmer needs the rain. His head may not always know it, but his heart does.

Mommy's admitted to the hospital. Her blood pressure is sky high, but the nausea and abdominal pain, we learn, are coming from gallstones. She has several small stones and a large one the size of a golf ball. The doctor performs surgery and removes them.

When Mommy returns home and things get back to normal, she finds that she's still fatigued and run-down. She worries about her health and continues leading me back to her stash, repeating her request. I reiterate my promise, but I ask that she take better care of herself. I point out that she's gained a lot of weight around the middle, and that isn't helping her.

Mommy agrees and decides to try a popular new diet by Dr. Robert Atkins. It allows her to eat all she wants and still lose weight. The catch is she can only eat proteins and fats, which means Mommy has to give up bread, one of her favorite things in the whole world. She loses some weight and begins to feel better. That's when I announce that my boyfriend, Sal, asked me to marry him and I accepted. I feel guilty, as though I'm turning my back on Mommy and my siblings, but Dad is elated because he thinks it's about time I found a man to take care of me.

Amid my wedding plans Mommy continues leading me to her stash. I promise that no matter where I am, married or not, I'll take care of my siblings if anything ever happens to her. I mean it. Having said that, I feel better about my decision to get married.

In a relatively short time Mommy drops an enormous amount of weight. Dad is so impressed that he decides to follow the Atkins diet just because it allows him to eat massive amounts of steak, shrimp and lobster. But no alcohol. He'll be on the wagon for a while.

****

There's a knock at the door, a pause and another knock. This is unusual because everyone we know walks right into our house without knocking. They just open the door and yell, "Is anybody home?"

Dad answers the knock. It's a man from the insurance company.

"Is Catherine home?" he asks.

"That's me," I say.

I follow Dad and the insurance man into the living room for a meeting.

"I want to close the file on your car accident," the man says.

"My car accident was over a year ago. I didn't know the file was still open."

"You didn't? Well, we're prepared to offer you ten thousand dollars for your pain and suffering."

I'm in shock. I had no idea that I was entitled to anything other than having the medical bills paid for.

Dad jumps on the offer.

"I'll take it," he says.

After the insurance man leaves, Dad says that the ten thousand dollars is *his* money because it's *his* insurance policy. I say nothing. A few weeks later the check arrives and Dad quickly reminds me that it's his.

"I was all banged up in that accident. I was in pain. My nose was mangled, and I had to have an operation because of it. Besides that, it took over a month to get my car fixed, Daddy."

"It's my goddamned insurance policy."

"But I pay for my portion of the insurance."

Dad's enraged. He curses and hollers before he finally relents.

"You should at least split it with me. That's the least you should do!" he says.

I look at Mommy and wait for her to speak up, but she doesn't.

"That's not fair, Dad. This money was given to me for my injuries."

"Go ahead, keep the goddamned money," he says. "You're ungrateful and greedy! I'm gonna remember this so you better not come running to me asking for anything."

I feel like a heel, so I sign the check and put it on the table in front of him.

"Here, Daddy, take it," I say. "I don't want it."

I really don't because it feels cursed and dirty now.

I go to my room feeling like a creep, yet I know I'm not greedy. I don't understand why Dad wants to keep the money. He brings home wads of cash. He's beyond his million-dollar mark, but he spends it so fast it's as if he's purposely sabotaging his own goal. If he didn't squander his money, he'd probably have an extra couple of million by now.

The other day he bought a summerhouse the way other people buy a loaf of bread. The house sits on a lagoon across from a bird sanctuary in Manahawkin. It's a perfect place for him to go fishing anytime he wants. *I just don't get it.*

The door to my bedroom opens and it's Dad. He slams the check on my bureau.

"Here, I'll let you keep it. Use it to pay for your own wedding and think of it as my gift to you."

I don't say a word. I just look at him. He repeats the part about it being my wedding gift because he expects me to express appreciation.

"Thank you, Daddy."

He leaves my room and I sit here feeling guilty and undeserving.

A Good Old-Fashioned Fistfight

Dad sold the rights for his windshield replacement kit to one of the Big Three automakers. The deal he made didn't pan out exactly as planned, but he did end up with a nice chunk of change to add to his stash. He dissolves that "on-the-side" company, but money keeps flowing in because his other scheme is up and running full speed ahead.

At age forty-five Dad's feeling pretty good because he lost fifty pounds on Atkins just as Mommy did, though it took her twice as long. She's been very careful not to put the weight back on, but Dad's back to drinking and he's slowly expanding. To add to his new style, he's grown an ugly, little mustache. He looks like Hitler with a thyroid problem—especially when he's angry. Evidently, he's still upset over the insurance money. He reminds me often that he's not spending a cent on my wedding. The insurance money is my gift!

I feel so guilty about keeping the money that I pay for every blessed thing having to do with my wedding, including the bridesmaids' dresses for my sisters, my younger siblings' clothing, my mother's dress, Dad's tuxedo and their shoes.

Sal wants me to find us a place to live and pick out some furniture, so I use my insurance money to secure an apartment, then I visit Oyving and he gives me "such a deal" I'm able to furnish every room.

My wedding day unfolds as planned. Hitler zooms me down the aisle and happily gives me away. My journeys down both aisles are now complete.

Our reception is the typical Low party—lots of music, dancing and drinking. Afterward, Sal and I do what every newlywed couple does first—we open the envelopes. I didn't want to believe that Hitler really meant it when he said the insurance check is my wedding gift, but he kept his word. His empty card says, "Congratulations, Love Mommy and Dad."

After the honeymoon Sal and I settle into our little apartment. I work during the day, and Sal works nights, which leaves me time after work to give Mommy a hand with whatever she needs. Often, she summons me home to take the kids during Dad's drunken tirades. These are the times I feel guilty about not being there. But feeling torn is something I'm used to.

****

Hitler sits in his chair bitching about gas prices doubling to over seventy cents a gallon. When he's tired of that topic he switches to the Watergate scandal, the Vietnam War, the goddamned hippies and his favorite subject of all—Women's Liberation. He's been averse to women's lib all along, but now he's so disgusted he hollers at news reporters on television.

"Women are ruining the world. They should shut the hell up and stay the hell home where they goddamn belong. They deserve equal pay like my ass deserves it," he bellows. "If they want equal pay they should grow a beard and a goddamned *jooje*."

"Give me a break," Mommy squeals.

"That's all you get is a goddamned break," Hitler says with his finger wagging at her. "You don't work—you sit home all day!"

Mommy's sick of listening to him, so she borrows Aunt Edna's slapstick.

"Joe," she says, "wipe off your mouth."

"Why, do I have crumbs in my mustache?"

"No crumbs, just a little bullshit, donkey shit and people shit dripping onto your chin."

"What do you mean by that?"

"You're so full of shit, Joe, you need toilet paper for both ends!"

Just as he does with me, Dad stifles his amusement. He won't give Mommy the satisfaction of laughing out loud. He tells her to stop being a smart-ass, and now he's on a roll again.

I just came over to tell my family that I'm pregnant, but Dad's familiar monologue makes that impossible. I'm beginning to understand why Mommy keeps her mouth shut. The writers of *All in the Family* must've met Dad in a bar and decided to model Archie Bunker after him. As Dad begins to harp about the price of gas, I wonder why it bothers him so. His bounty of cash is buying him a bar, which will save money on all the secondhand scotch that gets flushed down the toilet. But at least he finally buys something nice for Mommy—a mink stole. Maybe she'll get to wear it at some black-tie affair given in honor of stay-at-home, barefoot-and-pregnant women. If not, she can always flaunt it while she's peeling potatoes for a batch of pierogi.

****

Sal suddenly reveals that his parents hold title to the house *he* bought.

"If you're the one who bought it, why do *they* hold the title?"

"That's not for you to worry about. Just pack your things, we're moving."

The house is near his parents' home, a good hour or more southeast of our apartment *and* my job. Since I'm pregnant and my salary is meager, I quit my job and move.

Now that I'm not working, I spend all my time with Sal during the day until he goes off to work the night shift. He tries to direct every move I make. He doesn't like it if I contact friends or family and he doesn't want me going anywhere without his permission. He's even chosen a friend for me to visit: the wife of one of his friends. He sets up the day and time that I should visit her and I oblige. I hate every minute of visiting with someone I don't even know when I have so many people in my life I'm familiar and comfortable with.

Sal goes out drinking after work, then he wakes me up at three in the morning wanting to know why I haven't bothered waiting up for him. I've fallen short of his expectations, so he takes every opportunity to demean me. I'm beginning to feel suffocated.

Christmas is not far off. I promised my siblings that I'd come for a visit and make cookies with them. Sal, however, doesn't want me leaving the house. I explain that making cookies with my siblings for a few hours isn't going to affect him.

"You're not going!" he insists.

"Yes, I am."

I hop in the shower, and just as I'm washing my hair I feel something hit my head, then fall to the bottom of the tub. I look down to see my clothes; the outfit I ironed and prepared for myself is soaked. My waistline has gotten bigger and it's a challenge finding clothes that fit. This outfit was all I had to wear today. I feel as though I'm going to break down. I can't say no to the man without him flying into a fit of rage. He either throws something at me or pushes me up against a wall or pulls on me. I can't take it. I feel like a kid again, the one without a voice.

"Why'd you throw my clothes into the tub, Sal?"

"Because I don't want you going anywhere," he laughs.

"What in God's name is so wrong in going to my mother's house to bake cookies?"

He chuckles again and it sounds sinister to me. For the rest of the day I imagine how disappointed my siblings must be.

I feel like a slave, as if I'd been purchased. If I step out of line, he doesn't say much. He just laughs and pushes me or knocks me up against the wall.

"I'm pregnant," I tell him. "You can't go around hitting me."

"I didn't hit you," he corrects me.

To him, a push or a shove isn't a punch but it all feels the same to me. I decide to call for help but he grabs the phone, pulls the cord out of the wall and kicks me. My big, pregnant belly somehow gets in the way of his foot. I don't know what he was aiming at, but he says it's not his fault.

I, however, see it as an attack on someone other than myself: my baby. I have always jumped in to rescue the defenseless. The *kick* inspires me to *divorce* Sal. The word *divorce* feels like a curse word.

I'm supposed to lie in the bed I made, but the sheets are dirty, the mattress is lumpy, and it's crawling with bedbugs.

I tell Mommy and Dad that I want to have a talk with them and they agree to come and see me while Sal's at work.

"I'm going to divorce Sal."

"You're pregnant!" Dad shrieks. "You'll be ruining your life! Believe me, it's better to stay and work it out."

I'm stunned at how Mommy agrees with everything Hitler says. *Does she really agree?*

I feel alone and trapped, but I decide to wait and see what happens over the next couple of weeks. I'll remain agreeable and keep my mouth shut—just like Mommy does.

As the days pass I continue to feel like a prisoner, so after Sal goes off to work, I drive up to my parents' home. Once again, I explain my position, but Dad stands his ground. I don't know how to make him understand. After several explanations, he suggests that Sal and I seek counseling. I'm surprised at his suggestion because he *hates* head doctors, but I heed his advice.

I find a counselor and make an appointment. Sal comes along begrudgingly. The counselor talks with both of us for a while, then individually. Afterward, he gives us a questionnaire. Within minutes, Sal makes a big X on every page, then storms out of the office. I stay to complete the form.

At the next appointment, the counselor advises me to temporarily separate from Sal until we can air out some of our differences. In the meantime, since Sis is getting married, he tells Sal to take me to the wedding and use that time to prove to me that he can spend the night out behaving appropriately.

When I inform Dad of our temporary separation, he reluctantly allows me to come home. But only for a while.

"I don't like the goddamned yoyo, either," Dad booms, "but divorce isn't the answer!"

****

Now that Sis's wedding plans are under way, Dad comes up with a new family rule.

"From now on," Mr. Rockefeller boasts, "whenever one of my children gets married, I'm going to give them a wedding gift of two thousand dollars!"

Sis's wedding day arrives, and Sal meets me at the reception hall. I'm five months pregnant, but I look as though I'm eight months along.

"What have you been eating?" Sal shrieks.

"Everything in sight!" I say.

He laughs, but not at the joke.

It's a lovely Italian wedding. The dinner begins with rigatoni and before long the band is playing a tarantella. The music draws everyone onto the dance floor. We're singing, laughing, locking arms, encircling whoever has the nerve to be the first to dance solo in the center. That would be me! I don't get out that often so I take every opportunity to dance. Dancing agrees with me more than anything else so I shamelessly wiggle my *dupah* in the middle of the tarantella circle while Sal drinks at the bar.

Throughout the wedding Sal has been completely antisocial, and he's had more than one man's share of booze. Just about a half hour before the band plays its last song, Sal approaches me with disdain in his eyes.

"It's time to go!" he roars.

"The wedding isn't over yet," I say. "I want to stay and dance until the end."

"We stayed long enough!" he screams. "You're my wife. When I say it's time to go, it's time to go!"

As he's ranting, I notice a bulge in both sides of his jacket.

"What is that?" I ask.

He opens his jacket, exposing two bottles of vodka.

"I stole them from the bar."

"No, Sal. You stole them from my family, because they're paying the bill."

He slams the bottles onto the table, walks around to me, wraps his paws around my throat and starts shaking me back and forth. I reach up to pry his fingers from my neck, but I can't.

Within seconds my cousin Gerry's husband, George, jumps him from the side. George is smaller than Sal, but he's got tons of testosterone, which means, "Jump the son-of-a-bitch now and ask questions later."

Sal and George end up rolling around on the floor, punching each other. Sal's so furious it's hard to contain him. Before long, some of the uncles take turns throwing punches at him, along with many of the cousins who've had lots of practice at this kind of thing. Dad jumps in and he's all over Sal like whipped cream on a super-duper sundae. If Sal still has disdain, it's now in his underwear.

My cousin Moinie tries to get a jab in, but she breaks a nail on Sal's face. Rita's husband Johnny is getting his licks in, too. That's how you know it's a really good brawl. Johnny is a fun-loving kind of guy and the last person you'd expect to get in on a fight.

Now there's a pile of men rolling around on the floor. As the fight moves to another area, the group of men follows, exposing Johnny on the bottom. Rita wants to know what the hell he's doing down there, but he just laughs.

Now tables are being flipped, glasses are breaking, plates with cake are flying all around, the floor is sopping with mixed drinks, red wine and coffee, and the air is thick with flying éclairs, cannolis, cream puffs and cigarette smoke. The band stops playing "That's Amore" and pipes in a few notes from the "William Tell Overture." People are hollering and cursing and some are cheering and yelling, "Get him again!"

I'm horrified, and I can't help but notice that Dad, along with the other male relatives, are having a grand old time. A good, old-fashioned fistfight is right up Dad's alley. But truthfully, this is probably the first brawl in Dad's life that he himself did not initiate.

Within fifteen short minutes after the mayhem breaks out, the South River Police arrive and spoil all the fun. Dad tells them to get Sal the hell out of here.

"Wait a minute!" Dad shouts with a slur.

While the police are straining to hold Sal, Smokin' Joe Frazier throws him one more punch right in the kisser.

"Okay," Smokin' Joe tells the cops. *"Now* I'm done with the bastard. *Now* you can take the son-of-a-bitch away."

When he's gone, the men gather round to verbally replay, punch for punch, all the fun they had. They're laughing, snorting and patting one another on the back. They lift their glasses and drink to "a punch worth throwing, a fight worth fighting, and to the sorry-ass fate of the next son-of-a-bitchin' bastard who tries anything slimy with anyone's daughter."

As I look around the hall, it appears as though the Hell's Angels crashed a wedding hosted by the mob. It's not pretty. But then again, everyone who stayed late to witness the grand finale walked away with cake on their shoes and a mouthful of dirty gossip—more than enough to last until the next Low party.

In the morning Smokin' Joe tells me he knows what the problem is.

"Sal is probably an alcoholic and what's worse is his choice of booze," he says. "Vodka makes a man mean. Sal should switch to scotch."

Deep down I feel I need Dad's permission and approval for a divorce. I feel indebted to him, so I make my next visit with the counselor alone. I recount the sequence of events, and by the end of our session he asks me to bring my father to my next appointment.

"He probably won't come."

"Please," he says. "Try to persuade him."

A week later I muster the courage to ask Dad to come with me.

"What does he want to see *me* for?"

"I have no clue, Dad. I'm just passing on the message."

"The reason psychiatrists get into that profession in the first place is because they're so goddamned screwed up, they need to figure themselves out," Dad says. "But, I'll tell you what—if it makes you feel better, I'll go with you next time."

At the next session the counselor questions Dad about his methods of parenting.

"Spare the rod, spoil the child," Dad tells him.

He omits his unjust use of the rod, that he sees red, that he misses his target. He doesn't tell the counselor that he hits only some of his children. But I dare not contradict him. The conversation eventually leads the counselor to ask Dad if he drinks.

"A little bit."

"What's your definition of a little bit?"

"I have a few beers once in a while."

"What does once in a while mean?"

"I have a mixed drink or a beer or two, sometimes once a week, sometimes only once a month and sometimes months go by and I don't drink anything at all," Dad says.

The counselor's questions enlighten me. I realize that the definition of any word can be altered to suit a person's delusion. Dad's responses do not match my recollections, but they trigger my epiphany. *I married a different version of my father. Sal's personality is extremely different from Dad's, but there are similarities in their character that can't be denied. I married a man who treats me the way Dad does. It's what I'm used to. It's all I know. Indirectly, all of my life, Dad has been choosing the kind of man I'd marry.*

I'm in such deep thought I don't hear the rest of the conversation. The session ends.

During the next session it's just the counselor and me. I had previously explained to him that there have been so many times in my life I thought I was crazy. I wondered what was wrong with me. I always seemed to be doing something to upset Dad, Sis, and now, my husband. I earnestly want to know what it is about me or the things I do that causes so much conflict.

"It's not you, Cathy," the counselor says.

"Then why do I always feel as though I'm doing or saying something to offend my husband?"

"Because that's how he wants you to feel. Sal bullies you into getting what he wants. You feel bad and then *you give him* what he wants to make *him* feel better. But it only works temporarily. Soon, he'll make you feel guilty over something else. He's preying on your kindness, Cathy. People with narcissistic tendencies easily identify and target good-natured souls. I sense that you're so used to this kind of behavior you don't even realize how you end up with the bad end of the stick. You're not crazy. The problem is that you're dealing with self-centered people who don't care *how* they affect others around them."

The counselor gazes at me for a long moment.

"I've been counseling people for a long time, but I've never advised anyone in such a short span of time of what I'm about to tell you."

He pauses.

"Get a divorce, as fast as you can! Do it, then run in the other direction and keep running as fast and as far away as you can!"

Life Gets in the Way

Dad is so unhappy about my divorce, he feels compelled to warn me of the position I've put myself in.

"You'll be lucky if you ever get married again—men don't want a used woman, especially one with a kid. You just wasted all the insurance money on a wedding that didn't work out. You might as well have thrown it down the drain."

This becomes a regular chant.

Although my plan to move back home is temporary, Dad instructs me on the rules of my living arrangements. I'm to pay thirty dollars a week for room and board, clean the house, help with the kids and do any other chore that's asked of me because there's no free ride in this world. And when my baby is born I'm to buy the baby food and supplies myself because he's got enough mouths to feed. If I can't even take care of myself, what good am I?

I continue with my pre-natal check-ups to make sure all is well with baby and me. When the school year ends Mommy and Dad pack up the kids and head down to their summerhouse.

"This house better be in tiptop shape when I return," Dad tells me as they're leaving.

I don't mind being alone. I like the quiet, and when I clean the house, it *stays* clean. Mommy was nice enough to rearrange the bedrooms so that I could have some private space downstairs, and she gave me the crib that she used for her last five children. It's set up and ready, and I'm excited and frightened all at once.

It's late at night when my contractions begin. I get myself to the hospital where I end up in a cold, white room, with a large ticking clock on the wall, alone and twenty-four hours of painful labor ahead of me.

My beautiful daughter, Leah, finally arrives—on Father's Day.

****

Back at home the quiet time offers me the opportunity to think about how I'll raise Leah. I want to be a conscientious parent, not one who flies into thoughtless rages. I want her to feel loved, to be safe, and I want her to be educated.

To my surprise Sal comes for a visit. He awkwardly holds Leah for a few moments, then he informs me he won't be coming back. He says he doesn't want to live in two different worlds, so I remind him that Leah is his daughter, too.

"I don't want *her* living in two different worlds," he says.

"What worlds? Mars and Jupiter?"

"I can't come back," he says, then he disappears.

I feel sorry for Leah, knowing she won't have a father in her life, until I realize that the worst thing I can do is to pity her.

As the summer rolls on, I keep busy while Leah sleeps. I tend to the tomato garden I started for Mom. I mow the lawn, trim bushes, shampoo carpets, and wash windows and walls. When the walls don't come as clean as I'd like them to, I paint them. Dad wants me to keep the pool clean for their short visits home, so now I'm a champ at backwashing, vacuuming and treating the pool with chemicals. With summer almost over, the Low house is in tiptop shape.

"You painted!" Mommy exclaims as she walks through the door. "Everything looks great!"

"So what?" Mr. Clean says. "That's the least she can do in exchange for a place to live."

This might be the right time for me to tell Dad that I want to move out.

"Dad, my divorce was finalized on August 28th. I'm going to be receiving sixty dollars per week in child support and alimony. I've got about a thousand dollars in the bank and with a part-time job, I should be able to support myself. I want to get a place of my own."

271

"You can't make it on your own," Dad insists. "Who the hell do you think is going to watch your baby when you're working? Just stay here and pay your room and board and do your chores. You don't know how goddamned lucky you are. What the hell are you thinking?"

First he doesn't want me here. Now he does. My instincts are telling me to go, yet I still feel intensely obligated to my father.

****

When Dad finalizes the deal on the bar he bought, he quits his job at the chemical plant. Owning a bar has always been one of his dreams, and he seems to be realizing all of them. He has the two sons he always wanted, more than a million dollars from his "on-the-side" schemes, a summerhouse on the water for fishing, and a bar for drinking.

He also decides to buy two acres of property in South Jersey, but he doesn't bother to check it out before he makes the purchase. After the closing, he drives down to get a glimpse of what he bought. There aren't any roads leading up to his land; paper roads are just that —they're on paper because they haven't been built yet. Dad parks his car and, map in hand, begins walking through the woods. Without warning he finds himself staring down the barrel of a rifle, and soon we hear all about it.

"The guy wielding the gun was a goddamned redneck," Dad says. "And there were so many goddamned crumbs in his beard he could've made a meal out of it. His hair was greasy and he was missing all his front teeth. His blue jeans were black, and his red plaid shirt was torn and filthy—but his rifle was clean and shiny!

"When he sees me he yells, 'Get the hell off my land!' So I throw my hands up over my head. I try telling the son-of-a-bitch that I just want to see my property but he tells me if I don't get going, he'll blow my head off.

"'Yes sir,' I say, then I run like a son-of-a-bitch. By the time I reach my car, I'm so upset, I dig into my pocket for my cigarettes, but they're gone. They fell out and I was too goddamned afraid to go back and look for them."

Dad never gets to see the property, which he claims he bought with the bonds Joseph and Andrei received as gifts at their christening parties.

The title of the land is in Dad's name, so he says, "When I die, the boys are to get an acre apiece, and everything else I own is to be split equally among all nine of my kids."

****

Aunt Louise's husband passes away unexpectedly in October of 1974. I never got to say goodbye to the many people in my life who passed on and I want the opportunity to do that with Uncle Joe. But Mommy and Dad insist I stay behind to mind my younger siblings. Since I'm already babysitting, Sis drives by and drops off her two stepchildren. I ask her if she would take turns babysitting so I can go, too, but my request just annoys her. She's busy with more important things.

****

Now that Jane is married and Anya is away at college, I'm the only grown-up Low kid available to help Mommy—and she needs all the help she can get.

On the weekends Sis delivers her two stepchildren because she doesn't have to pay for the babysitting services. Dad says that's the least family can do for family. Now Mommy has seven children between the ages of four and twelve running through the house, and she can't control them. Between grocery shopping, cooking, laundry, her high blood pressure, and worrying about the shape Dad will be in when he comes home late at night, she's completely run down. She needs to nap to regain some of her energy, and even then she's not as quick as she used to be. Mommy is in a difficult position and I feel for her as much as I do for the children. They need more attention and guidance than they're getting. Although I'd rather be living on my own, I feel compelled to remain at home "just in case."

****

Dad soon discovers that his new business venture isn't turning a profit so the workload multiplies for Mommy and me. We go down to the bar early each morning to sweep, mop floors, and prepare food for the lunch crowd. We have no choice but to bring Leah and Andrei with us and work around them. We do these chores without pay for the good of the family. Bugsy doesn't do any of the down-and-dirty stuff because he's the brain of the operation. His job is to run things, which means he'll sit at the bar, drink and watch the bartenders. He says some of them might be "playing the piano" and although he expects them to, he wants to be sure that they don't break into a full sonata. He sits at the corner drinking scotch and water, shooting the shit with his bar buddies. After downing a few, he buys the bar a round, and with their free drinks they lift their glasses to "Joe Low, the best bar owner in town!"

Dad loves the attention, so he's easily swayed into buying another round or three before the night is over.

At home in the morning Mommy tells Bugsy he's playing his own piano the way he gives away the bar. Dad argues that you have to give to get.

"Maybe," Mommy says, "but you're giving more than you're getting."

"Why don't you mind your own goddamned business? I'm the one who makes the money, I'll run my business how I please," Dad spews, because it doesn't occur to him that Mommy *and I* have been working without pay for the good of the family. Mommy could throw this in his face, but she doesn't. Of course, I'm living in their house—I have no right to utter a word.

I do make it my business to be a good influence on my younger siblings. Dad often comes and goes without saying hello or goodbye to them, but when friends and relatives visit, they get a proper greeting from him. I don't want the children to feel forgotten so I pick up the slack every chance I get.

There's no hugging or kissing in the Low house so for no reason at all I hug and kiss my younger siblings. On special holidays the kids always kiss Mommy and Dad, but my siblings and I never exchanged those pleasantries. One Christmas after my younger sisters were born, I began a new tradition. I would look them in the eye and tell them "Merry Christmas" and give them their own special hug and kiss. This tiny gesture brightens each of them. I've been doing this with my older siblings as well. Sis hates my idea. She'll kiss her friends hello, but she won't even let me touch her, let alone kiss her. She gags and puts her arms up as I approach. The times I do manage to sneak a kiss onto her cheek, she wipes it off as if it's a disease.

****

Since Dad has owned the bar, his drunken tirades have increased, especially during the afternoons. My younger siblings are now experienced enough to know that when Dad comes home shit-faced, they've got to hide in a closest or under a bed. If they're in the vicinity of Lincoln's casket, they're lucky, because it never occurs to the grizzly bear to peek inside. The grizzly curses as he moves from room to room looking for someone to pick on until he gets tired and hungry, then he goes into the kitchen to hunt for a picnic basket. Once he's fed, he goes off to bed and snores like thunder, but little children can emerge from dark corners during the storm.

When Dad's not drinking he's usually on the run somewhere. Once in a while he melts into the couch and listens to the Mills Brothers while melancholy seeps from his pores. Tonight the Mills Brothers infuse the atmosphere with a song about how people always hurt the ones they love.

How true. But I refuse to hurt the ones I love, even if they hurt me.

Dad seems a bit sad tonight.

"Is everything okay, Daddy?"

"You know," he says, in a deep but soothing tone, "life passes you by very quickly. When you get to be my age, you don't have a lot of time to do the things you want to do."

"What do you want to do?"

"I always wanted to see the pyramids of Egypt, the ancient ruins in Greece, maybe do a safari in Africa, and I *really* wanted to go back to Japan to dig up my black pearl—it must be worth a pretty penny by now," he sighs. "Eh, someone else probably found it already."

"Where'd you get the pearl, Dad, and why in the world would you bury it in Japan?"

"By the time I was able to enlist in the Army, World War II was over, but we still occupied Japan—that's where they sent me. It was pretty easy to drum up a little cash on-the-side over there, only I made a lot of it. Just before it was time for me to come home I decided to make an investment. An old Japanese man who dealt with investment-grade jewels showed me a bunch of gems, but it was the black pearl that caught my eye. It was a lot of goddamned money. I didn't care. I bought it on the spot, and right then and there, I decided to bury it in Japan just so I'd have a reason to go back some day. I loved Japan!" Dad sighs. "Anyway, I put the pearl into a little wooden box, then I dug a deep hole under one of the structures on the Army base and that's where I buried it. Boy oh boy," Dad says, "I really thought that by now I'd have gone back to Japan for the pearl."

"How come you didn't?"

"Life gets in the way of what you really want to do. I didn't know life would always be so hard. Well, maybe someday we'll all have everything we need, and it'll all be easier."

"You already have everything you need, Daddy."

"No," he insists. "When I don't have little kids and bills to worry about, that's when things will be easier. That's when I'll be able to rest and maybe then I'll buy a sailboat and sail around the world. Right now, life is a struggle."

It seems that he only sees what he doesn't have, and that's the object of his constant discontent. I've heard Mommy tell him many times that he could have taken the entire family on ten trips around the world with the money he spent in bars. I want to remind him that he got everything he wanted—a bigger house, his sons, the bar, a summerhouse, lots of money. I desperately want to point out that the kids just need his time, his kindness and understanding. Those things cost nothing. But I zip my lips because my thoughts always incite Dad's anger.

"Someday," he says, "things will get better."

As he speaks, Leah crawls up to his feet and pulls herself to an upright position. He lifts her to eye level and instantaneously grants her a nickname.

"Hi, Mooky. What a little Mooky you are. You're Gampa's Mooky, aren't you?" He points to himself and says, "Me Gampa Low and you Mooky."

Leah sticks her finger on Dad's nose and he does the same with her. Now he's teaching her "nose, eyes, mouth." Then he growls and pretends to bite her finger.

I'm in awe of his loving reaction, but I wish he could find the same joy playing with his own children who ache for his affection. I see love in my father—it's there, hidden beneath a pile of secondhand baggage, but it's there. I'm touched and bewildered all at once.

Comedy and Tragedy

Another school year ends and the family heads down to Manahawkin. Dad invites everyone he sees to come and visit. In anticipation of his many guests he stocks the summerhouse with booze, transforming it into an alcohol candy store with various brands of whiskey, vodka, rum, scotch, green crème de menthe just in case you want a Grasshopper, and blackberry brandy for warming up.

Hardly a few days go by without Mommy and Dad having long-term company. As long as there's floor space, there's room in the Low house for a sleepover. And Mommy's home-cooked meals are an added bonus.

Dad runs back and forth to the bar and on errands for his "on-the-side" company, so he isn't always around during the week while visitors enjoy the beach, the fishing, nickel-dime poker and casual coffee talks around the kitchen table. In the mornings, especially on weekends, you have to step over people to get into the kitchen.

During coffee a few of Dad's cousins from Pennsylvania show up unannounced. The resemblance between Dad and his cousins is unambiguous—red hair, blue eyes and matching beer bellies. The overgrown blowfish plan to stay only for the day until they find themselves in the Low liquor store. Dad mixes their drinks while ordering Mommy to make them something to eat. The blowfish dive in to eat, gab, laugh, sing and drink into the wee hours of the morning until they tilt and pass out on the living room floor. My little sisters and brothers awaken to the snorts and grunts of a pig farm. In order to make your way to the kitchen, you've got to jump over men the size of grizzly bears—it's like navigating through a forest speckled with mines. Vulgar sounds come from both ends and you're terrified you might disintegrate because the ghastly combination of secondhand booze mingled with *jarts* shoot at you from every angle and bounces off the walls.

Soon Dad's cousins awaken and Mommy has the coffee ready, but they don't want coffee! They're ready to start the party all over again. Dad, who *always* drinks coffee in the morning, doesn't think it's right for a man to drink alone so he joins his cousins for a few more drinks.

This goes on for several days until Dad has to get back to business up north. When he returns to the summerhouse, he asks Mommy about his cousins and she explodes.

"I thought they were never going to leave!"

"What do ya mean?"

"All they wanted to do is drink," Mommy winces. "I couldn't stand it anymore."

Dad looks up at the shelves on the wall and sees that every last bottle of booze is gone.

"Where the hell is all the goddamned booze?"

"Your cousins drank it."

"That's impossible," Dad says. "No one can drink that much."

"Impossible?" Mommy replies. "If they could've cracked open the bottles and licked them, they would've."

"You mean to tell me they drank every different kind there was?"

"No!" Mommy laughs. "Just one kind! The free kind!"

"I can't believe it!"

"Well, believe it! And you're lucky I hid the rubbing alcohol because if I didn't they'd still be here."

"Goddamn sons-a-bitches! I can't believe it!"

"Listen Mr. Ripley, the next time you go around inviting everyone under the sun, tell them there's a cover charge and make sure you're here to wait on them because now *I'm* the one who needs a goddamned vacation!"

"They couldn't have drunk that much booze!"

"Go look in the garbage."

Dad goes outside and the next sound you hear is the crashing of glass against metal.

"Jeeeeeeeeesus Christ, where the hell did they put it all? What the hell! Do they have goddamned holes in their feet?"

"You mean to tell me you didn't know they drink like fish?" Mommy says.

"I didn't think they'd amaze me."

"Well I'm glad you're amazed because *you* usually amaze me."

For the next couple of weeks all we hear is how Dad's cousins drank all of his goddamned booze. Could you imagine that anyone could be so gluttonous?

We finally get a break from that subject when Grandma Low is admitted to the hospital. Although she went in just to have her gallstones removed, the doctor felt he needed to do exploratory surgery and inadvertently, he slit her liver. When the operation is over, the doctor goes on a long-awaited vacation to a cabin in the woods without any ties to the outside world. Within hours Grandma's health spirals downward as her liver releases toxins into her bloodstream. It doesn't look good so we pack up and head home to Sayreville.

On the last day of July a phone call brings the news of Grandma's passing. I curl up in the corner of my room to cry in secret as I recall my blue-eyed Grandma, her sugar bread, and the wooden swing where she taught me all about the virtues of stepping in dog shit.

On the first of every month Mommy says, "Rabbits." That's her way of wishing everyone good luck for the entire month ahead. It usually rolls off her tongue in a heady proclamation, but today, the first of August 1975, she whispers it more like a prayer. She serves Dad coffee and he sips it silently.

"I'm sorry, Daddy," I say as I hug him.

He doesn't hug me back. He barely nods his head as he quietly stares into space. The light from the kitchen window makes his eyes appear more blue than gray. He's awash with sadness and I don't quite know what to say. I lead the kids downstairs to keep them occupied, to keep the house quiet for Dad.

For Mommy and Dad to attend the services and the burial, they insist I stay home with the children. I do, but I'm disappointed because I so wanted to say my last goodbye.

After the burial everyone picks up where they left off. In Dad's case, he goes on a few more drinking binges and he decides to run away from home and explore South America because life is short and he doesn't want to miss out on anything. But he ends up coming back home in the small hours of the morning to all the people who will certainly forgive whatever he's done the night before.

Within weeks of the burial, Mommy's side of the family piles into our backyard for an end-of-summer bash. We kiss, hug, get squished in *dzidzees* and begin the festivities with an off-key version of "The Gang's All Here" led by none other than Aunt Mary.

There are twenty-four cousins here, plus friends, aunts and uncles—just a small gathering. Uncle Sava has a surprise for us. He's going to dole out five-dollar bills to all the kids today.

Dad puts a chair in the middle of the yard for Uncle Sava and brings him whiskey on the rocks. Uncle Sava perches himself in the hot sun, takes a few swigs of whiskey to wash down the pilaf, and now he's ready to dole out the fins. I'm embarrassed because I'm twenty-two years old, but I get in line with Leah because Mommy insists on it. As big as I am, Uncle Sava makes me sit on his lap and kiss his ten o'clock shadow. I don't know if it's his age or the whiskey, but he still can't remember who's who.

"And who are you?" he asks.

"I'm Cathy."

"And who do you belong to?"

"Joe and Lillian—uh, I mean Arms."

"Yes, Arms! She has enough kids to start an army. Have you been a good girl?"

"Yes," I say. I'm even more embarrassed now. When you wear a D cup bra it feels creepy to be asked if you're a good girl.

Next in line is my sister, Louise. She sits on Uncle Sava's lap but refuses to kiss him. At nine years old it's clear that Louise isn't afraid to stand her ground, but in spite of her protest, Uncle Sava kisses *her.* Her face is covered in his sweat, which she wipes off then pinches her nostrils closed with her fingers.

"Whose daughter are you?"

"Ninnian's Naughter," she says, still holding her nose.

"What's the matter with your nose?"

"What's the matter with your breath?" Louise replies, and thank God Dad's not in earshot.

Uncle Sava laughs, kisses her *again,* then hands her a fin. He throws back a few more gulps of whiskey to restore his energy because there's still a line of cousins waiting for their fin. Mildred steps up for hers. She puts it in her bra with her *dzidzees* for safekeeping, but I don't think it's safe. Her twins are big enough to win the boobie-prize *and* best-looking couple. If a dirty old man ever reached in to check out the merchandise, he'd get paid for doing it.

Since Uncle Sava can't remember who's who, he can't keep track of who may have gotten in line more than once. When that happens, *and it does,* the double dippers simply say they belong to Joe and Lillian.

Now Uncle Sava's happy because he's getting old and he knows there aren't any Greek restaurants or liquor stores in heaven. You can't spend your money up there, but he wonders out loud if you can break plates on the clouds in heaven.

"No, Sava," Mommy chimes, "but you can break 'em on your head."

"I love your ingenuity, Arms!" Uncle Sava shouts back.

A day like today, overflowing with family, the promise of a bag of herns from Aunt Chris, volleyball in the pool, the singing and laughing, is among all those engraved on my heart.

Between the tragedies of our lives there's always an abundance of comedy. Some people cry all the way home just because they lost a shoe. In the Low family, you could lose a leg or an eyeball, you could be punched in the face or on your deathbed. It doesn't matter. Someone will be rolling out the shot glasses, firing up the grill, and bursting out in song.

That right there is the epitome of comedy and tragedy.

My New Career

"This bar is just a monkey on my back," Dad complains over his morning coffee.

It doesn't bring in enough money to pay its bills, so he's using profits from his side scheme to cover them.

"Well, stop feeding it," Mommy quips.

"What do ya mean by that?" Dad asks.

Mommy hands him a banana from the counter.

"You're the lord and master of that monkey," she says.

As Dad chuckles I take the opportunity to ask, for the tenth time, if he can put me on as a bartender.

"I'll work for tips only—just a couple of nights a week."

"You'll get eaten alive. Just pay your room and board, earn your keep around the house and stop asking to work at the goddamned bar," he insists. Then he's out the door.

When Dad returns home in the evening, still grumbling over his bad investment, I take the opportunity to ask him once again to teach me how to tend bar. He relents and ushers me into his saloon early on Saturday to show me around and teach me how to pour a beer.

When I pull the tap handle I end up with a glass of foam. As I pour it down the drain Dad shrieks.

"What the hell are you doing? That's wasting, goddamn it! Give it to me. I'll drink the goddamned beer!"

At this rate, Dad'll be drunk before the bar opens. When I finally get the knack of tilting the mug just so under the tap, Dad moves on to martinis, old fashions and kirs. He tells me it's important to learn everyone's name and what they drink. When I see a customer walk through the door I'm to have their drink ready as they're sitting down. There's no reason they should ever have to ask for what they want. Dad also insists that I clean the glasses to a sparkle because even the slightest residue can ruin the head of the beer. Next he schools me on buying back. If a customer is having several drinks, I'm to comp every fourth or fifth one, and if he buys a round for the bar, I should get his next drink.

"Men have filth on the brain," Dad says as he shows me the ropes. "Don't pay any attention to them. Let it go in one ear and out the other."

I have to keep the bar clean, the ashtrays emptied, light cigarettes for the customers, and if someone orders a burger and fries, I'm expected to go into the kitchen and cook.

After a couple of weeks I get the hang of it. Dad rewards me with three late shifts a week. Mommy gets an extra ten dollars for each night I work because I leave Leah with her, so my weekly room and board goes up to sixty dollars. Lucky for me, I pull in about sixty dollars a night in tips. And better yet—my new career allows me to be with Leah during all of her waking hours, while earning a living at night.

Now that I'm on my own behind the bar, the customers are putting me through an initiation. They melt stirrers together, they use the f-word as an adjective, and every other comment drips with sexual innuendos. I'm not sure what to make of it, but I wouldn't think of complaining to Dad because he'd tell me to "get out of the kitchen if I can't take the heat."

When Dad comes into the bar at night, I race to make his scotch and water the way he likes it—mostly scotch. He sits at the corner and as I place his drink in front of him he commands me to buy the bar a round. Under Bugsy's orders I'm to bring the customer his next drink just before he finishes the one he has. This rule includes Dad so if there is an inch of liquid in his glass, I better get him another drink, *quickly,* or he'll embarrass me in front of everyone.

As the night unfolds, Dad becomes one, two, three-sheets-to-the-wind, and he commands me to buy the house so many rounds, I can't even use his buy-back rule.

What bothers me the most is that I'm the one making Dad's drinks. I decide to reduce the amount of scotch I pour into his drinks, little by little, hoping that he won't notice. Just as I think I'm getting good at it, he pounds the bar.

"Hey, what the hell's a matter with you? What the hell are you trying to pull? I drink *scotch* and water, not water, goddamn it!"

Before he finishes his tirade, I set another drink in front of him. I'm between two boulders: my employment is improving my own financial circumstances, and Dad's, but now I feel as though it's my fault he drinks, then goes home and causes a ruckus. Since Mommy is home alone with the kids, I worry even more.

Before the night's over, Dad and his buddies take off and end up at another bar. After giving away his own profits, it's baffling that he'd spend his money in some other establishment, but at least I don't have to continue serving him.

I'm acquiring a unique education "behind the stick." I meet garbage men, teachers, policemen, judges, lawyers, truckers and CEOs. Most are wonderful people, but there are always a few rotten apples so I've had to toughen up. If I'm going to continue working as a bartender I'll have to figure out how to handle the jerks, especially the guy who keeps telling me he has something hard that needs to be rubbed. I hear about his hard thing a hundred times. Finally, I pick up his beer and pour it over his hand. His hand is soaked, his money's soaked and he's furious.

"What the hell did ya do that for?" he growls.

His friends lean in to listen.

"I was just getting your date drunk!"

His buddies fall off their stools, roar with laughter, and Mr. Hard turns red. I tell him if he can behave himself, I might allow him to buy another beer. I hand him a bar rag, he takes it and remorsefully cleans up the mess.

****

Dad's been coming home drunk four or five times a week. While most of his drunkenness is hidden from the children they still see far more than they should. And now the girls aren't the only ones he goes after —he's added his four and five-year-old sons to his target list. When Dad booms through the door, pickled in the middle of the day, it isn't unusual for him to grab Joseph by the collar and swing him around in circles while the poor kid musters everything he's got to keep from choking to death. And if Andrei is in reach, he'll go after him. The environment continues to fuel the obligation I feel toward my five youngest siblings. I can't bear the thought of turning my back on them, yet my duty to protect my daughter from the madness has begun to invade my thoughts.

Tonight I'm at home. The children are tucked into bed, and Mommy is exhausted so she turns in. Not long afterward, the phone rings. It's bad news about Dad. Wherever he goes a story follows him, and he's always the main character. I hang up the phone and wake up Mommy to tell her that Dad's in the hospital on life support.

"His heart stopped. He was out cold—dead—and he had to be revived."

As she dresses, I explain that Dad was out bar hopping with his buddies. Before entering the next saloon, he decides he wants to play punch-for-punch—a testosterone-fired game where men take turns hitting each other to see who's tougher. Dad wants to prove he's as tough as a rhino.

"Come on, punch me," he begs his friend. "You can't hurt me. Come on, punch me!"

His buddy is younger and stronger than he is. He doesn't want to play that stupid game, but Dad refuses to take *no* for an answer. He hounds his buddy until he changes his mind.

"All right Joe, just one time."

He slams Dad in the face and as he tries to step back, his heels lock up against a curb. Dad hits the concrete like a grand piano, and stops breathing. While someone tries to resuscitate him, an ambulance is summoned, and just as it arrives, his heart kicks in and he begins breathing.

"He's not in good shape, Mommy."

"Don't worry," Mommy says. "He's not going to die. God doesn't want him in heaven because he'd start fistfights with all the angels and all hell would break loose up there."

She grabs her purse and rushes out the door. I do everything to stay awake while waiting to hear from her, but I fall asleep at the table.

The phone rings and it's Mommy. Dad has to stay in the hospital for a while. He's weak and he lost some feeling in his legs, so he couldn't get out of bed if he wanted to. But he'll live.

I'm really angry with Dad, but no matter what he does wrong, I don't want to lose him. Over the next couple of weeks Mommy and I hold everything together—the kids, the house, the bar, and the phone messages for Dad's "on-the-side" company. We do it all for the good of the family.

By the time Dad's released from the hospital he regains most of his motor skills. But one of his legs isn't quite the same. He hobbles up the steps and into the house with a cane and he resolves to give up drinking for good this time. Starting now he's on the wagon.

He resumes his routine, coming and going as he pleases, but over time he begins to disappear for two days at a clip. Because Mommy and I clean the bar most mornings, we discover shot glasses wet with the residue of scotch. We know that Dad's still drinking, but for the first time in his life he's sneaking it. When he gets really drunk, instead of coming home, he drives south to the summerhouse.

Amid all the madness, Mommy keeps me updated on her cash-stash. I, in turn, reiterate my promise to care for all the kids "just in case."

Because death came knocking on the door, the topic of having a will pops up. Dad doesn't want a will nor does he want Mommy having one.

****

"When it rains it pours," Mommy says. "Your father should've bought an ark."

Dad calls to let us know that he's in a motel somewhere in Manahawkin. He couldn't come home because he was drinking and too tired to drive. Then the real story unfolds.

He drove his shit-faced self to the summerhouse where he rolled into bed, lit a cigarette and fell asleep. He awakens in a cloud of smoke and he can't see a thing. He chokes as he runs to the sliding-glass doors and the instant he cracks them open, the house turns into an inferno.

As a child, Dad escaped countless near-death episodes. When he and his brother Frankie were trolley-car-hopping in the city, Dad fell and was run over by a trolley car. He was also hit by a city bus, and attacked by a pack of rabid dogs on Staten Island. He almost starved to death when a tapeworm hosted on him for over a year, and after using the family couch as a trampoline, a sewing needle that was carelessly stuck in the cushion, shot into his back. It wasn't until an entire year later that an X-ray revealed the needle was only a hair from his left lung.

Normally, when Dad falls asleep after drinking, nothing can rouse him. In this instance something divine saved him—again.

The fire company, the cops, and an ambulance show up, but Dad refuses to go to the hospital. After the fire is put out, he drives himself to a motel where he sleeps like a baby.

"Is there anything left to the house?" Mommy asks.

"It's shot to hell."

All Mommy can do is shake her head back and forth.

When Dad arrives home he announces that he's going on the wagon.

"Which one?" Mommy inquires sarcastically.

"The little red one."

"The *little* red one? No wonder you're always falling off."

Lessons of Our Forefathers

As much as it pains me, I decide to move out.

"What the hell for?" Dad explodes. "You'll never be able to make it on your own. If you leave, don't come back! And," he adds with his finger wagging in my face, "there's no way in hell I'm helping you move, so don't bother asking me for anything."

Despite his anger I find an apartment in a complex a few miles from the house. It's known as "the slums of Old Bridge." There are some nicer places, but no one wants to rent to a single mother. On moving day Dad keeps his word. He doesn't lift a finger to help me, yet he never ceases to remind me of what I should be doing for the family.

Dad doesn't see that I help Mommy with her chores every chance I get *and* whenever he falls off the wagon I bring my siblings back to my sanctuary overnight.

Mommy and I still clean *Dad's* bar, but not for long because he finally put it up for sale. Mommy is practically doing flips—she never wanted him to buy it in the first place.

Luckily, it isn't long before Dad finds a prospective buyer for the bar, but the bank will lend the buyer only a portion of the loan as first lien holder. So the buyer talks Dad into holding a note for him as second lien holder. Dad agrees, as long as it's paid up in a minimal number of years. The deal is sealed, the new owner takes charge, and I feel relieved because I get to keep my shifts at the bar.

Within a short period, things begin to go awry. Dad calls to inform me that the new owner is defaulting on the note. Since his side scheme is drying up and his cash has been dwindling, Dad's been counting on that monthly check. He wants to know what the hell is going on at the bar and asks me to discreetly find out as much as I can. Over the next couple of weeks I hear rumors that the new owner has his house up for sale. He's moved all his assets into someone else's name, and suppliers are complaining about being paid late or not at all.

Instead of waiting for his check to come in the mail each month, Dad confronts the owner, who makes empty promises and is now evading him. Dad needs an informant so he enlists me to keep him updated on the guy's whereabouts.

Suppliers are refusing to deliver new goods, and to compensate, the owner is out shopping for booze and physically bringing in supplies by the crate. He's pocketing all the cash that the bar takes in, and none of it is showing up on the books.

During my next shift the bar is unusually crammed with customers. By the looks of this place you'd think we were giving away free drinks. I don't understand what the draw is, but I'm not questioning it. The tips are good, and an hour into my shift, I learn why.

Colored lights begin to flicker from the back of the bar, and suddenly the crowd of men are howling like a pack of wolves. I turn toward the lights to see a set of pink *dzidzees* flapping around, changing color in midair to blue, then green and pink again. The dancer isn't even in sync with the beat of the blaring music, but the wolves don't care because their brains are made of *jooje*. *I don't think Dad would like this.* In this instant I decide to quit. I grab my tips and head toward the door, but I can't get it open. It's padlocked.

"Where the hell are you going?" the owner asks.

"I didn't sign up to work in a nude bar. I quit. I'm leaving."

"You have to finish your shift first."

"If you don't unlock the door I'll call the police."

"You bitch!" he says as he lets me out.

When Dad learns of this, he doesn't care about the nude dancers. He's upset because my leaving ends his inside information.

I've got to find another job quickly. Since I'm good at organizing and cleaning I put an ad in the paper for a housekeeping position. I get several jobs in homes nearby. The money isn't as good as bar tips, but I won't have to worry about being harassed. Or so I think.

Most of my new employers treat me like old gum stuck to their shoes. By contrast, one goes above and beyond in the compassion department. I'm not used to being treated with such kindness, and at times it almost brings me to tears. Besides my pay, she always sends me home with something extra: children's books, or shoes and clothes for Leah. I feel grateful and ashamed all at once, but I put everything to good use.

The books enable me to give my daughter one of the things I didn't have as a child. Now Leah and I share a special reading hour every day and together we discover Shel Silverstein and Dr. Seuss. I want to meet the boy who loves a tree as much as I do. And how could I have lived so long without knowing Dr. Seuss? I never knew there was a Horton, I never knew there was a Who—here I sit, all grown up, without a freaking clue.

****

By the time Dad goes to an attorney to have a lien put on the assets of the guy who bought his bar, it's too late. Bugsy's been scammed. In short order the bar is shut down and auctioned off. Dad lost a ton of money on that deal and now he thinks there's a black cloud over his head.

"It's not what's over your head," Mommy says. "It's what's in it—rocks."

****

My child support and alimony checks are coming in a bit sporadically. If a check is even just a few days late, it's a hardship for me. I'm not being reimbursed for Leah's medical expenses, and now the engine in my car blows up.

I end up at a used car lot belonging to a friend of a friend where I spend every cent of my savings on another used car. I hop in my new clunker and head home, but it breaks down about a mile from my apartment. It's raining and I don't have a damn umbrella, there's no phone booth around, and even if there was, I don't have a *dime* on me! I brave the wind-driven rain, squishing all the way home in my cheap shoes.

As I'm dripping all over the kitchen floor, I call to make arrangements to have the car towed to a mechanic. All my grocery money goes toward the towing.

Later the mechanic calls.

"I hate to tell you this honey, but you bought a piece of garbage. What you've got here are two different cars pieced together. They were both probably total wrecks. Whoever put them together to make a buck is some kind of something or other that I can't say because it's not very nice. Technically, this car is illegal."

"So what do I do?"

"The car can't be fixed. Period. Call the guy who sold it to you and tell him you want your money back."

I thank the mechanic and I call the car salesman to explain the situation to him.

"There's nothing I can do," the salesman snaps. "You bought the car as is. *You* figure it out."

Now I'm walking about a mile back and forth to my cleaning jobs. I can't spare a penny for groceries, and I don't even have an extra quarter for laundry after I pay my monthly bills. But I recall how Mommy once scraped the bottom of the barrel and came up with delicious homemade meals. If she can do it, I can too. I use the cheese grater to grate a bar of Ivory soap into flakes, which I use to wash our clothes by hand in the bathtub. I sing at the top of my lungs while I scrub my underwear because "time flies when you're having fun." I use one tea bag to make a pot of tea and I water down everything else so that it'll last longer. You can stretch a lot of things, but you can't stretch a pair of shoes. Leah has outgrown the secondhand shoes my employer gave me so I swallow my pride and call Sal. His mother answers the phone. I explain to her that Sal has yet to reimburse me for medical bills. I need the money to buy shoes and other essentials for Leah.

"Can you please give Sal the message?"

"If you can't afford to buy your daughter shoes, it's your own fault," she spits. "After all, you're the one who wanted the divorce. Now you can just sleep in the bed you made. How do you like that?"

Arguing with a rotten tomato is fruitless. I settle on calling the Probation Department to explain my dilemma. The phone clerk suggests I sign up for welfare. If I do, my child support and alimony will go directly to the Welfare Department, and even if Sal's payments are late, they'll send me a check on time every month. I quickly realize that's my only choice.

As I'm hanging up the phone Leah is sliding an end table across the wood floor. The lamp on the table falls and shatters, and I lose it. I grab her by the arm, smack her behind with all my might— five, or six times, maybe more—then I throw her onto the couch. She cries herself to sleep, and I sit on the floor in the middle of the broken glass weeping. I suddenly realize that I just treated her the way Dad always treated me, and I'm shocked at my behavior. The only other people I've ever raised my hand to are Sis, and Dad—that time I punched him in the arm when I thought he had drowned in the pool. Leah's just a toddler. She didn't know the lamp would break. *I'm so angry with myself. I wish I were the last berry on a bush beneath a flock of starving birds.*

At this moment I hate my father and I hate myself. I call Jane to tell her how I'm feeling.

"I understand," she says, "but it isn't good for you to feel this way. You have to forgive Dad."

"How do I do that?"

"The French have a saying, Cathy. They say, 'To understand is to forgive.'"

When our conversation is over, I ponder her simple advice. I realize that I'm guilty of the same thing I hate in Dad. That makes me a hypocrite. Dad hated the beatings he got from his father, but it didn't stop him from repeating the same behavior. If I point my finger at Dad, he can point his at Grandpa Low, and so on until the finger ends up in the eighteenth century. You just can't go back that far. Dead people can't change anything.

293

The next few weeks aren't easy for me. I'm in my own head trying to unravel everything, separating the good from the bad, trying to understand. I'm working hard and barely scraping by. I pull myself together enough to fool the people around me, but on the inside I'm crumbling. Too much is happening all at once. While dealing with my own problems, which I can't seem to resolve, the circumstances of my siblings weigh heavily on my heart. I love them more than flowers love the sun.

I pace the floor as I consider how to change my circumstances. Memories, good and bad, flash-flood my brain and I do my best to separate them because I want to keep the good stuff fresh and clean and shiny while clearing out the dusty clutter of crap.

I've lived my entire life trying to please Dad and I'm still not good enough for him. The lessons he taught me weren't necessarily true. They were just his beliefs. The direction he gave me didn't work out as planned. *Find a man to marry who will take care of you.* His voice echoes in my head, but I don't want to hear it anymore. No one's going to take care of me—except me.

Every emotion I wasn't allowed to feel as a child suddenly explodes. I fall to my knees and curse God. *You played a fine joke on me! Where are you and why don't you ever hear anything I say? I need a car so that I can get a better job. I can't have one without the other. Why do I even bother talking to you? You haven't heard me in over twenty years!*

"Go to hell, God! Go to hell!"

While drifting off to sleep, I have a realization: I reacted reflexively. Had I given the situation some thought, I would have responded differently. I realize how easy it is to react the way you were taught, to carry on something that you never intended. Starting now, I'm trashing that part of my legacy. I promise myself to count to ten before I take action.

****

The phone rings and stirs me awake. It's my brother-in-law.

"Cathy," he says, "I ran into some guy who's giving away an old car. He told me to ask around to see who might need one. You want it?"

"You're kidding me?"

"It's not a joke, Cathy. He's just giving his car away. You want it?"

"I'll take it."

The hairs on the back of my neck stand on end. *Is God really listening, or is this just coincidental?*

The car is old but it'll get me around long enough to save the money I need for repairs. I thank my Good Samaritan and he laughs.

"No big deal. It's just an old piece-of-shit."

The "old piece-of-shit" changes my life. It enables me to take a baby step in a new direction. Within days of receiving it, I get a job as a bartender. In short order, I buy Leah a decent pair of shoes and I splurge on some books and a *Reader's Digest* magazine for myself.

Now I'm equipped to begin my secret mission: fix me!

I figure if I start reading, I'll cure my stupidity. Over time I keep all the promises I made to myself. I never mistreat my daughter again. It's the first link in the chain that I crack. The second link fractures when I realize I was never stupid to begin with. Reading offers me insight into the inspirations of other people. Previously, my thoughts were saturated with Dad's beliefs, but now I can measure up and compare my understanding of things with some phenomenal minds: Norman Vincent Peale and other inspiring authors, including Dr. Seuss. Their writings gift me with a whole new perspective *and* a new vocabulary. I even learn that *shit* and *goddamn* aren't common nouns or adjectives. Well, in New Jersey they are, but hardly anywhere else. Now I can rhyme *shit* with *fit* and confidently refuse to "eat it in a box." The more I read, the more I see how little I know, how much I have to learn. I'm a broken toy, inside and out, beaten down, stunted. I have so much catching up to do.

Mere words had me believing things about myself that aren't true. *Why didn't I understand the power words can wield?* Rooted in ignorance, greed and injustice, words can break hearts and create wars but they can also move mountains when inspired by truth and light.

The Prayer of Serenity now hangs on my wall to remind me that I can't change the past, I can't change anyone else, but I can change me. I accept Dad and all his ways but because he is the way he is, I'm even more concerned for my younger siblings and Mommy. I can't change their circumstances, but I can support them.

****

Dad has had his share of bad years, but his journey throughout 1977 "has potholes at every goddamned turn."

Grandpa Low dies suddenly of a pulmonary embolism, yet Dad swears he died of a broken heart because he missed Grandma so much. I attend the wake expecting to see a somber swarm of Lows but with all the chatting and moving about, it feels more like a cocktail party. As I kneel down beside Grandpa my gut tells me he isn't in that stiff body. I just know he's somewhere else—probably floating around in heaven with his pigeons.

Hey Grandpa, have one of your birds send me a message. If a pigeon poops on my head, even if I don't like "da prrresent," at least I'll know you're thinking of me.

Grandpa's funeral is the end of an unsettling chapter in Dad's life, and to close it for good, he says, "When people die, they're dead and gone and that's the end of them."

Mommy argues that they live on through the next generation. I think she's right. The doctrines that shaped us in early childhood survive into our adult lives, which ultimately mold the foundations of our offspring.

We rarely challenge principles that are carved into our young minds, perhaps because we're taught not to question authority, and possibly because we were just too young to even remember when or how we embraced our ideals.

Beliefs are the most powerful forces on earth. Yet, true or false, right or wrong, as they are inadvertently handed down from one generation to another, history often repeats itself—both the good and the bad.

The Baron's childhood was destroyed because of the beliefs of madmen, yet he carries that destruction forward on the wings of his anger because *he* believes that letting it go will excuse the atrocity. So even as an old man, the Baron remains their prisoner. And if Grandpa Low, who so deeply loved Russia yet hated its government, could've peeled away his anger, perhaps he would've shaken the dust off his shoes and bought some new ones for *his* children.

****

Dad's bar is history, but he still tips the bottle, and there's no rhyme or reason to his patterns. After going weeks without a drink, he switches gears and ends up shit-faced several times a week. Mommy still desperately tries to hide his behavior from the children. When Dad's in a stupor, the kids often end up at my place for sleepovers. Her efforts to protect her children were more successful with most of her older kids. But the five younger ones have already experienced more than their fair share of abuse, so much so, to protect themselves from further heartache, much the way I did, they often abandon their souls. My heart breaks for them, but isn't that what hearts are for? It seems kind of senseless to have a heart at all, if it can't even break for another when it ought to.

As broken as I am, I also feel privileged to be there for my sisters and brothers, to lift them up and to let them know they're loved.

Curiously, I recognize that in many ways, my role as family caregiver, although beyond the scope of what parents should expect from a child, has often saved me. My love and concern for my siblings has kept me strong.

This Thing Called Life

Without the help of a contractor, Mommy, Dad, and the kids gut the charred remains of the summerhouse, and little by little, they rebuild it. Dad's on-the-side schemes have dried up and their year-round home is up for sale. Dad's looking for a regular job and in the meantime they're living off Mommy's cash stash.

Except for the traveling Dad wanted to do, he achieved all of his dreams, including the first one on his list—make a million dollars. Over the past ten years he says he actually made almost two million. But he spent the money as if it really did grow on trees, he gave it away, lost it on bad deals, and pissed it away in the bars.

The five-bedroom bi-level in Sayreville sells for about $55,000 in 1978. After living there for almost ten years, our family leaves behind a place in time that holds a multitude of wonderful memories and sorrows. As for Bugsy, moving into the summerhouse adds to his pile of regrets. He sees it as taking a hundred leaps backward.

Dad's helping Mommy set up their summerhouse with newly purchased metal-framed, triple bunk beds for Joanne, Hanna and Louise. Joanne says it's old prison furniture, and the mattresses came from an old motel. The triple bunks are put into the smallest bedroom. It doesn't have a closet, but an old metal rack from the dry cleaners will do. Joseph and Andrei, however, are given the largest bedroom and new beds.

The small house has one bathroom for all seven of them. It's not exactly a comfortable year-round residence. The plug-in electric heaters Dad installed are woefully inefficient. To supplement his make-shift heating system, he buys a kerosene heater that leaves the air dry and dirty. In the freeze-your-butt-off winter chill, we exhale steam—inside the house. But it will have to do for now, because Dad's too preoccupied fighting with *his* siblings over Grandpa's will. In the meantime, my siblings awaken in the morning with black nasal mucous.

Because of Grandpa's will and all the controversy it's created, Dad says he's *never* going to write one of his own. He reminds me that when he and Mommy die, the boys are to split the two acres of property and everything else is to be divided equally among all of his children. There's one exception: if any of Dad's children predecease him and Mommy, their surviving children are to inherit their parent's equal share. Simple! His *word* is his will.

Dad gets a job in a chemical plant in Hoboken. He's fifty, but in order to get hired, he instantly grows ten years younger. He has a ninety-mile drive each way, so he usually doesn't come home during the week. He finds various places to stay, and sometimes it's my apartment. Often, he doesn't head home until Friday nights.

Mommy's smile doesn't hide her depression. She still cooks and does the laundry, but she has great difficulty dealing with her growing children, and with Dad's unpredictable emotions and drunken tirades. The abuse and neglect flaunts its ugly head in the behavior of their five youngest children—and in ways my parents never saw with their first four. Joseph, one of the favorites, can do no wrong in Dad's eyes and most of the others can hardly do anything right. Both extremes work to the detriment of *all* the children. Dad tells them all who and what they are. They believe him and act accordingly, either superior or inferior. There's no balance, no common sense, no justice.

****

It's a Friday night and I drive down to Manahawkin to find Mommy lying on the couch watching television. She can't sleep. Between worrying about Dad's whereabouts, *and* the hot flashes she gets because of her change of life, she awakens often. While we're talking, Dad barrels into the house, shit-faced, looking for an argument. Mommy jumps up and runs into the kitchen to get the grizzly bear a picnic basket while he's growling, calling her names, making false accusations. He grabs a coffee cup from the table and flings it at her. She ducks, it hits the wall and shatters. Mommy leans onto the counter with her back toward Dad and me. She doesn't say a word.

Enough is enough!

"Daddy," I scream. "Dad, Dad!"

He turns toward me as he sways back and forth breathing and snorting. The odor of secondhand scotch surrounds him like chintzy cologne. The grizzly bear's false teeth come loose as he tries to answer me. He pushes them back into place.

"What the hell are you yelling about?"

"I have something important to ask you, Daddy. I need your help," I lie.

"Important?" His eyes light up because he likes it when people come to him with *important* questions.

"Yeah, it's really important and only you can help me. But it's private."

His demeanor instantly changes and he follows me to his bedroom. As he stands between his bed and me, I push him full force. What I really want to do is beat the living shit out of him. I want to grab his belt and whip him as if *he's* a horse pulling a wagon. I could've cracked him over the head a million times in his sleep, but I really don't want to hurt him. What I want *more than anything* is for him to stop hurting everyone else! He falls onto the bed and barely bounces because he's a solid mass of over three hundred pounds. His glasses fall off. I hand them back to him as I stick my pointer inches from his face.

"I'm sick of your drunkenness, your nastiness, your injustice, and your physical abuse. It's all got to stop! You can't keep doing this to Mommy and the kids. How much do you think they can take?"

He doesn't answer me. He lies there peering at me with his false teeth hanging out of his mouth. I stand here waiting for an answer, but his eyes slam shut and he snores.

Mommy is teary-eyed, sitting motionless on the couch. It's painful to look at her. I can't help but remember what she used to be, who she used to be. The beautiful vessel is now a shipwreck. I want to do something to make it better, but I feel powerless. I get her a napkin to dry her eyes and I hug her. She leans forward and bursts into tears.

"Mommy, you've got to put your foot down with him."

"It won't matter," she whispers. "Nothing I say matters with him."

The thought crosses my mind to tell her to leave him, but I stop myself. I already know her answer. I quietly sit on the floor with my arm resting on her thigh until sleep takes her away.

In the morning Mommy has the coffee perking while she dutifully fries up eggs for everyone. As they dip their toast into the yolk, they all chime *"Motzi!"* And Dad adds, *"Homa, homa, homa."*

Both Mom and Dad pretend nothing happened the night before. Not a word is uttered about it, but I see its effects in Mommy's lackluster pearls.

It's all so tragic. But the kids smooth it over with a little ditty they call *Shut-the-hell-up.* That is the song's hook *and* title. They mimic Dad as they sing mostly profanities, laughing themselves to tears. Sounds of laughter spawned from adversity cannot be topped.

After breakfast Dad sits in his easy chair writing in a red spiral binder. Later, when he hands me the binder, I find a story he wrote for Leah, his little Mooky. It's called "The Village That Santa Couldn't Find."

"Leah," I tell her, "Grandpa wrote a story for you."

"Grandpa made me a story? Grandpa," Leah calls out, "you're a story maker?"

"Yup," Dad says, "I'm a story maker and I made one just for you, Mooky. Come here and I'll read it to you."

Leah climbs onto Dad's lap. As he reads, I hear a tale of hope and I see a gesture of love—another flicker of light that reminds me of how much I love Dad.

When it's time to go home, my heart breaks into a million pieces. I want to stay, to do something more for Mommy, for my siblings, but I can't.

****

Now that I'm on my own, I'm raising Leah differently than I was raised. I don't curse her, or label her, and I don't compare her to other people. I'm learning as I go because there really isn't any rulebook when it comes to raising children, but I do know the importance of balance and justice.

At the same time, I'm re-raising myself—it's the only way for me to abandon the destructive part of my father's legacy. It's not easy. I can't silence Dad's voice, the one that said so many hurtful things, the one that still echoes in my head.

As I begin to acknowledge that legacy of abuse, I'm more aware of what I should avoid: relationships with the kinds of men who expect more from me than they're willing to give; the kind who belittle me and make promises they have no intentions of keeping. If I ever get married again, I don't want that man to be another version of my father.

I'm way behind most people my age. I know I'm lost, broken and stunted, but I'm committed to getting it right—this thing called life.

As for my family, I'm sticking by them. They're my blood. I love them deeply. I hate many of the things Dad does, and maybe I should hate him too, but I don't. I love him, even after everything he's done to Mommy, my siblings, and me. I don't know why, I just do.

And as for Mommy, I *love* her madly. The fabric of her spirit is like no other, but it needs mending. I hate what she's become: a whitewashed wife and mother who once promised "to obey" and did so even amid the ever-changing, self-serving rules Dad designed for himself.

Somewhere over Dad's bottle of scotch Mommy lost part of herself. She never got to enjoy the high, but she certainly ended up with the hangover.

PART FIVE: SIDES TAKEN

Making Lemonade

Twenty-some years fly by faster than leaves on a windy day. By the early 1990s all of my siblings are adults and most of them have children of their own.

The events of my life—the best ones and the worst ones—are written on my heart like etchings on a tombstone. The Baron would say that having a memory is a curse, but I see it as a blessing. Old memories mingle with newer ones and teach you things you can't learn from a book.

Except for a few occasional beers, Dad gives up drinking. While his drunken tirades have ended, his demeanor is still the same. He is what he is, he insists, and if anyone doesn't like it, they can shit in his hat.

Hanna's son, at three years old, sort of takes his grandfather up on that. He sprinkles sugar in Dad's fishing cap, the one that says, "Fish fear me—Chicks dig me." Dad flips it on, and a moment of silence is followed by an explosion.

"What the hell is on my goddamned head and neck? It's sticky! Jeeeeeeeeesus Christ!"

Mommy jumps up to see what's on Dad's head. The sugar crystals sticking to his sweaty head and neck send her into a laughing fit.

"What's so goddamned funny?" he snaps.

His rant is tiring, but Mommy cleans up his head and his hat because he's in a hurry to get down to the surf to do some fishing. He flips his cap back on and complains that it's wet.

"Good," Mommy says, "it'll keep your head cool."

She still can't figure him out. If he keeps this up, he'll drop dead of a heart attack.

Dad's had many close calls with death and it's probably his bad health more than anything that helps him curb his drinking. Sometime in the 1980s, he suffered from heart failure. He was told he didn't have long for this world, but as with all his other close calls, he defies death. He has an enlarged heart and an aneurysm behind his stomach—one he's told is growing and can burst at any moment.

My relationship with him is better than when I was a child. I've worked hard at it, and we've had some tender moments, but I'm still careful about what I say because I'm in tune to the ticking of his internal bomb. Usually, he talks and I listen. If there's anything about me that makes him proud, he keeps it to himself.

But one evening he accidentally slips up.

I've got this crazy habit of starting sing-a-longs at every family affair. It begins with me standing on a chair with a candle or a lighter in hand belting out "God Bless America." Before I finish the first note, almost everyone in the room is singing as if their lives depend on it. "Over There" follows, then "Yankee Doodle Dandy," and many other old favorites. Before long I'm taking song requests, which is ironic because my voice still sucks.

At one wedding my cousin, Joey, nudges me and whispers, "Hey Cathy, do the *Marine Hymn,* Cathy. Can ya do it, Kahtee Schmahgatee?"

"This one's for you, Joey." I salute the U.S. Marine for taking a bullet in his gut while on the frontline during the Vietnam war, for his bravery, and for his never-ending kindness. Together Joey and I belt out the words, and everyone present salutes him as they join in.

Even the waitresses who are eager to go home join in. We all do, because every minute that we sing together is a moment untainted by worry—we're one, we're happy.

But during another affair, I don't feel like singing. That's when Dad slips up. He's drunk, but only one-sheet-to-the-wind. He walks over to my table, puts his arm around me and looks me in the eye with a hopeful gleam as he hands me a lighter. The silent language that passes between us tells me this is a precious moment not to be squandered—they're too few and far between. I take Dad's cue and as I hop on a chair, Dad scoots in beside me with another lighter in hand. He sings the first note with me and stays until the last note of the last song. He's proud of me for my sing-a-longs. Imagine that.

****

Life comes full circle in the 1990s. The Baron joins Grandpa six feet under and Yaya quietly passes away at the age of ninety-five. I don't have grandparents anymore, but my children do. Mom and Dad are the new Grandpa and Grandma Low. Dad doesn't do killees or pigeons; he does bluefish and stories—real ones and fishy ones. Mommy doesn't do sugar bread; she does pierogi and silliness, even when she isn't feeling her best. Her blood pressure is out of control, her arteries are clogged, she has trouble walking, and she's had several mini strokes. Yet in between Dad's tirades I see flashes of her natural exuberance.

She and Dad moved out of their summerhouse long ago and live in Howell near most of my siblings and me. Shortly after the move Mommy took a job in a bank and began saving hefty amounts of her pay in her company retirement plan. Dad retired because of his heart condition, so his Social Security benefits supplement Mommy's income.

Miraculously, all nine of us Low kids made it into adulthood together. In addition to the holidays, we gather together in my backyard nearly every weekend in the summer. Save Andrei, all my other siblings are married with children of their own. I remarried in 1980 and I now have three daughters. Even if only half the family shows up it's still a party. The deck that meets the above-ground pool in my backyard is a perfect setting. Burgers sizzle over the coals, oldies blare from the stereo, and grown-ups reminisce around the table under my big blue umbrella.

Our family screw-ups, especially Dad's, induce uncontrollable laughter. Say a word, any word, and most likely we'll have a song or a story for it. For instance, *carrot*. Dad almost dies when he gets a carrot stuck in his lung, but he coughs it up on the operating table and it goes flying at the surgeon just before he makes his cut.

"The goddamned doctor was so pissed off because he couldn't get paid for an operation he didn't perform," Dad snorts with a chuckle.

Mommy remembers going into Andrei's walk-in closet and finding a fluorescent lamp shining down on a multitude of leafy plants. She can't figure out why he's growing plants in his closet. When she calls Dad in to see the plants, he kicks them over, then launches into a tirade. There's enough marijuana in Andrei's closet to fly a hundred hippies to the moon.

We each have our own recipe for when things go wrong. We've learned how to make lemonade, and we laugh because Mommy taught us to, because that's the best medicine of all.

We don't reminisce about the horrible ghosts of our past. We don't talk about the broken coffee cups or the broken hearts because if you cry over every little thing, you might as well lay down and die. Where there's life, there's adversity, so whatever doesn't make us laugh gets buried.

But there is something we do not yet know. The absence of accountability ensured the survival of repetitive destructive behavior, so everything that we thought was dead and buried, is alive and about to come back and haunt us.

****

Andrei, my youngest sibling, now twenty-eight, has been reaching out for help. He needs to talk with someone about the remarkable experiences he's been having. Joanne and I are all ears.

"I've been abducted by UFOs," Andrei says.

He suddenly looks up, suspiciously eyeing the airplane flying overhead.

"They're watching every move I make. They're stealing my thoughts, my inventions. They're getting rich off of me."

"Who?" we ask.

"The FBI, the government, people on television. They steal my ideas. I invented EZ-Pass and they stole that. Evil people are out to get me."

My sister and I convince him to come along with us to the hospital. Andrei repeats his story to a doctor and is given some pills, a prescription, then he's released.

Dad hollers and curses at Andrei, and Mommy tries to reason with him. Neither approach works, so they do as they've always done —they call and ask *me* to do something.

Andrei rents a room in a house two blocks away from mine. He's almost six feet tall and two-hundred-forty pounds of solid muscle. He has large, strong hands and his feet are size fourteen. He has a full head of thick, curly red hair that hasn't been cut in months and a ten o'clock shadow. It's a hot summer day, but he's wearing wrinkled jeans, a red plaid flannel shirt and work boots. Colored rags are tied to his head, the same kinds of rags Grandpa used to tie at the top of his pigeon pole, except that Andrei's rags are specifically designed to keep evil away. As I peer out my kitchen window, I see him approaching my house. *And so do my neighbors!* Andrei's on his way here to cleanse my home of evil spirits. His voice is deep and strong like Dad's—and my neighbors have big ears.

"I've been abducted again and this time they've planted a chip under my skin," Andrei proclaims as he stomps up my driveway.

"Who?"

"Aliens," he says.

"What do they look like?" I ask, but I shouldn't have because my question angers him.

He leaves my house, and before the day ends, Andrei drives over to Earle Ammunition Base and attempts to break in with a screw driver. He's picked up and sent to the hospital, where they give him meds and release him.

Each time he's released, he stops taking his meds and the pattern repeats itself.

Today I find Andrei thrusting his fists into the air. He thinks he's beating up the devil. His beliefs fuel intense anger and he blames his lot in life on evil people.

"Who's evil?" I ask.

"Evil people can disguise themselves as anyone, even as a baby," he roars.

"Let me help you, Andrei," I say. "Who can I call to help you fight this evil?"

"You better not call the hospital," he shouts. "If you send me to the hospital or make me take medicine, I'll bring you down."

****

I wait alone on a dark street corner, one block from Andrei's house. He's going to be picked up and taken to the hospital, and I want to be sure he's okay. The sun begins to rise when the police finally arrive, and then an ambulance. They remove Andrei from the house on a stretcher, strapped down at his ankles, arms, and waist. He's crying out in desperation as they lift him into the back of the ambulance.

"I'd rather die than live like this! Let me go!"

Andrei is among the kindest of the Low children. If you were in need of help, you never had to ask him twice. He would surely give you his umbrella on a rainy day. It kills me to see him going through this. His illness has stolen him away. It just isn't fair.

Hours later Andrei calls me from the hospital and says he's watching the Puerto Rican Day parade on television, and they're celebrating his capture.

"It's your goddamned fault I'm here," he tells me.

"It's not my fault, Andrei."

"Who put me here?" he demands to know.

He has so much anger. It's best he doesn't know who made the call.

"I don't know who put you there, Andrei."

As usual, he calls our brother and sisters and blames each of them for his capture. Most of us react to Andrei's accusations by ignoring them or joking about them. How can you not when he imagines that every Puerto Rican in New York City is doing the salsa in honor of his capture?

Sis, however, becomes enraged. She tells me it's *my* fault that Andrei accuses her of putting him there. She knows better, but I'm compelled to remind her that Andrei accuses everyone in the family, not just *her.* My explanation is rejected because it doesn't satisfy her voracious emotional appetite. Her habit of running to Dad to complain about me never lost its velocity. In response, Dad shows up on my doorstep to defend her—again and again.

The pecking order Dad created many years ago remains completely intact every time we gather as a family or interact individually. I still fear Dad, but my fear of Sis has intensified. I recognize that her discontent over anything she might imagine is the spark that ignites Dad's fury. To keep from angering her, I have to agree with her, do whatever she asks of me, and regard her and her unpredictable emotions with the utmost importance while remaining insignificant.

That's a lot to ask of a nobody.

Because all of us Lows have remained in our order of predetermined importance, there were never any insurmountable squabbles. Until now. Being regarded as a tool finally wears me down. I realize that as long as Dad and his favorite children are getting what they want, and the rest of us stay in our places, without an opinion, without any rights, our family remains intact. Dad's definition of *for the good of the family* never included *all* of us—just himself and his favorite children. Even when they tell outlandish stories, he believes them without question, and defends them unconditionally.

In an attempt to get along with Sis, I suggest we have a talk about Dad's frequent attacks on me.

"It's not my fault that Daddy treats you like shit," Sis says.

"You treat me the same way. It's got to stop. Otherwise we can't have a relationship. To move on, I'll let it all go, Sis. I'll chalk it up to bad childhood habits."

"That's *all Daddy's fault,*" Sis says. "I can't help it that he always loved *me* the best."

"Enough, Sis! We're not kids anymore. You're almost fifty years old and you're still using his partiality to your advantage."

Afterward, Sis goes running to Dad—again.

In turn, he attacks *me* because he thinks I'm the one who said it's *"all Daddy's fault"* that we don't get along.

The Civil War

When Mommy calls and asks me to come over and do some cleaning, I quickly grab my broom and fly there.

In the early years the order of my parents' home was comparable to Yaya's, but now it's more like Grandma Low's. I step into the smoke-tinted living room onto the brown matted-down carpet. Dad is perched in his worn, musty easy chair. No one wants to sit there —it's that bad. Once in a while people forget and plop themselves down, but the puff of air from his cushion sends them flying to their feet as a few expletives shoot across their lips. Dad didn't marry his first love, Harriet Lipschitz, but he sure managed to turn Mom into Armenouhe Sniffschitz.

Above the chair are photographs—Dad in his Army uniform, my parents' wedding picture, and all nine of us kids in our high school graduation caps. My photo is twenty-nine years old.

Dad's side table is littered with candy wrappers, an ashtray overflowing with cigarette butts and empty glasses. He's busy hollering about women again.

"You have it easy today, all you women," he snaps. "Today a machine washes and dries your dishes *and* your clothes, the freezer defrosts itself, microwave ovens cook in two minutes what used to take hours, and you've got disposable diapers, too! Women today don't even know how to straighten out their goddamned bratty kids. A good old-fashioned lickin' is what these kids need. Women ruined the world! If you don't believe me, look around!"

He's quiet for a moment.

"Hi, Daddy."

"What the hell do you want?"

He sees that I have my vacuum with me. He won't fix Mommy's vacuum.

"Mommy asked me to come over and do some cleaning."

He stares me down for a long moment.

Mommy serves him lunch, running back and forth from the living room to the kitchen as Dad continues his tirade. I want to tell him to give Mommy a break, but as always, she puts her finger up to her lips.

"Shhh," she says. "Don't say anything to him, it'll only cause trouble."

I take a sip from my big old cup of shut-the-hell-up and get to work cleaning upstairs, downstairs, and all around Bugsy's chamber. When I'm done with the chores, I make tea for my parents and me, and just as we're relaxing, the phone rings.

"Hello," Mommy says. That's all she says. She can't get in another word.

Sis is complaining about me. She's loud and I can hear her crying. Mommy's expression reeks of pain as she listens before passing the phone to Dad, who gets a repeat performance.

"Don't you worry," he says with conviction, "I'll take care of this!"

He hangs up and turns to me.

"What the hell is the matter with you? Who the hell do you think you are going around to all of Sis's friends and saying such goddamned awful things about her?"

"That's not true, Daddy. I don't talk to her friends. I'm afraid to —and what you're accusing me of right now is a perfect example as to *why* I keep my distance."

I'm so sick of Dad acting like Sis's soldier. I feel no different from when I was a teenager. Only Dad can't hit me anymore. Not that it matters because his words pack a more powerful punch. Unlike his aim with the belt, his tongue always hits the target—my heart.

Dad's neck veins are popping, he's breathing like a dragon, and his hands are shaking. Mommy's head is drooped in defeat. As upset as I am, I'm more worried about the pair of them having a heart attack after I leave. Mommy's seventy-three, Dad's seventy-two. They're both ill. *They shouldn't have to live out their last years like this. It's cruel.*

I grab my vacuum and head toward the door. As I open it I say, "Everything you just heard is a bunch of bologna, Daddy."

"Just get the *fuck* out of my house and don't come back!" he spits.

This is the first time I've ever known him to throw anyone out of his house. And although I'm sure he's said it before, it's the first time I've ever heard *fuck* cross his lips. You remember firsts—your first kiss, your first beating. You remember them because they take your breath away.

The next day Mommy shows up at my house wanting to know why I'm so mean to Sis, why I'm so cruel.

"You were never like this, Cathy. What happened to you? You used to be such a *good* person. You were *never* like this!"

I'm stunned. Mommy is suddenly convinced that I'm not who I am. I feel violated, cheated, defamed. I don't want to argue with her. She shouldn't be using her energy to spew Sis's anger. Ten years earlier I would've just taken it on the chin, apologized and pretended the situation never happened. I can't anymore. If I do, I'll completely die inside. Nothing will be left of me but a tattered shell, and I'll be a casualty just like Mommy.

On behalf of all that Mommy once was, I refuse to keep pretending. I refuse to be her failure. All she ever wanted for her children was love, peace, and happiness. She took nothing and gave everything. Of all people, she deserves the outcome she strived for. That's what I'm trying to give her—even if she can't see it.

"You're right, Mommy. I was never like this."

She freezes bug-eyed, staring at me curiously.

"Think about what I was like," I plead. "Think about what everyone else *was* and *is* like. Who was I yesterday? Last week? Ten years ago? You're right, I was *never* like this."

She doesn't answer me. She quietly turns and I watch her shuffle away. Halfway to her car she stops to catch her breath. When she reaches it, she leans on the trunk to rest. It's too much for me to see her this way. Mommy doesn't have long for this world and the little time she has left is being sabotaged with lies.

The following day Dad calls. He's enraged over what Sis tells him about me.

"You're not *my* daughter!" he informs me. "You're no longer part of my family and anyone who sides with you is no longer part of my family, either!"

Not everyone sees it Dad's way. His proclamation forces every family member into choosing a side, instantly splitting us in half like the North and South.

In an attempt to pressure me into jumping back into the confines of their expectations of me, Dad and his southern regime quickly load their tongues with toxic words, aim, and fire.

I go down for the count. Depressed. Fetal. And as I lie in a pool of blood, my brother Joseph takes a cheap shot at me.

"It's your fault the family is broken up, Cathy. You're nothing but dirt, and when thrown into water, you fall to the bottom!"

His words cut to my core. My family has always meant *everything* to me, but now I wonder why. All that I have in this world is *Who* I am, but I'm not even allowed to be a *Who. I wish I was never born. I want to die.* For days *I am* dead on the inside—yet again.

I've worked so hard at fixing myself, but it wasn't enough. It never is. I take another deep look into my soul and in my silence and stillness, I see that I never really fixed myself at all. I never thought enough of myself to *truly* stand up and walk away from the abuse—to keep from being broken in half over and again.

I don't want to give up my family, yet when I peer down the road, into a future with more of the same, all I can see is *me*, surrounded by "lions and tigers and bears." The part of me that was born wanting to live, and love, and sing, and dance in a pair of ruby heels—that part rises up and shrieks, *Get off the carousel, you stupid ass!*

I have danced around the anger in my family as if it were a minefield. Going forward, I refuse to accept emotional rage as par for the course. That's as bad as embracing it. Neither Dad nor his southern regime have an ounce of regard for me. In coming face-to-face with

314

this reality, I come head-to-head with a past that was never buried, and I'm confronted with the fact that I'm standing in the same place I stood at age ten, and fifteen, and twenty, and thirty.

I've been lying to myself on the frayed strands of hope that someday all those I have loved would love me in return.

Rather than concede, I accept my pink slip.

That enrages the southern regime even more.

"You changed," they scorn, as if *change* is a disease. "You ruined everything, Cathy, and because of you, our family will never be the same again!"

I'll Miss You Most of All

Some old ladies get their hair done once a week and wear brightly colored polyester clothes. Not Mommy. She keeps her wavy salt and pepper locks short and combed back. Her black shoes and black matching slacks are ten years old, but her newest wardrobe addition is a gray sweatshirt with a big orange triangle on the back that says "Caution—Slow Moving Vehicle."

Her blood pressure has taken its toll, so she's back and forth to the doctor, and in and out of the emergency room. She takes so many pills she can't keep track of them. She's trapped in her body and worried about our family, especially Andrei.

Dad tells her she better not have a stroke and end up in a wheelchair. He says he's not taking care of an invalid. He flips on his cap, picks up his keys and leaves. When the door slams behind him, Mommy sings "Jimmy Crack Corn" because her master's gone away.

She smothers her pain with a song the same way you protect a gash with a bandage. Eventually the gash heals, but there's always a scar. After all these years I realize that Dad expects Mommy to be strong enough to take care of his needs and submissive enough "to obey" his commands. In accommodating him she's had to shield her spirit—dimming the light that sustained us all. In spite of the scars, now at her weakest moment, her humor rises above Dad's insensitivity, making her ten feet taller in my eyes. Dad appears to be strong, but he is brittle. Without Mommy's flexibility he might've cracked years ago. No matter how grim the circumstance, her generous spirit oozes from her center, giving Dad a soft, forgiving place for his infinite reckless landings.

She's the glue that kept us together, the *Arms* who made us strong, and some of us embrace her manner while others cuddle up to Dad's.

****

With Dad out of the house today, Mommy wants to talk about her cash stash. She leads me into her bedroom and we sit on her lumpy mattress. Because of Dad's unrelenting rage, she's afraid of what he'll do with their assets after she passes away. Dad still refuses to have wills drawn up, so Mommy will likely pass on without one.

She gives me an accounting of their assets. After estimating the value of their estate, and considering the hits they took, it's substantial enough to provide a small income to supplement their social security benefits. Had it not been for Mommy, she and Dad could've ended up with nothing. The wishes Dad repeated throughout his life still stand— the two acres of property in South Jersey go to the boys, and all nine kids are to share equally in everything else regardless of whether each of us has one child or ten. Dad's last wishes never deviated, but given the current climate, Mommy's worried that in a fit of rage he might pass everything onto his favorites.

She acknowledges that only a few of her children received the lion's share of what she and Dad handed out over the years. She recalls how often they had to help Dad's favorite kids with overdue taxes, court, and lawyers. She makes a gesture of love, hoping to equalize the imbalance for those who were left out. I'm to hold her stash until Dad dies, then split it with the underdogs. It's a little over ten thousand dollars—a pittance compared to their combined total assets, but it's the only thing Mommy controls.

"I want you to take the money," she says.

"No, Mommy, I'm not taking it now. You're not dead. You're still here."

Our friendly quarrel ends when she shows me her new hiding place. A huge leather bag sits in her closet. She directs me to reach into the pockets and slide my hand all the way down. I do, but I can't find the money.

"It's a good hiding place, isn't it?" she says.

As it turns out, there are secret pockets beneath the actual pockets.

My fingers find their way to hundred dollar bills rolled so tightly, I wouldn't have guessed there are thousands of dollars here. After counting it, I slip it back into hiding.

"Where'd you get this bag, Ma—from a drug dealer?"

Mommy laughs and begs me not to forget about the money. I promise to honor her wishes. But I don't like being the only one who knows about this. *What if I drop dead?*

I let my gut decide who to tell. And without a thought, I share my secret with Jane.

The next day Mommy tells me she's not feeling well. I drive over to the house to find her looking extremely pale. Dad is in his easy chair shouting at the television.

"Hello Daddy," I say, but it falls on deaf ears. I'm no longer his daughter.

I drive Mommy to the hospital, where she learns her blood pressure is alarmingly high. Among the parade of doctors to appear at Mommy's bedside is a young, intense-looking proctologist who tells me to step outside of the curtain because he needs to do a rectal exam. Before I slip out, I cup my hand over Mommy's ear and whisper, "Don't make cocky on the doctor's finger."

I leave her giggling on the bed.

When I return, the doctor is making notes on his chart. Mommy nudges me and points to his hand. As I spot a scar on the tip of his finger, Mommy clears her throat.

"I see this isn't the first time you stuck your finger where it doesn't belong," she says.

The doctor looks at his finger blankly and continues writing.

The bed vibrates as Mommy laughs.

"So how do I look at the other end, Harvey?"

"You called me by my first name. You can't do that! I'm a doctor! That's personal!"

"Listen, Harvey," Mommy says, "you're the one who got intimate with me first."

Harvey jumps up, swings the curtain open and zips past the nurses' station, whining to the nurses that the lady in number three called him by his first name.

Mommy and I laugh ourselves to tears.

While Mommy's in the hospital, Sis, who also lives in the vicinity of our parents' home, complains that she was the *last* to find out about Mommy being there. She tells me it's all my fault that she didn't know. The next time Mommy goes into the hospital, Sis insists that I call *her* first.

Mommy's blood pressure is stabilized and she returns home weak and fatigued. There isn't much anyone can do for her. All I can do is give her my time and tell her some dirty jokes. During my daily visits with Mommy, the phone rings, and it's always Sis. She doesn't ask about Mommy's health because she's busy complaining about me. Dad grabs the phone from Mommy for Sis's recap, and when he hangs up, he curses me and tells me who and what I am. The scenario repeats itself everyday.

I ignore it. I have no choice, because someday soon I'll *never* see my mother again.

****

For my forty-seventh birthday my children give me a plane ticket to Florida for a visit with Jane. While I'm gone, Mommy's sister, Louise, comes to take care of her and do her chores. They reminisce about their days in the orphanage, they bicker and call each other silly names. They laugh when Dad acts like Archie Bunker, and when he leaves the house to go fishing, they knock over his chair, pick up the coins that fall out and use them to play nickel-dime poker. They tease each other like they did as kids, and momentarily they're young again.

I return from my trip and resume my daily visits. Since Dad's out fishing today, Mommy and I are free to talk without any interruptions from Bugsy.

"What happened between you and your sister?" Mommy asks with a longing.

I look at her curiously. She already knows the answer.

"She treats me terribly, then she cries to Dad as if *I* did something to her. And she's convincing. You should know, Ma!"

"I know," Mommy admits. "She likes to be the best, but maybe it's because she's the oldest."

"That's an excuse, Ma. I know you're trying to keep the peace, but it isn't working."

"What can I do?" she asks.

"I'm not asking you to *do* anything. But excuses are part of the problem. She's always treated me badly."

"Can't you just ignore it?"

"I've let it go all my life. That never stopped it, did it, Mommy?"

"No, but can't you forgive her?"

"Who says I didn't? I forgive her! I've been forgiving her all of my life, yet she has never apologized or taken responsibility for anything, which is a pretty good indication of what's to come. So what choice do I have other than staying away from her?"

"I don't know. Why don't you try to work things out with her?"

"You know I've tried, but things got worse instead of better. It's been a one-way street all my life, Ma. Why am I less than her? Tell me why I'm less!"

"You aren't less," Mommy says as she drops her head. "I know what that feels like. I can easily name a few people who've treated me like crap."

"Besides Dad, who?"

"When I was a kid," Mommy recalls, "my aunt made me all kinds of promises that she never kept. Yet I looked up to her. I wanted to become a corsetiere."

"You did?"

"Yup. And even though I should've known better, I believed her when she promised to teach me. I spent a nickel for the bus ride to her house every day—that was a lot of money back then! Every day she'd give me the broom, the mop and a *totslot*, then order me to clean her house. Every few days I'd ask her when is she going to teach me. 'Soon,' she'd say, and then she'd tell me that I have to work from the ground up. I believed her. But without fail, she'd put me to work scrubbing her house and showroom and after more than two weeks, every nook was spotless."

"Did she at least pay you?"

"Not one red cent, and I hadn't learned a thing about being a corsetiere."

"So what did you say to her?"

"Nothing. I said nothing. But I never went back there again. I didn't call her. I didn't visit her. Through the years the only reason I ended up seeing her again is mostly because of our family gatherings —I wanted to see her sons. I loved my cousins. Other than that, I gave her the same effort she gave me."

"So you understand where I'm coming from?"

Mommy nods her head yes. "But how did it get to be this bad?" she asks.

"I think Dad's favorites emulate him because it works for them. Simple as that. I'm not one of them. I'm one of the 'big mouths' who have to 'shut up and listen,' like you, Ma."

"But when did all this happen?"

"It didn't *just* happen. It's been like this as far back as my memory goes. You tell me, Mommy. You were here long before I was."

Mommy's biting her upper lip. She's not sure she should say what she's thinking.

"Way back when you were just a baby, your father would come home from work and tell *me* what I did all day. I couldn't figure out how he knew."

"Maybe he had ESP."

"EPS! Extra People Spying! He was questioning Sis. She spoke well, so he was able to get information from her. I didn't think too much of it until the day I lent out my car to the neighbor. His son was sick and he needed a car to get him to a doctor. Your father knew what I had done before I even had a chance to tell him. Without considering that I was helping someone in need, he went into a rage and gave me such a hard time about it. If *he* was the one who lent out the car, it would've been okay, but he didn't want me having the same authority."

It all begun before I had a memory. I've been doing the same dance as Mommy for forty-seven years. How could she stand it without going crazy?

"Your father rewarded Sis with treats. Sometimes he brought home a cheap little toy or he'd give her a cookie. Even if there was no treat, the attention Dad gave her was just as good. There was always something in it for her and she looked forward to it so much that after a while he didn't have to ask her anything. The minute he got home she'd run to him with a story."

"You're kidding!"

"Oh no! And if Dad didn't like what she told him, he'd give me hell. They formed a special bond with each other."

"A bond? Come on, Mommy, she was only three. He was messing with a baby's head."

"I don't think he meant to. I think it's because he was insecure."

"At this point does it matter what he *meant* to do? Geez Mommy, he's still doing it. So is she. And a cookie isn't enough anymore. Now she wants the whole damned bakery."

"I really made a mess of things," Mommy says after hours of vomiting bottled-up memories. "I'm sorry. I tried speaking up."

"You're not the one who made this mess! You did your best, Ma!"

"Maybe if I tried harder, things wouldn't be *so* messed up."

"It's not your fault!"

Mommy leans forward to cup her hands over her face, to hide her anguish, to hide her tears.

It's painful knowing the full extent of heartlessness that Mommy endured. And here she sits beating herself up and taking the blame.

When I was a kid I wanted to be just like Mommy. I am.

****

In the middle of the night Mommy thinks she's having a heart attack. She wakes up Dad and he calls an ambulance. At the hospital, Dad gets tired so he drives himself home. In the midst of the family war, he lays down his weapons when he calls me to take his place at the hospital.

By the time I arrive Mommy has had a stroke. Later, when the entire family is present, the doctor recommends that Mommy undergo surgery, which involves implanting a shunt into her brain to drain the excess fluid. When the operation is done, she cannot communicate.

In an attempt to get a reaction from Mommy, her sister, Louise, rubs her feet as she speaks to her in Armenian.

"Armenouhe, Arms, I know you hate it when I touch your feet."

Mommy's eyes open at the sound of her native tongue. When she sees her sister, tears trickle down the sides of her face. Aunt Louise continues speaking Armenian and Mommy hangs onto every word with a longing to escape the broken body that imprisons her.

When the doctor suggests we remove Mommy from the ventilator, we agonize over his recommendation. My siblings and I agree that it's the best decision, but Dad needs more time. They've been married for over fifty-one years. It's clear he cannot bring himself to make the decision.

Dad sits in the corridor staring at the painted concrete wall. He seems to be gazing into the past. I take the seat beside him.

"Daddy, when I was a teenager you took me to a movie. Do you remember what it was?"

He thinks for a moment.

"No."

"You know, it was the one about the dance marathons of the 1930s."

"Oh," Dad says, "with Jane Fonda. Red Buttons was in that, too."

"You remember?"

"Yeah," he says. "They Shoot Horses, Don't They?"

"I remember asking you why they shoot…"

I don't have to finish reminding him. Dad looks at me and as tears flood his eyes, he nods his head.

****

323

Jane is staying at Mommy and Dad's house. She makes coffee and breakfast for Dad, does the laundry, and cleans the house. While she's watching television in the evening, Sis comes over and saunters in and out of Mommy's bedroom. Jane hears her opening drawers and closet doors.

After she leaves, Jane calls me.

"I saw Sis searching through Mommy's stuff. When she realizes I caught her, she says, 'Look what I found! Coupons!' as if that's what she'd been looking for."

"Coupons?"

The absurdity of it sends Jane and me into fits of laughter. We can't even speak. We're cackling the way we did when we were young and Grandpa accused us of killing his got-dem killees.

I want to wait until after Mommy passes to take her stash, but Jane thinks I shouldn't. While everyone's out I drive over to the house. I feel like a thief in the night, yet I know I'm following the orders of a woman who had very little say throughout her married life. Her little cash stash is the one and only thing she feels she has control over.

I quiver the entire drive back home, where Jane is waiting for me. My hands tremble as I show her the cash.

****

Dad reluctantly makes the decision to allow the hospital to pull the plug.

"When we remove the breathing tube, she may continue to breathe on her own for a while," the nurse says.

"How long is a while?" Dad asks.

"No one can say. It could be a minute, an hour or days."

"What time are you going to remove it?" Dad asks.

"We're just waiting for the doctor. We'll let you know when he's ready," she says, and disappears behind huge wooden doors.

We wait in the hallway—Dad, my siblings, Aunt Louise and I. Because of the family war, we separate ourselves with the side of the corridor we choose to lean on.

"I can't go in there when they pull the plug," Dad says.

Then he turns to me and tells me to take care of the funeral arrangements. He knows I'll be careful with his money.

"No!" Sis yells.

She thinks I'll botch up everything and embarrass the family.

It's another one of those delicate moments. Mommy is dying, Dad's a wreck and Sis is angry just because Dad asked me to handle the funeral arrangements. *She* wants to do it!

Once again, I say nothing.

Inevitably, Dad agrees with her, so she settles herself down.

"You can get the church, Cathy," Sis says in a tone that insinuates getting the church is unimportant.

"It's time," the nurse interrupts. "Who wants to come in?"

"I do," I say.

My siblings, Aunt Louise and I follow the nurse into Mommy's room and minutes later Dad appears.

A curtain separates Mommy from us as the breathing tube is removed. The nurse draws the curtain back. We all pile in around Mommy while Dad is frozen up against the wall.

Mommy is still breathing, so I sing to her.

"You Are My Sunshine…"

Before long, we're all singing—off-key the way Mommy used to, and anyone happening by would never guess we're in the midst of a civil war.

We put our hands on Mommy. There's a hand on her head, on her chest, her arms, legs, feet. We say the Lord's Prayer and then Aunt Louise speaks to her in Armenian.

The clock ticks and Mommy breathes. I break the silence with a song, one that Father Farringer sang to the melody of "Danny Boy" way back at Incarnation Camp.

"I Cannot Tell…"

And as we sing of how the angels worship Jesus, a Catholic priest wanders in—drawn by the song. He hopes we don't mind the interruption. We don't. We tell him the priest at the Russian Orthodox Church refused to come and bless Mommy because she was technically not a member. She grew up Episcopalian, but stopped attending church years earlier.

The priest prays and blesses Mommy as if she was a good Catholic. It doesn't matter to me that he's Catholic. I don't care what church he's from. I believe there's only one God and I don't think He gives a hoot where you pray.

"I can't believe Lillian has nine children," the priest says after he blesses Mommy. "You're all so wonderful. She must be an amazing human being to have such a wonderful family. You're all so loving. Bless you all."

"Bless you, too, Father," we say.

Mommy's breathing is labored now. We chat, sing, and remain at her side. She brought us into the world and we're going to see her leave it.

We recite the Lord's Prayer in unison, and as we say "Amen," Mommy takes a huge breath and it's her very last one. It's 10:05 p.m., September 23, 2000.

After a good long cry, one by one, the room empties out until Aunt Louise and I are the only ones left at Mommy's side. I watch Aunt Louise climb into Mommy's bed to lay beside her—the older sister who raised her during their mother's long and frequent absences. She cradles Mommy and cries out her name.

"Arms. Armenouhe, I love you. You're my best friend. What am I going to do now?"

I leave them be.

I'm happy only because Mommy's out of pain. I didn't want to see her go, but she deserves some peace. I'm forty-seven years old, yet I feel as though I'm five. *I want my mommy!* When I was young she used to say that little birds come and sit on our windowsill to share their secrets. That's how she always knew what I was up to. Back then, I'd sit in my sandbox, crooning, and suddenly someone would be singing along. I'd look up to see Mommy smiling, leaning on the windowsill and singing along through the screen.

"You Are My Sunshine…"

How sweet she was to put her chores aside just to sing with me. *Go get your wings, Mommy, and fly away like a bird, but don't forget to come and sit on my windowsill.*

★★★★★★★★★★★★★

A day passes by. I go to see Dad and it's just him and me.

"Did you get the church?" he asks.

"Saint Mary's by the Sea in Point Pleasant. It's Episcopalian. What about the eulogy, Dad?"

"No one said anything about that. I won't be able to do it—I'm too drained," he says.

"May I?"

"Sure. You can do it," he says.

"That means the world to me. Thank you, Daddy."

I hug him, and kiss him goodbye—and he *lets* me.

The morning of the funeral Dad motions me over to Mommy's casket. He takes her wedding band and hands it to me.

"I want you to have it," he says.

Given our history, I'm deeply touched. The *gesture* is so precious—it's all I need.

"Dad," I say, "I'm luckier than my younger sisters. I got to have Mommy longer than they did. Why don't you give it to one of them?"

"You take it," he says. "You can keep it or give it to whomever you want."

I take Mommy's ring and pass it to my sister, Louise. Of all us girls, she's had the least time with Mommy.

Now I'm supposed to say my last goodbye to Mommy as I lean into her casket—but I don't.

"Hi Mommy," I say instead. "Wake up and sing with me. Just one more time. Please!"

But she doesn't, so I stand there looking at her until I hear a bunch of relatives yelling at me to hurry up and get to the church. I wipe the *schmotchkies* off my face and head out.

327

Saint Mary's by the Sea is packed with friends and relatives—an awesome testament to the life Mommy led. Doreen, my lifelong friend, is seated near the back. From the podium I can see her face shimmering with tears, and in an instant I recall the banter between her and Mommy and how it always ended in uproarious laughter. Dad's up front with my siblings. Their eyes are puffy, and their faces glisten in the morning light.

When I first open my mouth I can't speak because I'm about to cry, but then I remember what Mommy told me to do the last time I had to speak in front of a group: *Think of a shit story.*

Lillian Low was born March 23, 1927. Her given name was Armenouhe Kartalian, but her sisters called her Arms, for short. One time someone phoned our house and said, "Hello, is Legs there?" Mommy replied, "No, but Arms is."

Armenouhe means "I am Armenian," and she sure had enough kids to start her own country. At the very least—a baseball team. The name Armenouhe is bold and proud, but the manner in which she lived her life can only be described as humble.

Mommy always told me that when she dies, she'll live on through her children. She's absolutely right. I know I wouldn't be who I am had it not been for my funny mom.

She taught my siblings and me how to work hard and do it with joy. She taught us how to laugh in the face of adversity. She made us want to sing. She made us want to dance. And while she had many talents that could've brought her fame and fortune, she committed herself to being a loving wife and mother.

Of all her gifts, her ingenuity is unsurpassed. She fixed toasters and radios. She sharpened pencils with knives, and truly, she was the barber, the butcher, the baker, the seamstress, the athlete, the comedian, the accountant, the mechanic and the doctor.

She made her own chuck-cherry wine to cure our real illnesses and she had some unique cures for our faked ones. The cure for wanting to stay home from school was: clean the house. Haircuts: soup bowl on the head. Bubble baths: Tide detergent. Splinters: red-hot needle. Broken nose: thumb press. Sanitary cooking: underwear

328

on your head. If you stepped on a rusty nail or had a boil: raw onion. It burns but it works. Removal of ticks: lit cigarette. Bumps and swelling: coin press. How many times have you sported an image of George Washington on your forehead? Yup, Arms was the doctor to call if you were ailing.

When I reveal that Mommy's definition of a dozen donuts is as many as you can fit into the box, laughter erupts and echoes off the ceiling. I have to stop because they're laughing and crying all at once. I've never heard a sound quite like that before: joy and sorrow blending like a milkshake. Only Mommy could sweeten such salty tears…

…All kidding aside, no words exist that are fitting for Mommy, Wife, Arms, Aunt Lillian, Friend, and Grandma, that can render her greatness.

All I know is that my mom made room for some other comedian to command applause from a packed auditorium. Some other seamstress won the praises of the elite because she chose to make clothes for little children who had no clue how hard her loving hands worked. And for sure, some other lady won the Olympic Gold Medal in track because Mommy chose to run after us instead.

Red, the tough "individual" from the 1st Platoon of Company A, the one who buried his precious black pearl in Japan many years ago, appears to be a frightened soldier. His pearl is nothing but a speck of dust compared to the treasure he's about to bury today.

****

Months later I bring Aunt Louise to visit Mommy's grave.

"I love you, Arms," she whispers somberly. Then she puts a kiss in her hand and transfers it to the etching on the gravestone.

"Arms," she continues, "say hi to my husband Joe, and to Mama, and to Peppy. Life won't be the same without you, Arms. Our little trips out to Las Vegas will never be the same without you.

Everyone in Circus-Circus will miss your jokes. But I will miss you most of all."

Me too, Mommy.

A Feather in the Wind

With Mommy laid to rest, the family war resumes. It's a cold winter, so instead of fishing, Dad uses his free time to hit the casinos in Atlantic City. He also finds plenty of time to call and belittle me, and when he's really bored, he shows up at my house yelling profanities. I haven't seen Sis for months, but her complaints, channeled through Dad, confirm that staying away from her was a smart decision.

My attempts at letting Dad know that he's upsetting himself for no reason falls on deaf ears. I resort to writing him a few letters, but they're useless. I suddenly realize that it's impossible to fix an imaginary problem.

****

Andrei's imagination always gets him into trouble. After learning that he's been in jail for three days, I head out for a visit with him.

"What happened, Andrei?"

"I was driving up Route 88 when an ambulance came up behind me. It was going to abduct me. I would've disappeared and no one would've known what happened to me."

"That doesn't make sense, Andrei."

"I had to get rid of the ambulance so I sped up and swerved back and forth over the line to lose it," he confesses.

The police report says Andrei led the cops on an erratic chase through Point Pleasant. Suddenly with cruisers in pursuit, he slowed down, sideswiped a police car, forcing it off the road, then skipped across two lanes of traffic, went over the railroad tracks and turned into a 7-Eleven parking lot. I stop reading and look up at Andrei.

"Why'd you stop at 7-Eleven?"

"To buy a pack of cigarettes."

"Cigarettes?"

"Yeah," he says. "But I didn't get the chance. The goddamned cops surrounded me with guns as if I was a goddamned felon."

When Dad gets wind of what happened, he shows up at Andrei's hearing and bails him out. Instead of being sent to a hospital, Andrei's *free* to do as he pleases until the next hearing.

He moves into a cheap motel along the Jersey Shore where he drapes his coat over the television to keep it from stealing his thoughts. His bed looks as though he had a fistfight in it, the floor is ankle deep with dirty clothes and garbage, and dried tea bags hang from the ceiling.

I bag up his garbage, gather up his dirty clothes, and he follows me out the door for our weekly ritual. First stop, the grocery store.

"Let's go to the cereal aisle," Andrei shouts. "I love Captain Crunch!"

Eyes gape at me, then Andrei and back at me. They see a tall, conservative brunette and a six-foot, wild-looking, thirty-one-year-old redhead. *They think he's my husband.* They laugh and whisper, and I laugh and sing "Jimmy Crack Corn" because I don't care.

Next stop, my house. On the way there I sing a song that Andrei knows because *I know* he'll sing along. Drenched in its melody, there isn't the slightest hint of sadness, anger, or insanity in Andrei. *It's impossible to think an awful thought when you sing a happy song.*

After the last note Andrei asks, "You gonna make me a seven-course meal, Cathy?"

"Yup, Andrei, but first I have to start your laundry."

King Farouk Jr. seats himself at the head of my kitchen table. A seven-course meal makes him happy so I figure out how to pull it off. It's *only* once a week. The first course is sliced oranges, followed by cheese and crackers, then a salad. Next comes deli ham rolled around a pickle. For the fifth course I serve him three giant stuffed cabbages, mashed potatoes, and string beans because that's what I served my family for dinner. Andrei's still hungry so I give him seconds. When he's done, I slip him a bowl of sherbet.

"This is better than a restaurant. What do you have for the last course?"

He counted! He knows it was only six courses. I have to think of something, so I tell him to rest his stomach while I check his clothes. As I'm folding them he yells from the kitchen.

"Can you make some of your *fine* coffee?"

"Okay, Andrei. Give me a few minutes and I'll make you some *fine* coffee."

I mimic the way he drags out *fine* and he laughs as if I told a joke. I don't have any cake, so I toast some bread, butter it and sprinkle it with cinnamon and sugar like Mommy used to do. I serve it with his *fine* coffee.

"Guess what, Cathy?"

"What, Andrei?"

"I've got billions of dollars overseas," he whispers. "When I get my hands on that money, I'm going to build you the house of your dreams."

"I know you will, Andrei."

****

It's the night before Andrei's hearing so I go over to the motel to check on him. His radio is smashed in the parking lot below his room. He's sitting on the bed in a pair of shorts that expose nine toothpicks stuck in the flesh above his knees. The toothpicks are on fire and some have burned all the way down to his skin. He has nine slashes at his wrists and at his ankles—each one represents a Low kid.

"What the hell are you doing, Andrei?" I ask in alarm.

"I'm cleansing our family of evil spirits."

"Why is your radio all smashed up?"

"It was stealing my thoughts!"

"Andrei, a radio can't steal your thoughts."

My comment infuriates him, so I apologize just to calm him down.

In the morning Andrei sits quietly in court while his public defender speaks on his behalf. When Andrei rises to address the judge, he answers his questions in a clear and humble manner. Andrei is smart. He doesn't share any of his secrets with the judge. He doesn't want him knowing about his billion-dollar deals, or that the government is stealing his thoughts.

The judge follows the letter of the law. He must release Andrei pending his trial date, and before the judge excuses my brother, he asks me to stand up.

I rise and acknowledge the judge.

He tells me to be sure that Andrei takes his medicine everyday. Andrei usually becomes hostile when he hears the word medicine, but since he seems composed, I tell the judge I'll try my best. The judge brings down his gavel for recess, and Andrei's free again.

Before anyone in the courtroom has a chance to leave, Andrei comes flying at me. He grabs my neck with both of his massive hands. At that, no one leaves.

"You're not gonna make me take medicine!" he screams desperately as he shakes me like a dirty throw rug. "I'm not taking medicine!"

Guards come rushing toward us. I'm in shock, but he didn't hurt me. He didn't have the chance. The guards were quick, and now, the judge's two-minute lunch break is over. He confers with the prosecutor and public defender while the guards move us out to the foyer.

Andrei is eager to leave and is clearly agitated. To compose him, the guards tell him he'll be able to leave after the paper work is processed. Andrei physically stifles himself, but emotionally, he cannot. Now he's barking at the thirty-plus courtroom spectators who failed to leave for lunch. The guards order them to leave, but they don't. They'd rather watch a live soap opera.

Each minute feels like ten. Soon half a dozen police officers encircle Andrei, and after a long struggle, they cuff his wrists to a leather waistband and shackle his feet. The chains at his ankles look heavy. It's painful to watch, but I don't look away—I *never* look away.

"What did I ever do to make you people treat me like an animal?" Andrei roars.

His voice hustles up the stairs and down the hallway. People are hanging over the railings. They multiply in the corridors like cockroaches looking for water.

"What?" Andrei screams. "What did I do? You want to lock me up so you can steal my ideas! Stop treating me like an animal or I'll starve myself! I'll pee on you! I'll shit in your food!"

Except for my tears, I blend among the spectators.

Andrei is sent to the hospital again. Within days he calls to chastise me for breaking up our wonderful, loving family, and he demands to know why I won't talk to Sis, why I'm so mean to her. I hold the phone three feet from my ear until he runs out of steam.

"So how you doin', Andrei?" I ask.

"Shitty," he says. "The medicine robs my strength and stamina. Without that, I'm nothing. They're stealing my manhood!"

"I hear what you're saying, Andrei—I'm sorry."

I end the conversation with, "I love you."

"I love you, too, Cathy."

My heart aches for him even more. I can't comprehend why anyone would offer him upsetting information. *How could anyone have a heart filled with so many cobwebs?*

****

It's winter and the snow and ice have piled up on the steps of Dad's Howell home. He slips and breaks his shoulder. Now he has to wear a sling. Dad's been so irrational and cruel that when Jane hears the news of his fall she says, "Dad didn't slip on the ice—Mommy *pushed* him!"

We cackle as we imagine Mommy swooping down from heaven to give Dad that nudge.

How could she help herself? Especially now!

Dad always resisted creating a will. He didn't want to deal with all that "legal mumbo-jumbo." Instead, he recited his wishes like a parrot, so we'd know what to do when he passes. Sis, however, convinces him that making a will is the right thing to do. He follows her lead, placing all his faith and trust in her.

The will is drawn up in January 2002, and every wish Dad repeated throughout his lifetime is tossed out like a feather in the wind.

****

Andrei is out of the hospital and temporarily living in a halfway house. In the spring he appears in court to answer the charges of eluding the police and endangering pedestrians. The judge finds Andrei "innocent by reason of insanity." He's ordered to live in a psychiatric institution for a period of up to ten years. Under New Jersey law, Andrei may be considered for early release based on the success of his treatment.

****

Dad sells his home and moves in with Sis. Their unyielding hostility toward me is reason enough to refrain from ever stopping by for a friendly cup of tea, yet amazingly, the southern regime accuses me of not being decent enough to visit with my dying father. It doesn't seem to matter to them that he's not on his deathbed. He's strong enough to fish in the surf and to sit at a black-jack table at Caesar's Palace for hours on end.

I pretend it doesn't hurt as I struggle to stay out of the line of fire. If I ignore their accusations, maybe they'll get tired and stop. But it *doesn't* end! The badgering is vile and relentless, and the siblings who've rejected the ridiculous stories about me are often bombarded with information designed to convince them of my cruelty. Some of the rumors land on my doorstep.

The phone awakens me, and it's Jane calling to clue me in on the latest gossip.

"Sis is telling everyone that you pushed Mommy while she was on her hands and knees begging you for something," Jane says.

"Oh my God! I've never raised my hands to Mommy in my life."

"I know," Jane says, "but I wanted you to know what people are saying about you. To back herself up, Sis is telling everyone that Dad was there and *he* saw it too."

I've gotten better at ignoring the products of Sis's imagination, but it sickens me that others may believe I pushed my mother. Mommy was so ill and her legs were so bad, there was no way she could even get down onto her knees, yet the southern regime embraces this crap.

It feels as though Sis is desperately trying to recreate my image. Why?

In a letter to Dad I remind him that he was sitting at the table during this so-called pushing incident.

You know I didn't push her, Dad. You were there when this allegedly happened. How can you allow such awful things to be said about your own child when you know they're not true? You're breaking my heart, Daddy.

My note moves Dad. He sets the record straight.

"Cathy *never* pushed Mommy."

Sis extricates herself from this messy episode by telling everyone that it just came out all wrong. What she *really* meant to say is, "It was *as if* Cathy pushed Mom."

And along with all the others, her little mistake is flicked away like a piece of lint.

Bridge to the Past

I'm perched in a rocker on my front porch enjoying the bright summer morning, when Dad's silver Mercury Grand Marquis pulls up in front of my house. There are countless dents in the front and rear bumpers because he has a habit of bumping into things. I wonder how he can see out the windows because his car needed a wash six months ago. He turns off the engine and just sits there. He's wearing his white baseball cap that's no longer white. I needn't walk to his car to know what's in there: an ashtray overflowing with cigarette butts, a urine bottle which he's probably using right now, a bunch of old hats, a fishing box, empty coffee containers, and a KFC bag filled with bones.

The door opens and out pops his cane. He pulls himself out of the car and slowly makes his way toward the porch with an expression that insinuates shame. I watch every step—his cushiony rubber shoes soften his slight limp. His short-sleeved shirt has stains all over the front where he drips his food. My family calls stains on a shirt "a Joe Low." He's lived such a colorful life—it's inevitable that something would be named after him. His polyester pants lost their creases ages ago and they're littered with lint balls. Dad lost a lot of his muscle mass this summer. He was once strong and solid, but now he appears feeble. He moves slower and he looks as though he's aged ten years in the three since Mommy died. As he approaches the steps I offer my arm to help him up. I could ask him to leave, but amazingly, I still have hope that his kinder side will surface.

I pretend nothing's wrong. I can't believe he's not telling me what a piece of shit I am. He grabs me and hugs me, and I can hear that grunting sound he makes when he's trying to hold back tears. But he

338

weeps. We hug, cry, and say nothing for a while. His grip is firm but tender, and I know he's come to a realization.

He sits in the rocker on the far end of my porch and lights his cheap menthol cigarette. He used to smoke Kools, but he buys the generic brand now.

"Do you want some breakfast, Daddy?"

"I'll have some eggs, and some fresh coffee."

Ten minutes later I return with eggs over-easy, fried ham, toast and coffee. I place it on the table in front of him. His eyes fill with appreciation. He removes his baseball cap because it's impolite for a man to eat with his hat on. He's got a good head of hair for a man of almost seventy-six years. The red locks from his younger days have turned to salt and pepper. Except for his sideburns, he's still got a lot of pepper. He looks a lot like Grandpa now. He rips his toast, dips it into the egg yolk, takes a bite, and chimes, *"Motzi!"*

I bring him another cup of coffee just the way he likes it, with lots of milk and one Sweet'N Low. He lights another cigarette and tells me he was practically weaned on coffee. It's remarkable that he's still alive considering his dietary habits and lack of exercise.

There's silence for a moment as we watch a family of white domestic ducks hobble by. The sky is decorated with cardinals, finches, sparrows and humming birds, but Dad spies a hawk.

"He's a *big* son-of-a-bitch," he says.

We laugh and continue our nature watch in silence.

"One of my favorite places in the world is your front porch—sitting in a rocking chair," he says suddenly.

"Me too, Dad."

After another long moment of silence, he asks me to hold up three fingers. I know what he's going to say. I've heard it dozens of times, but I oblige.

"At the end of your life," he says, "if you have three people who are willing to give up their right arms or jump into a fire for you, consider yourself the luckiest person alive."

I quickly think of three people to match my fingers. Dad's not one of them. I keep that to myself.

"Phew!" I say as I wipe my forehead. "It's getting hot, Mr. Lucky!"

Dad bursts out laughing and it's contagious.

Dad loves telling stories as much as he loves fishing, so I ask him to tell me more about his childhood.

"When I was a kid, I never had the support of extended family," he says. "And Pop—no one messed with him. Right or wrong, I had to do things Pop's way. There was no winning with *my* father. He was one tough son-of-a-bitch."

"What made him so tough?"

"It was where he came from," Dad insists. "The Russian peasants had no choice but to work like goddamned slaves. They were shit-scared of the nobles, kids were shit-scared of their fathers, and women were terrified of their husbands. Men beat the crap out of their wives to keep them in line the same way the nobles kept all the peasant farmers in line. It all came from the top. Pop did the same with me as his father did with him and his family. It's all *he* knew. And all the goddamned work *I* did as a kid was for the good of the family. Even when I was in the Army I had to send my paychecks home to Pop."

"Did he save the money for you?"

"Not a goddamned cent!" Dad roars. "When I got home from Japan I learned that Pop spent all my money on a bunch of goddamned pigs and chickens. All the pigs became diseased and they died before I even got a chance to see them. All Pop had left were the chickens, and I had to feed them, collect eggs, and make repairs around the goddamned shithouse we lived in.

"He never gave me an inch. One night, I'm sound asleep; he shakes me awake and tells me to get the hell up. It's the middle of the goddamned night! He tells me that one of his chickens is missing. So I ask him, 'What the hell am I supposed to do about it?' He says he thinks it was a farmer who lives about a mile or so away and he wants me to help him avenge the man. He doesn't have any proof whatsoever that that man is the culprit! What's worse is, Pop couldn't possibly have known he was missing just one chicken—he certainly couldn't count them because they never stood still long enough. Besides that, they all looked alike!"

"Did you tell him that?" I ask.

"I told him. But he didn't care. He didn't need any 'got-dem proof,' he said."

"It's pretty crappy when people act on assumptions," I say.

Dad stops as if a truck hit him. He looks me in the eye for a long moment. Then he drops his head.

"Nothing's worse than that," he says as he gazes up at me.

He knows. I knew he did. It was horrendous having to bear the burden of his rage and his despicable behavior when he knew all along that I deserved none of it. I hate to think it, but Dad is emotionally stunted. I'm beginning to see how untamed emotions can trump intelligence.

I look up in the midst of our quiet reflection and ask, "So what happened next, Dad?"

"What?" he asks as I break his mental reverie.

"What happened after Grandpa woke you up?"

"Pop wanted to get the farmer back ten times. He thought a pig for a chicken would do the trick. So we walked through the blackened woods until we reached the farmer's pigpen. Pop chose the biggest goddamned pig the farmer had. He clubbed the son-of-a-bitch over the head and made me drag it home through the woods!" Dad shouts as if he's reliving the ordeal.

"You don't know what hard work is until you dragged a goddamned gigantic dead pig through the woods for over a goddamned mile in the middle of the goddamned night!"

His face reddens, his neck veins bulge, and he's wagging his finger at me as if I'm the one who made him drag home the pig. His false teeth fly out in the midst of his story, and with all his gasping and spitting all I can do is laugh out loud. I can't stop.

Dad replaces his teeth and roars, "Do you want to hear the goddamned story or not?"

"All right, Dad. I'm done laughing. You can finish."

He repeats the part about how hard it was dragging home a dead pig—three times!

"Geez, Daddy," I say as I control my urge to laugh. "Why didn't you just put a rope around the neck of a live pig and walk it home?"

"Pop didn't want to cause a commotion. If he took the time to try and rope one of them big bastards, they'd grunt, squeal and wake up every animal on the farm, including the farmer. And besides that, them goddamned pigs have nasty teeth. When they bite into you, they don't let go," he says.

"Wouldn't it have been easier to steal a horse and ride it home?"

"Yup," Dad says, "that would've been easier, but you don't steal a goddamned horse to butcher it. With a pig you get to eat the evidence."

"Did you hate your father?" I ask.

"Nah. Not anymore. He had a miserable life, too. He lived his life the way he was taught as a child: no crying, no complaining, do whatever the hell you have to do and shut your mouth. It's all he knew. Times were tough, even after he left Russia. Things weren't much better in America. It was the same shit, just a different toilet. He couldn't get a decent job because big business screwed the working man back then. So what the hell difference did it make that he was in a free country? Life was hard, and it got worse during the Depression. Pop just did what he had to do to get by."

Dad puts the story of his childhood into perspective by adding bits of history. Living on the run and sleeping on lumpy mattresses with bedbugs was far better than the cardboard boxes other folks slept in during the Depression Era. Grandpa may have been crooked, but Dad and his siblings never slept in the street.

There's been no cease-fire between the North and South, but Dad secretly lays down his weapons against me. All he wants now is some peace, someone to talk to, and he knows I'm all ears.

****

While I'm cleaning up the house I hear a bang, scraping sounds, and someone yelling Jeeeeesus Christ, goddamned son-of-a-bitch! It's Dad.

342

He speaks two languages: English and Foulish. He probably wants to make sure all my neighbors know that he's bilingual. I look out the window to see that he hit the curb and now his tires are scraping the concrete as he tries to back away from it.

I quickly pour a cup of coffee and fix it just the way Dad likes it. As he's hobbling up the steps I greet him with the coffee.

"For *me?*"

"Just for you, Dad."

He takes the rocker on the far end of my porch, lights his menthol, sips the coffee and ever so gently rocks back and forth, peering into the sky. I notice that he taps his heels twice as he comes forward, the way Grandma Low did. He suddenly stops and leans toward me.

"Kids have it easy today," Dad says. "It's nothing like when I was a kid. Pop sent me out to work on the goddamned streets of New York when I was only five years old. Everybody was goddamned poor during the Depression, and when you sprinkle poverty onto the goddamned streets, it grows a lot of tough sons-a-bitches! I know, I was one of 'em!"

"And you still are," I tell him.

Dad shifts his blue-gray eyes up to the canvas in the sky. It seems as though he sees the story of his life up there.

A cornucopia of birds flutter by, cars pass in the street, and a boy zips by on his bike.

"It must be the kid's birthday—looks like a brand new bike," Dad guesses.

My mental shit-file snaps open. I want to ask Dad about the bike he bought for my ninth birthday. *I'm still afraid to ask. I don't want to mess up this beautiful moment. They're always too few and far between.*

"You're probably right, Daddy. It must be nice to get a birthday bike."

Dad looks me square in the eye as he draws his brows together. Just as he's ready to snap at me, his brows separate and rise, his mouth opens and his jaw drops—the same way everyone else's jaw drops when they remember something that they had long forgotten. I suspected that Dad took the bike back to the store for a refund. Now I'm a bit more convinced of it.

A few days later, on my birthday, a card arrives in the mail. It's from Dad. His note says he knows I've had more than my share of ups and downs in the first fifty years of my life. He hopes my next fifty years will be *all* ups and *no* downs.

I weep uncontrollably. My father's words—the gentler ones from long ago—rise up like the sun on a summer morning. *Before you know it, life passes you by.* As I take stock of my life, I see all the things I didn't do. I didn't go to college, I never had dance lessons, I haven't traveled, I've hardly done anything. I'm going to change that.

Ironically, the first thing that pops into my head is: *memorize the second half of the Gettysburg Address.* I haven't attempted to study it since the fourth grade. I know the first half better than I know myself, but the second half is a blank. I need to fill it in.

****

Dad shows up on my porch more often now. When I'm not home he sits and waits for me. I can always tell because I find three or four menthol cigarette butts in the ashtray, which means he waited for a while. That melts my heart. When I miss him like that, I'm disappointed.

The little time we have left is no longer wasted on anger, not his or anyone else's. He arrives on my porch dressed up in his kinder side, and he treats me civilly.

"Boy, oh boy," Dad says. "If only I had my life to live over again."

"What would you do differently?" I ask.

"Well," he says, "I would've bought you kids some books when you were little, and I would've let you read in bed every night for as long as you wanted. The new rule would be, when you're done reading, lights out."

"That's a good rule, Dad."

"Yeah," he says, "too bad you don't think of these things when you should."

"What else would you have done differently?"

"I wouldn't have pissed away all the money I made when we lived in Sayreville. I wouldn't have done a lot of other stupid things I did."

"What other things, Dad?"

"I wouldn't have sold the Howell house after your mother died. I regret that. Giving it up was like throwing away my independence."

Another question is bouncing around my head. I want to know the *one* thing he *really* wanted to do but never got around to doing. I'm half expecting him to say he would've sailed around the world or returned to Japan for his pearl. But his answer surprises me.

"I would have written the story of my life. Maybe you can write it," he chuckles.

"Maybe," I say. "I can call it Calamity Joe."

"You can't call it that! Calamity Joe was a horse thief. I wasn't a goddamned horse thief. I stole goddamned pigs!"

As Dad laughs at himself, coffee from his mug splashes onto his pant leg. His false teeth slide down and he grunts and roars uncontrollably. I laugh with him until the laughter fades to a sigh.

As Dad continues digging up his past, I begin to understand him as a human being rather than *just my father.* It's easy to see how he was broken to bits before he even had the chance to become a man. All at once, I'm released of the lifelong anguish he heaped on me. He didn't have to tell me anything, but then, he always said it wasn't fair of his grandmother to take her words to the grave, leaving his abandoned mother with unanswered questions.

"There's always more to a story than meets the eye," Dad says. "Sometimes, the stories of our lives begin long before we're born."

"So that's why you followed in your father's footsteps?"

"Yes and no," Dad says. "I'll admit that I purposely made you fear me. Fear keeps people in line. I wanted to keep my kids in line and that's the only way I knew. It's what I learned from my father."

"You went way overboard, Dad."

"I know I was a tough bastard, but I wasn't as bad as Pop. He had no mercy on me. He'd beat my ass if he didn't like the look on my face, and he always expected me to work his shady schemes, then hand him all the money."

"Dad!"

"What?"

"The apple doesn't fall far from the tree."

"It rolled down the hill a little," he says with a chuckle.

"Maybe an inch or two. C'mon Dad, you had plenty of shady action going on yourself."

"Right or wrong, at the time, I believed I did what was best for my family. I wanted you kids to have the things I didn't. That's why I was always hustling for a buck."

While Dad rocks back and forth, gazing out into the very blue sky, I search my mind for meaningful questions to ask him, ones that I'm sure won't anger him.

"What's the most important thing you've learned about life, Dad?"

That catches him off guard. His eyes appear bluer as they search the sky for an answer.

"Taking the time to stop whatever the hell we're doing to look at ourselves. And a little self-control to go along with that. Without self-control, no matter how fortunate you are, you could end up with nothing. And if you can't see yourself, you may never see your own fortune, or your own ugliness."

"If you can't see your own ugly, you can't fix it."

"True," he sighs, "but that's easier said than done. No one wants to admit when they're wrong. It's too hurtful to the ego. That takes more courage and fortitude than most people have."

"Mommy had it."

"Yeah, but she was a one-of-a-kind. She didn't need much to be happy. You'd think she hit the jackpot just because she cracked open a double yolk egg."

"Or if you said just one word that made her think of a song."

Dad laughs, but only for a second. Tears of sorrow and longing follow. If he sheds just one tear for each painful memory, and one for everything he's sorry for, there will be many more.

****

In the days to come Dad tells me about a share of property he has in upstate New York. Collectively, it's owned by a group of Russians and years ago when shares were made available to the Lows, he bought one. He doesn't know what it's worth but he wants me to know that it's part of his estate.

He recently had a couple of big hits in Atlantic City and he regularly withdraws money from his checking account whether he needs it or not. His cash is growing because he doesn't get around to spend it like he used to, so he keeps it in a metal lock box, which he's thinking of hiding in the trunk of his car.

He reminds me that he has always wanted his children to have an equal share of his estate, but he's not sure how things will pan out.

"I made some mistakes," he blurts out.

"So fix them."

"I'm trying, but it's not that easy," he says as his voice trembles.

"Are you afraid of something?"

He doesn't answer, so I ask him three times before he concedes.

"Yes," he says, "I'm afraid! Besides that, it might be too late."

"As long as you're alive, it's never too late for anything."

He doesn't say a word. But his eyes tell me he's still listening.

"You might think I'm not very smart, Daddy, but there's one thing I know for sure."

"What's that?"

"The right words can move mountains."

His thoughts paint worry on his face as he kisses me goodbye. He knows he helped orchestrate the family war and his hostile approach made matters worse. Now he wants to undo the damage. With all the schemes he had going throughout his life, he never got caught red-handed, but his own personal schemes robbed him of the one thing money can't buy—a loving family, connected and loyal.

But no one wins the game when some are allowed to play by different rules. You can't change the definition of "all for one and one for all" and expect infinite loyalty from the underdogs.

Dad doesn't know he's teaching me that we all have our own way of searching for answers, that we find them only when our hearts are open.

My conversations with Dad cause me to reflect on the mysteries of life. In many ways we're all the same. We're all searching for *that something*, often looking in all the wrong places, never realizing that the simple answers lie deep within ourselves.

The kid in me who learned the first half of the Gettysburg Address is buried beneath the one who failed to learn the second half. I clung to the part of me that played the game of life by Dad's rules. Not that it was ever a game. But even without a chessboard, life has rules. Until this late hour, Dad hadn't realized that I have the right to play by the same rules as my peers. Without an honest game, it doesn't make any sense to play at all.

Fear prevented me from asking myself the right questions. Perhaps Dad's fears were more deeply rooted than mine. Maybe the part of himself he's been searching for is stuck somewhere in time before he had a memory, or perchance before he was born.

Our reminiscent journey into the past exposed strengths and defects in the bridge that led us to the here and now. Turning a blind eye to the flaws gave them free reign to intensify and thrive—and no matter how much time went by, the past was always present. It was buried alive by the blind eye, and it came back to haunt us.

The Passing of a Legacy

Most of the Low kids on the North side of the family have hardly seen the kinder side of Dad since before our mother passed away. Nor have we celebrated a holiday with him since then. But the lights are on in Dad's attic. Like Mommy, he's enlightened himself in the telling of his own story. To begin healing and connecting with the rest of his children, he announces that he's going to spend Christmas in Florida with Jane. Some of us kids on the North plan on joining him for the holiday, but *immediately* following his announcement, Dad's health declines. He ends up in the hospital, and after a brief stay, he's sent back home to Sis's house.

In the New Year, while I'm visiting Jane in Florida, we get several calls from a couple of our siblings who report that Dad is terribly ill.

"He may not make it to the morning," Joseph's voice shrieks through the receiver. "It's despicable the way you've treated Dad! He's dying, Cathy! He can go any minute, and you don't even have the decency to be at his side!"

"If Dad's that ill," I tell him, "call an ambulance!"

"I can't. Sis isn't home. I have to wait till she gets here."

"If your dog was sick, you wouldn't wait."

He hangs up on me. He doesn't make the call, nor does anyone else. They're all afraid of Sis. They don't want to upset her. They believe they need her permission to make that call, so they wait.

Jane grabs the phone and dials 911. As a matter of routine, the police department is dispatched along with the rescue squad. The police arrive at Sis's house first. By this time she's home and thoroughly enraged that Jane had the audacity to make that phone call.

"Jane called the cops on me!" she cries.

As Sis's tirade continues, not one person in her presence dares to challenge her. Dad listens to her rant, and because he's afraid to arouse any more anger than already exists, he tells the emergency team he'll wait—maybe he'll feel better soon. The paramedics are sent away.

As Jane and I drive to the airport to board the first flight we can get, "Dance With My Father" blares from the radio. Jane is forced to drive through her tears.

I wasn't always sure that Dad loved me, but at least I don't regret the kind of daughter I've been. I have no illusions. I know that as a father, Dad fell short in many ways, yet I've loved him as if he was the greatest father in the world. As the song pipes through the speakers, I remember being a kid, standing on his shiny shoes as he whirled me around the dance floor—before he was three-sheets-to-the-wind. *I'd go back there if I could.*

****

The next day Dad is so ill, he's got to be taken to the hospital immediately. By the time he's checked in, he's extremely dehydrated and his kidneys are severely affected. Between that and his heart ailments, he needs intensive care.

Sis steams like a searing teapot as she claims we accused her of intentionally withholding medical treatment. It doesn't seem to matter that no one accused her of that. She chose those words.

I call the hospital where Andrei lives to arrange his visit with Dad. When he arrives he's shackled and two guards follow him into Dad's room, which is already crowded with eight other Low kids. We convince the guards to unlock the cuffs at his wrists so he can enjoy the sandwich we have waiting for him.

After lunch, Andrei wants to cleanse Dad of evil spirits. His freed hands move over Dad's head, chest, back and arms as if he's a fortune-teller. Dad squirms, but the rest of us explode with laughter—

all of us, the North and the South. Because of Andrei we are briefly connected. Tears spill from our eyes, our bellies rumble, and unidentifiable sounds replace the words we attempt to speak.

Andrei ignores us as he continues to perform his ritual.

"Scha ka ma doo," he says. "Moolasha koodem ohraha akama. Cleanse Dad in the name of Christ. Make him live! Schama toorah ho-ho-ho, akama!"

"What language was that?" Joseph asks.

"I speak almost every language," Andrei says. "German, Italian, Chinese, Cantonese, Russian, Greek, you name it."

"Where'd you learn all those languages?"

"I have the intelligence of the universe."

"Can you speak Spanish?" Joseph asks.

"Oh, no," Andrei says, "I had trouble with high school Spanish so I had to drop it."

****

As we Low kids surround Dad, friends and relatives come and go. Among them, some Dad included when he counted the many people who'd give up their right arms for him. An unlikely visitor arrives, as well.

"Joe Low," she whispers as she leans in closer to Dad.

Aunt Louise always says his first and last names as if they're one word. In happier times she visited my parents frequently. She and Dad would sit at the kitchen table, sipping their morning coffee, discussing world events, laughing and teasing each other. But after Mommy died, Dad ousted Aunt Louise from his life merely because he chose to *believe* rumors. Her loyalty to the Low kids on the North and her outspokenness made her yet another target for the southern regime.

Not knowing what to expect, she took the long trip from North Jersey, because in spite of it all, she remembers the kinder side of Joe Low.

Dad opens his eyes to see his old coffee buddy, Louise. He had thrown her away, yet here she is, in his final hours.

"You came *all* the way here to see *me*?" he asks with an endearing crack in his voice.

"You're my friend, Joe Low."

"*You* are *my* friend, Louise!" he whispers emphatically.

****

Visiting hours are almost over, but I decide to hang out in the hospital with Dad until the nurses chase me home. It's just the two of us, so I cuddle up next to him and hold his hand—the giant hand that used to frighten me. Now it feels safe, warm and loving.

Dad says he's tired. He wants to lie quietly and watch the evening news. In short order I hear footsteps approaching. Sis enters the room and makes her way to the other side of Dad's bed. Although we're estranged I acknowledge her.

As Dad drifts off to sleep, Sis demands to know why I'm so quiet. I explain to her that Dad had asked for the quiet time, but my answer is unsatisfactory. She begins telling me who and what I am, and how unforgivable it is that Jane and I called the cops on her.

With just a twist of a few words, I see how she rewrites an entire story and how it commands attention and pity. Her empathizers are so touched, they're eager to come to her defense—not knowing that there isn't anything to defend. What a cruel and selfish way to take advantage of the kindness of others.

I peer at her from across the bed in a much brighter light. I don't respond. I don't want to argue over Dad's deathbed. But her voice grows louder and her angry words shoot out like machine gunfire. Dad is sleeping like Grandpa Low, with one eye open. He raises his head and turns to Sis.

"Enough, already! Leave her alone, goddamn it! Stop being so sarcastic for no reason!"

She's too angry to stop. I'm not even sure she hears him because she's still carrying on about how mean I am to her.

"Stop! Enough!" Dad interrupts her. "You're always picking on Cathy. When is this going to end? Once and for all stop picking on her!"

Dad's words not only shock me, they leave *her* stunned. It's the first time he's ever admonished Sis over something she's said about me. She's so surprised her mouth falls open but no sounds escape. She flops into her chair and I drop my head onto Dad's bed. I sob.

Sis's silence doesn't last. She begins to rant again. This time Dad doesn't say a word. Although it's a huge effort for him to raise his arms, he pulls his hand out from under the sheets and strokes my head from the top to the nape of my neck, over and over.

Sis isn't used to seeing Dad show me affection. She cannot bear the sight of it. She jumps up, scoots around the bed, grabs my arm, and begins pulling on me. Now the bed is shaking.

"Stop," I say. "You're making Dad uncomfortable."

But she continues—without a grain of consideration for our dying father, without a speck of empathy for the man who jumped into all of her fires.

"Please stop!" I ask again.

She doesn't.

She cannot embrace the ounce of tenderness our father is finally showing me. Her fury swells as she relentlessly tugs on my arm. To make her stop, I get up and walk to the back of the room. I'm up against the wall and with her face inches from mine, she furiously recites all the mean things I did to her, the imaginary ones. In the same breath, she wants to know why I'm so unforgiving.

"I love you!" she shouts angrily, and it's the first time she's ever said that to me.

"If you love me, stop making up lies about me. That's all I'm asking for."

"I *never* lie," she fumes. Her eyes are bulging, her entire body is pulsating with anger.

Her rage is so intense I can spoon it out of the air and slurp it up like soup. I want to call her Pinocchio, and a few other things, but I hold my tongue. It's another one of those fragile moments. Without a word, I take my seat next to Dad. Sis quietly glares at me while putting on her coat. I don't expect her to say goodbye to me, but she doesn't even say it to Dad. She just hustles out the door in a huff.

Her anger toward me has always made me feel guilty for merely hoping that our father might love me, too. It's so blatant, I have no choice but to remain detached from her.

I slip my hand back into Dad's hand. It feels good for a daughter to hold her father's hand.

Dad drifts off to sleep and murmurs, "Anna, Anna."

He's dreaming about when he was a kid. When his father was busy making bathtub gin, and his mother was three-sheets-to-the-wind, his sister Anna would hold and comfort him.

Suddenly Dad looks up from his nap.

"Katrrrinka—you're still here."

He grunts as if he's holding back tears. "I'm sorry," he says.

"What?" I ask.

"You've been picked on long enough," he admits. "It's about time it ended. Enough is enough."

I lay my head on his bed and a river of tears soak his sheets. With great effort, he lifts his arm, puts it around me and says, "I love you."

"I love you, too, Daddy."

★★★★★★★★★★★★★

In the midst of the family war, at 8:32 a.m. February 8, 2004, Dad falls asleep forever. Directly afterward, my siblings and I meet at a diner for breakfast—the North and the South *together* at the same table. As the waitress is pouring coffee, Sis breaks the silence.

"All that's left of the money is Mommy's IRA. That's it!" she blurts out.

That's a bunch of bologna.

There's no reason for her to be bringing up our parents' estate when we haven't even processed the passing of our father. But now that Sis brought it up, we have some questions.

"Show us the will," my sister, Louise, says.

"I can't believe *you people* have the audacity to ask to see the will! Dad's body isn't even cold yet!" Sis snaps.

Nevertheless, we plan another meeting because a couple of my sisters live out of state and soon they'll have to go home.

Sis begrudgingly shows up for this meeting and reminds us that Dad's body isn't even cold yet.

"How dare you disrespect him like that," she scorns.

She nervously pulls out the will, and angrily reads half of the first page before tossing it aside. She recites the remainder because she says she knows it by heart. Five minutes later she swears this is the first time she's seeing Dad's will.

Her information doesn't jibe.

Finally, we all take a peek at the will. Only three of Dad's nine children are mentioned by name in the will. The blow intensifies when the names of Sis's stepdaughter and step-grandson leap off the page. Many of us ask questions, but her cryptic answers leave us baffled. Sis hates being questioned, so the meeting degenerates into a verbal boxing match between the North and South.

"It doesn't matter what you people think," she says. "*I'm* the one who knows what Dad wanted. And there's some things he forgot to do."

With that, Sis grabs her pen and writes in what she claims Dad forgot to add.

In addition to overstepping her authority, the will contradicts her earlier statement about the IRA being all that's left. When the meeting ends, we barely finish round one of our boxing match.

Days later Sis produces another version of the will—a copy of only page one, which contains additional handwritten corrections.

"Dad changed his mind about some things," she swears.

Now there are three wills—one with no changes, one that *she says* "contains Dad's changes," and the one she altered in our presence.

More questions follow, inconsistencies pile up, and rumors fly around.

On the surface, it appears that the North is squabbling over money, but there's more than meets the eye here. Dad's legacy of emotional abuse, anger, and injustice has been successfully passed on. The southern regime is using anger to defend the noble status Dad bestowed upon them throughout their lives simply because we on the

North have questioned the discrepancy between Dad's verbal wishes and the words presented to us on paper.

For the Good of the Family

Andrei arrives at church, shackled, with guards at his heels. He's humiliated at having to walk up the aisle this way, but like a good Low, he holds his head up high.

Joseph takes the podium and memorializes the real Joe Low, turning Dad's blunders into the most humorous and heartfelt eulogy I've ever heard. I especially love the way he says, "If it wasn't for Joe Low, a lot of people wouldn't have gone fishing." Although I barely got to experience fishing with Dad, I'm grateful that he shared his stories with me. Joseph obviously inherited Dad's storytelling abilities. I offer him a look that says, "I'm proud of you." He acknowledges me with a swift smile, and I understand why he turns away so quickly.

We proceed to the graveyard to leave Dad with a prayer at his final resting place next to Mommy. As I carefully place a rose on Dad's casket, I hear his voice echoing *Katrrrinka, Katrrrinka.* That's how he said my name only a few times in my life, and it made me feel loved.

Afterward, dozens of friends and relatives join our family for lunch at a local Italian restaurant.

Upon entering the restaurant, Andrei stands motionless, shackled, with a guard on each side, but his face radiates with joy at the sight of the family he loves so dearly.

We convince the guards to free his hands so he can eat with dignity. Andrei savors his meal with a gleam in his eye and a *homa, homa.* But as dessert is being served, the guards prompt Andrei to leave. They begin to secure his wrists to the thick leather waistband when Andrei says he can't leave yet. He has something to say. He walks to the center of the dining area with his guards only an arm's length away.

"May I have everyone's attention?"

There's instant silence, a stillness that spreads as if we are flashed frozen. The only movement in the room is the shifting of eyes, induced by expectations of a bizarre speech.

Andrei has gained almost one hundred pounds since he was sent to live in the institution. His bulky, brown winter coat makes him appear even bigger. He's thirty-three years old and he's been reminding me that he's the same age as Christ when *He* was crucified. His darkened red hair is streaked with gray, and his long, thick curly locks are secured at the nape of his neck with a rubber band. The chains at his feet rattle as he adjusts his position.

"My dad was the greatest father," Andrei shouts. "He taught me everything I know. He's the smartest man I know. Once in a while he had to give me a lickin' to straighten me out, but I deserved it. My best memory of him is when he took me fishing. I know you all have many good memories of my father, too. I just want to thank all of you for coming here to honor him. It means a lot to me. You had to get up really early and you got all dressed up and went through a lot of trouble to get here…"

As Andrei continues to speak, the conflicting image of his presence and his solemn words shatters the expectations of everyone present. They weep and moan, almost as if they're ashamed of their thoughts. In an unassuming way, Andrei reminds us of our humanity. Even those few who've never met him are moved. The guards, strong and tough, stand at attention, but their eyes are glistening, too.

"…Aunt Chris, you came all the way from the Bronx. That's a long drive. Hey, Aunt Chris!" Andrei yells, "Where's my bag of herns?"Our salty tears are sweetened with laughter.

The bag of herns that Aunt Chris never gave us is nothing more than an invisible bag of shit. As it turns out, I had my own bag of herns all along. Everyone has one. It's our birthright, and the longer we live, the bigger, heavier and smellier it gets. Aunt Chris wasn't forgetful, she was just kind enough not to give us hers.

"I'm not done yet!" Andrei roars above the laughter.

"…Aunt Lena, it's good to see you. I'm glad all my aunts are here. It was nice of you to come. Too bad Uncle Frankie, Uncle Harry, Uncle Johnny, Uncle Bill, Uncle Peppy and all the Uncle Joes couldn't be here. Dad outlived them all. My father was the last Joe standing! Hey, Sandra, how ya doing Sandra? Hey, Joseph! Hey, Michael-Michael-Motorcycle! I wanted to say hello and goodbye and thanks to everyone individually, but that would take too long. I miss you and I love all of you. Maybe sometime you can come by and visit me, and I wouldn't mind if you brought me a pack of cigarettes—Marlboro, the red ones."

Before he can finish, our blubbering family and friends rise to their feet, unleashing their emotions in applause. Amid the sobbing and clapping, they line up in front of Andrei as you do for a bride and groom after the ceremony. As each person hugs and kisses Andrei, *he* apologizes to them for not being able to return their hugs.

I watch as the line moves ever so slowly, and I weep.

****

Two years pass before the will is settled, and with that, I split Mommy's cash as she wished. She knew it wasn't enough to establish financial parity, but it wasn't really about the money. It was simply a message meant to say, "I love *all* of you."

****

Our family is still shattered. It's a shame we ended up this way because, in spite of the negatives, our good was too precious to be tossed out. It was strong enough to overcome most obstacles but too fragile to conquer rage, injustice, and the loss of trust. That gorge is too deep and wide to traverse. Over time, though, bridges can be built and gaps can be filled—with simple words of acknowledgment, heartfelt ones bound by the contract of loving deeds.

Dad never intended for his family to be split in half. His partiality, untamed emotions, sense of entitlement, and many other negative characteristics all too often overshadowed the greatness in him. Sadly, it sabotaged his aspirations of family harmony.

He seemed to have a clear view of his father's shortcomings, the ones that burdened him with a lifetime of resentments, yet he repeated many of the same offenses that offended him. Perhaps his own fear and insecurity prevented him from reversing his legacy of abuse. And in the last winter of his life, when he finally came to understand that his hostile approach and toxic words had taken root and sprouted up like weeds in his own flowerbed, there was little he could do to right the wrong.

But he's gone now. Dead people can't change anything.

It's up to us who bury the dead to learn from them. Dad did the best he could with what he knew. There's no doubt he left us with a mess—perhaps more than one man's share. But he also left us with a choice. We can stumble forward along the course of his legacy and walk among the ruins in the shadows of his fractured spirit, or we can muster the courage to take a new path—fully illuminated—allowing us to see the past, to accept it and acknowledge it, to understand it and learn from it. Not in spite of Dad, rather for *the good* of his future generations.

Facing North instead of South never meant I loved my father any less, although for a time, he may have seen it that way. But in the end, he loved me. As often as I've doubted that, I now know he always did. And although I never expected him to be happy with my rebelliousness, his final acknowledgment soothed my heart and restored my hope, proving that love eventually rises to the top and overflows.

When you stand up for justice, you risk a lot. I know I did. But you never really risk losing who you are, and you never risk losing love—unless love wasn't there to begin with.

If you enjoyed Secondhand Scotch,
please consider leaving a review at <u>Amazon</u>.
Thank you very much!

About the Author

Cathy Curran is a baby boomer and a native New Jerseyan. She graduated from the school of Do-As-I-Say-Not-As-I-Do and went on to study at the University of What's-Your-Problem. Now that Curran is retired, she plans on traveling a little and dancing a lot.

Contact the Author and Links

Email: 2ndhandcathy@gmail.com

Facebook: www.facebook.com/secondhandscotch/

Twitter: @2ndHandCathy

Website: www.secondhandscotch.com

Chat with me and other memoir authors in our Facebook group,
We Love Memoirs:
www.facebook.com/groups/welovememoirs/

Acknowledgments

Secondhand Scotch is the third complete version of my memoir. After tossing aside the first two versions, along comes Yvette Blackman, a lady I met at a dance studio, who unbeknownst to me, was an editor at The Associated Press. After becoming fast friends, she suggested that I write a memoir. That's all the encouragement I needed to merge my story with my father's. I worked on it for almost a decade, and if not for Yvette's feedback, guidance and support, the current version of Secondhand Scotch might still be sitting in a box atop the first two.

I now believe Secondhand Scotch was meant to be written, that all the stars lined up to make it happen. Yvette is the first of many stars who've helped me along the way. My sisters Jane, Joanne and Louise are three stars who kept me going. They inspired me and encouraged me to speak up, and they, too, offered valuable feedback. My children are a part of the galaxy for their input, and my husband, Jack, for offering me his blessings, and for a few bits of his snappy wit. Friends, who, early on, gifted me with their feedback are: Ginny Peterson, Debbie Conochan, Lynda Fischer, Beverly Fiore, Emily Santiago, Kelaine Conochan and Melissa Santiago, and my American beta group who read Secondhand Scotch with keen eyes: Bunnie DeLancey, Pauline Elting, Eileen Ruszala and Ed Gaffney, are included in the galaxy of stars, along with the beta group from Ant Press: Beth Haslam, Joy Hughes, Susan Jackson, Paula Hilston, Julie Freed and Kate Pill.

Another star in the lineup is Susan A. Schwartz, my editorial consultant, who offered me suggestions that enriched Secondhand Scotch. Sue Clamp, the final editor, who took on my project amid her busy schedule, did a fantastic job with all the finishing touches.

Victoria Twead, who put her faith in my project, and Joe Twead, who, along with Victoria, spent many hours working on my memoir, helped to light my way.

Thomas Ranieri and his team at Blue Star Multimedia shine bright for the amazing job they did with my photo shoot, video, website, book cover and marketing materials.

Taner Akcam, historian, sociologist, and author of **A Shameful Act: The Armenian Genocide and the Question of Turkish Responsibility** and other books, obviously has a busy schedule, so I was deeply touched and grateful when he responded to my email with a lengthy phone call to discuss the Armenian Genocide.

Last, but not least, another very important star in the lineup is my lawyer, Lawrence D. Mandel, Intellectual Property Attorney of Gertner Mandel & Peslak, LLC, who patiently counseled me.

To all those mentioned here, and to the many others who have inspired me to spread my wings—you are all my teachers.

Thank you, thank you, a million thank yous.

Ant Press Books

If you enjoyed Secondhand Scotch, you may also enjoy these Ant Press titles:

MEMOIRS

Chickens, Mules and Two Old Fools by Victoria Twead (Wall Street Journal Top 10 bestseller)

Two Old Fools ~ Olé! by Victoria Twead

Two Old Fools on a Camel by Victoria Twead (thrice New York Times bestseller)

Two Old Fools in Spain Again by Victoria Twead

One Young Fool in Dorset (The Prequel) by VictoriaTwead

Midwife - A Calling by Peggy Vincent

Into Africa with 3 Kids, 13 Crates and a Husband by Ann Patras

More Into Africa with 3 Kids, some Dogs and a Husband by Ann Patras

Fat Dogs and French Estates ~ Part I by Beth Haslam

Fat Dogs and French Estates ~ Part II by Beth Haslam

Simon Ships Out: How One Brave, Stray Cat Became a Worldwide Hero by Jacky Donovan

Smoky: How a Tiny Yorkshire Terrier Became a World War II American Army Hero, Therapy Dog and Hollywood Star by Jacky Donovan

Instant Whips and Dream Toppings: A True-Life Dom Rom Com by Jacky Donovan

Heartprints of Africa: A Family's Story of Faith, Love, Adventure, and Turmoil by Cinda Adams Brooks

How not to be a Soldier: My Antics in the British Army by Lorna McCann

Moment of Surrender: My Journey Through Prescription Drug Addiction to Hope and Renewal by Pj Laube

Serving is a Pilgrimage by John Basham

FICTION

Parched by Andrew C Branham

A is for Abigail by Victoria Twead (Sixpenny Cross 1)

B is for Bella by Victoria Twead (Sixpenny Cross 2)

CHILDREN'S BOOKS

Seacat Simon: The Little Cat Who Became a Big Hero by Jacky Donovan

The Rise of Agnil by Susan Navas (Agnil's World 1)

Agnil and the Wizard's Orb by Susan Navas (Agnil's World 2)

Agnil and the Tree Spirits by Susan Navas (Agnil's World 3)

Agnil and the Centaur's Secret by Susan Navas (Agnil's World 4)

Morgan and the Martians by Victoria Twead

Chat with the author and other memoir authors and readers at **We Love Memoirs:**

https://www.facebook.com/groups/welovememoirs/

Made in the USA
Middletown, DE
21 August 2017